A PENTECOSTAL PILGRIM'S PROGRESS

From a doctrine founded on assumption and a misapplied
religious experience to the purpose of Pentecostal
'tongues' clearly defined by Scripture.

R. Glenn Brown

For my grandkids, Cody and Zoe, their mother, Celia, and dad, Steve.

To Donna who has lovingly and patiently shared 57 years of my Pentecostal pilgrimage.

Dedicated ultimately to the glory of God who welcomes repentant sinners like me into his royal family.

INTRODUCTION

This autobiography is written primarily for my family. However, in eighty-seven years aboard planet earth I have had the privilege of intersecting many lives. How their lives impacted me has become part of my story and a small fragment of theirs. I am indebted to each one.

During these nearly nine decades I have embarked on four different careers. Perhaps I should say, one career divided into four segments. First, was my segment as a U.S. Navy chaplain. I had the unique privilege of serving with all four branches of our military service, Air Force, Army, Navy/Marines. I never planned it that way but, in God's providence, that's what happened. I share my experiences in each of these. My over-riding career or calling was to be a proclaimer of the gospel of Jesus Christ.

After graduating from high school in 1946 I enlisted in the Army Air Corps before the Air Force existed. In 1947 the

Air Force was officially launched as a separate branch of our armed forces. I completed my three year enlistment in 1949 and enrolled in Denver University in January 1950. In June 1950 the Korean War started and I joined the advance ROTC program. Upon graduation in summer of 1952 I was commissioned a 2nd Lieutenant and called to active duty. I served five years as an Army Reserve officer, two years active, three years inactive. After four years of Seminary I was called to active duty as a Reserve Navy Chaplain in 1960. In 1962 I accepted a commission into the Regular Navy. I served eighteen years as a Navy chaplain, mostly with the Marines. In 1978 I retired from military ministry with twenty-six years combined service.

The second segment of my career was as a pastor. I was the founding pastor of Central Assembly of God (name since changed) in Granby, Colorado from 1955 to 1960 before entering the chaplaincy. After retiring from the chaplaincy I was inducted as pastor of Faith Chapel in Pleasanton, California in March, 1978 and served until end of November, 1991. My career segment as pastor covered nearly nineteen years.

In January, 1992 the Soviet Union collapsed and the iron curtain was demolished. New democracies were being established that were at last open to the gospel. God spoke to Donna and me about making ourselves available to minister in Eastern Europe. We did and exciting things began to happen. I was personally invited by General Zoblotny to help introduce Christianity to his military Command in W. Ukraine. I accepted his invitation and in 1993 began a ministry that has continued for nearly twenty-two years. Since then I have made thirty-seven trips to Ukraine. You will rejoice as you read what God has done in this segment. It is in a separate book called: **BIBLES, BORSCHT AND BULLETS.**

In 2008 I felt the Lord nudging me to begin a writing ministry. In 2009 I published my first book entitled **PENTECOST REVISITED.** I challenged my church's doctrine that there was no valid baptism with the Holy Spirit unless it was initially physically evidenced by speaking in tongues. I had seen clearly that this teaching was based entirely on unsupported assumptions and a religious experience wrongly interpreted. Speaking in tongues is a valid spiritual gift but its scriptural purpose at Pentecost is to symbolize all the languages and people groups of the world to which the gospel must be proclaimed. Joel makes that very clear in his prophecy Peter quoted. (Acts 2:16-21) Our Pentecostal insistence that speaking in tongues is required evidence of being filled with the Spirit is wholly without merit. It has resulted in great confusion and division within the body of Christ. It will continue to do so as long as American Pentecostals hold fast to their unbiblical tradition.

I have rejected a central tenet of American Pentecostalism for reasons explained at length in books I have written. Nevertheless, I am thoroughly Pentecostal in the sense that I firmly believe in the supernatural manifestation of God's presence in the body of Christ today. Such manifestations did not end with the death of the apostles as many American Evangelicals insist. Missionaries attest to their present global application to the church. Sadly, it is primarily in America that their absence is noted..

I agree whole-heartedly with my friend, Dr. Allen Anderson, foremost scholar of global Pentecostalism: *"Pentecostalism has taken on many forms quite different from those of North America, and in a global context the North American types are not really meaningful...Many Pentecostal groups, including some of the largest Pentecostal churches in Europe and Latin America and many in the so-called Charismatic Movement, do not insist on the 'initial evidence' of tongues."*

He goes on to say: *"It may be very difficult to tell what is meant by 'Pentecostal' today, but perhaps the term is best understood as referring to those movements with an emphasis on the experience of the power of the Holy Spirit with accompanying manifestations of the imminent presence of God."* (Quotes from *African Pentecostal Churches and Concepts of Power,* a paper read at Africa Forum, April, 1997)

I applaud and support Dr. Anderson's characterization of "Pentecostal." It is something all Evangelicals should rally around. We will never defeat the forces of humanistic materialism and the ideology of rampant Islamist terrorism without the demonstration of the supernatural power of the Holy Spirit. I see all too little of this power in my own life. I long for and pray for more.

I have continued writing six more books and hope to write until the Lord calls me home. I would like to augment my writing segment with personal appearances for seminars and preaching as the Lord opens doors. You can obtain more information concerning me and my ministries at: http://pentecostrevisited.com

TABLE OF CONTENTS

PROLOGUE

My Ancestors

When I was a youth I don't recall that I had a great deal of interest in my ancestry. Occasionally I would hear my parents refer to some ancient relative but it sparked no particular interest in me. Of course, my four living grandparents were special people whom I treasured well into adulthood. But beyond them the past, with its dead forebears, seemed too remote to excite my curiosity. It was much later in life that I developed more interest in the generations that had preceded my own. Unfortunately, my interest was aroused too late since the primary sources for obtaining information about family history had passed on. Consequently, the information I have is fragmentary and partial. Since I am approaching the age when I may soon become one of the deceased ancestors in our family history I decided to pass on to my grandchildren a

more complete resume of my own life. Included in this pro-
logue is some partial and incomplete background material
relating to our family tree.

MY DAD'S ANCESTRY

The Brown family ancestry was Scotch-Irish. I am not sure
when they immigrated to America but it was probably in the
late 18th century. I heard reports that they originally settled
in Pennsylvania and then migrated to Kentucky and then on
west to Missouri. My great-grandfather (great, great, great
for Cody and Zoe) William A. Brown was born in 1837 but
I am not sure of the location. He married Dianah (maiden
name unknown to me) during the Civil War period. They
eventually settled in Lathrop, Missouri where my grandfather,
George William Brown, was born February 17, 1873. In 1881
the lure of free land under the provisions of the Homestead
Act of 1862 drew William and his family to western Kansas.
Two years later in 1883 Dianah died. William eventually married again and continued to farm the homestead until he died
in 1925.

My granddad, George William Brown, followed in his
dad's footsteps and eventually homesteaded a Kansas farm in
Ness County. On September 24, 1896 he married my grandmother, Dora Maude Everhart. They reared eight children,
five boys and three girls. My dad, Robert, was child number
four with two boys and one girl older than he. My grandparents lived together on the same farm until Granddad
died on December 10, 1959. They had celebrated 63 years
of marriage in September. Grandma continued living until
October 1964.

MY MOTHER'S ANCESTRY

My mother's dad, Dennis Lewis Bluhm, was of German extraction. Her mother was Laura Mathilda Monsees. Her people came from the Alsace region between France and Germany. It was sometimes under French sovereignty and sometimes German, depending on who won the most recently fought war. The last name indicates her father, at least, was probably French. The Bluhm clan emigrated to America in 1840 and the Monsees sometime later. Both settled in western Missouri. Dennis Bluhm and Laura Monsees were married April 27, 1906. They became parents of six children, three girls and three boys. My mother, Eunice Mae, was the oldest.

MY DAD

My dad, your great grandfather, Robert Brown, was born on the homestead farm in Western Kansas on September 16, 1902. He completed the eighth grade in a one room rural school house and after graduation went to work on the family farm. He was the fourth of eight children with two older brothers and one older sister followed by two younger brothers and two younger sisters. I have good memories of each of these uncles and aunts.

To the best of my knowledge, dad was the first in his family to profess faith in Jesus Christ. At age fourteen he surrendered his life to Christ in a Methodist revival meeting that met in the school house where he attended eight grades of school. My dad grew up during the beginning of what is popularly called the "Pentecostal Renewal". To understand this I will have to share a little church history with you. But this background is necessary in order to understand our family history. For many years most of the Protestant churches of this era taught that the supernatural miracles and gifts of the Holy Spirit described in the New Testament had ceased with the death of the original Apostles. I think this teaching had developed for two reasons: (1) The culture was becoming more humanistic and materialistic. The supernatural was popularly discounted. Much of the church bought into these cultural assumptions. (2) This teaching that miracles had ceased with the death of the Apostles served as a convenient theory to explain why the Church displayed little supernatural power.

In 1900, not many miles from where my dad was born, a small group of Bible School students in Topeka, Kansas began a serious study of the ministry of the Holy Spirit to the Church. Their study convinced the students that the popular teaching about the Holy Spirit was not true. They began to earnestly seek God to manifest His power in the church as described in the New Testament. God answered their prayer and the students experienced a powerful manifestation of the Holy Spirit. It was similar to the original outpouring of the Holy Spirit at the feast of Pentecost described in Acts 2 in which the Holy Spirit enabled the disciples to speak all the national languages of the Roman Empire. That is why it is called the "Pentecostal revival".

Across America more and more Christians were attesting to the reality of the supernatural activity of the Holy Spirit. All the spiritual gifts described in Scripture such as miraculous healings, tongues and interpretations, prophecies, words of wisdom and knowledge and discernment of spirits were once again in operation throughout Christendom. The gift of supernaturally spoken languages is valid and scriptural but the purpose assigned by the students and Charles Parham, their instructor, is sheer assumption and invalid. These students assumed that the gift of speaking in a foreign language under the inspiration of the Holy Spirit was proof that they had been filled or baptized with the holy spirit. There was no Scripture to support this conclusion but it was widely accepted and soon created a sensation in the religious world.

Centuries old assumptions were suddenly invalidated. The news of the Holy Spirit once again demonstrating His power in the Church reached dad's local Methodist church and he became hungry for more of the power of the Holy Spirit in his own life. When he was 21 years old he was baptized in the Holy Spirit in the same schoolhouse where he had asked Jesus Christ to be Lord of his life. It was a turning point and led to his call to be a preacher of the gospel. Two years later he met Eunice Bluhm and after a whirlwind courtship she and dad were married on December 20, 1925. In 1926 dad and mom began an evangelistic ministry with friends, a young couple named Hoovers. They traveled about in twin motor homes conducting services in Oklahoma and Arkansas, sometimes among the American Indians. Later in 1926 and early 1927 mom and dad moved to Colorado where dad worked on a bridge construction project near Boulder. In the late spring of 1927 they moved back to a farm in Kansas. I was born at this farm on January 7, 1928.

From 1928 until 1935 dad interspersed preaching and farming, mostly in Kansas. My sister Alliene was born in July, 1929. During this time we sometimes lived in a rented house and sometimes in the motor home (truck house.) I can recall living in both.

MY MOTHER

As you know, mothers are very special people. Eunice Mae Bluhm, my mother, your great grandmother, was born in Smithton, Missouri on June 30, 1907. She was the oldest child of Dennis and Laura Bluhm. Around 1914 her family moved from Missouri to a farm in Ness County in western Kansas. It was as a ten year old that she committed herself to Jesus Christ. Two years later she was baptized in the Holy Spirit. It was the defining experience of her life. In 1919 the family pulled up stakes again and moved to a small fruit farm near Boulder, Colorado. This four hundred mile trip took several weeks since they were traveling by covered wagon. Automobiles had been invented but were not yet widely used. Mother adapted quickly to her new home. She was an excellent student and enjoyed learning and intellectual stimulation. Dad's courtship of mother began in the summer of 1925. He was singing in the choir at a Pentecostal camp meeting in eastern Colorado when the Bluhm family walked in. When dad saw Eunice he said to himself, "I'm going to marry that girl." And he did a few months later.

Mom said about her marriage; "Actually, this should have been a very poor marriage because it had everything going against it and we did everything wrong:

1. A teenager (me) marrying against her father's wishes.
2. I should never have quit my job.
3. We honestly knew we should have waited.

"My father had warned, 'If you get married you're just going to go out traveling all over, preaching, and then have a bunch of kids.' And that's exactly what I did . But we always had fun...always. And we were married for over sixty years before Bob went to be with Lord." Mom voiced regret that she had married too soon but she never voiced any regret about marrying my dad, your great-granddad.

Mom was an ideal preacher's wife. The only person she loved more than her husband was the Lord. She loved Jesus Christ intensely, she loved people and she knew how to communicate love in words and action. She was a good speaker and teacher in her own right. She understood young people and was the popular teacher of her church's "Young Married Couples" class up until the time of her stroke in her late eighties.

Mother treasured each of her eleven children. She viewed each of them as a gift from God and loved each one as if he or she were her favorite. Three of them preceded her in death and each loss brought her terrible pain. Only her deep, deep confidence in God enabled her to prevail over such sorrow.

Dad and mom were both disciplinarians but their styles were sharply contrasted. Dad, especially with the boys, was convinced that "to spare the rod was to spoil the child." He didn't hesitate to use a switch or his belt if he thought punishment was called for. Often he would have me go cut the switch that he was going to use. I learned to cut a long, limber switch. Then if you stood close to dad as the whip was applied the butt end was largely ineffective and the limber end would wrap around your legs with little pain. I don't remember ever getting undeserved punishment. I don't recall mom ever using a switch or other corporal punishment. Her technique was to call you in for a private talk. After mother in her soft voice had expressed her disappointment or concern about some action I left with a determination not to repeat the offense or, at least, not to get caught at it. If I had a choice I would choose dad's whipping to mom's "little talk". But mom was quick to express her delight for good action as well as her disappointment for bad. She would sometimes leave a little note expressing her pleasure at something worthwhile I had done. I didn't get many of these notes but each one was treasured.

I'm nine months old in western Kansas where I was born.
1928

CHAPTER 1
GLENN'S STORY

I made my appearance on planet earth at a small farm on the windswept plains of northwestern Kansas in Norton County. I am told it was a cold, snowy day on January 7, 1928. Herbert Hoover had just been elected president of the United States. The "roaring twenties" were still roaring. The disastrous stock market crash and the following great depression of the 1930's were still more than a year in the future.

EARLY MEMORIES

I don't remember anything about the Norton ranch where I was born. Some people speak of memories as early three or even two years old. Not I. My earliest memory is when I was about five years old. We had moved from the lonely plains of western Kansas to Boulder, Colorado, a beautiful town in the shadow of the towering, snow-capped Rocky Mountains.

I have several distinct memories of the year or so we lived in the little house on 28th street on the east side of Boulder. I remember climbing the big willow tree in the back yard. I particularly recall the day the limb I was standing on broke and I plunged to the ground. I was knocked unconscious and suffered a dislocated elbow. My parents took me to the doctor and got my elbow back in its socket. I was forced to keep my right arm in a sling for about two weeks. I faintly recall some pain but I vividly remember my awkwardness as a "lefty", especially at mealtime.

Another vivid Boulder memory centers around my little sister Alliene, who was eighteen months younger than I. Our parents had left us alone for a short time and had given us strict orders not to get into something (I've forgotten what but I'm sure it was something we were not to eat). Well, you know what happened. We did exactly what we had been told not to do. Of course, we were caught and had to give an account for our disobedience. I was such a coward and tried to blame my sister although I had probably been the ringleader. Allien took her punishment like the brave little girl she was. I thought I was home free until she blubbered through her tears, "Glennie did it, too." And then I caught a well-deserved paddling.

Other brief flashes of memory include: my displeasure at having to take an afternoon nap. I was sure "nap time" was my sister's fault because she was a little girl and needed extra rest. I didn't need rest but had to lay down so Alliene wouldn't feel picked on. I recall how I envied the "big kids" who got on the big yellow bus to go to school. I had to stay home and take naps. I remember once we had a heavy rain that flooded the little irrigation ditch that ran near our house. There were fish swimming in it and I caught one with my bare hands. That was pretty exciting. By far the most significant thing that happened during our sojourn in Boulder, and the most exciting for my parents, was the birth of my brother John on September 15, 1933. I remember absolutely nothing about it.

ON THE RANCH IN WESTERN KANSAS

Sometime not long after Johnny was born, likely in the late fall 0f 1933, we moved back to a cattle farm in western Kansas south of where I had been born. I was past 5 years old and had not yet started first grade. But I was big enough to have my share of chores, probably much like the chores performed by the kids on the TV program "LITTLE HOUSE ON THE PRAIRIE". Our house was heated by an old fashioned stove. There were scarcely any trees on the prairie so we had to burn whatever fuel was available. It was a cattle ranch so you can guess the fuel that was available. There was lots of "cow patties" out in the pasture. This manure, when dried, made an excellent fuel which was cheap, plentiful and renewable. It was my job to take my little red wagon out in the pasture and collect the dried cow patties.

Another chore was to help herd our cattle. Dad would put me on a horse and designate an area where I was to keep the cattle grazing. There wasn't much to it, really. The horse did most of the work. It was really very boring and sometimes my mind wandered. If I neglected to keep the reins secured on the saddle horn the horse would lower its head to get some grass. This would jerk the reins out of my hands and without the reins I had no way to control the horse. If I got off the horse to secure the reins I was too small to climb back in the saddle. Consequently, I had to lead the horse back to where someone could help me remount or let the horse wander aimlessly wherever he chose. I made quite a few trips back to the house for help.

But the chore I like best involved riding around the pasture with my dad in our Model T Ford. Whenever we came to a gate, dad would open the gate and ask me to drive the car through. The old 1923 Model T was a pretty simple machine. I just had to push a foot lever and it would move forward. But driving through pasture gates was the full extent of my car exploits as a six year old. I have two other sharp memories of life on the Kansas ranch. Like all Kansas ranches ours had a windmill to pump water for the cattle and horses. Dad had to do some repair on our windmill so he climbed up the ladder to the platform where he could work on the mill. I was standing below watching. Suddenly dad cried a warning and before I knew what was happening something hard and heavy hit my head. Dad had dropped his hammer and it plummeted down, cutting a gash on my scalp. It bled profusely and I wailed loudly, crying for mama. Dad tried to come to my aid but I had had enough father-son bonding. I wanted my mama.

The other memory has to do with Rex, the German shepherd dog we had on the ranch. Rex was trained to round up cattle and drive them into a corral. Unfortunately for the cattle, Rex had a bad habit of biting the tails of recalcitrant cows. We had numerous bob-tailed cows in our herd. It was great fun watching Rex round up the cows but it was no fun for the cows who had their tails nipped. It was especially hard on the tailless cows during the warm summer days when flies were abundant. With their "fly swatters" removed by Rex they had no defense against their pesky blood-sucking enemies. This reduced their ability to gain weight. Dad solved the situation by selling Rex to a traveling salesman. A few months later we heard that the salesman, accompanied by Rex, was involved in a bad car accident and Rex was killed. I don't remember the fate of the salesman.

DEATH STRIKES OUR FAMILY

By far the most traumatic event of my young pre-school life was the sudden, unexpected death of my little sister Alliene. She was eighteen months younger than I and was my closest friend and playmate. Isolated as we were, she was often my only playmate. In the spring of 1934 our parents had left the ranch and dad was conducting evangelistic services. In May the weather was warm and we were living in a small motor home which had been constructed on a Model-T truck chassis. In those days it was called a "truck house." Before I was born dad and mom had conducted evangelistic services in Kansas, Oklahoma and Arkansas, living in the truck house. One night near the end of May in 1934 Alliene complained of a bad headache. As the night progressed her headache kept getting worse. In addition she got violently sick and threw up repeatedly. She began to hallucinate and spoke of seeing beautiful white horses. Mother believed she was seeing a vision of some heavenly scene that spoke to the heart and mind of a little ranch girl. A doctor was summoned and arrived early on the morning of May 26 but there was nothing he could do. Alliene had inexplicably been called to walk through the valley of the shadow of death and was now in the arms of the Good Shepherd. The cause of Alliene's sudden death after only a few hours of illness was never satisfactorily explained.

The doctor theorized that her violent vomiting may have ruptured a blood vessel and she may have bled to death internally.

As much as I missed Alliene and mourned her death it was nothing compared to the devastating sorrow it brought to my parents. My dad was particularly overcome by the loss of his only little girl. He became ill and went into deep depression. He spoke of dying and actually called me to his bedside to tell me good-bye. He didn't have much to leave me but told me that he wanted me to have his hammer after he was gone. Through this whole episode my mother was the steady rock of the family. She had an eight month old baby, a six year old son plus an ailing husband for whom she had to stay strong. Mother's personal relationship with Jesus Christ was the source of her strength. The comforting, empowering presence of the Holy Spirit was a sustaining reality that enabled her to triumph over the forces of death and sorrow. She also had many Christian friends who comforted and encouraged her. I recall a black Christian brother who came to us and prayed for dad's recovery and encouraged mom. Mom's faith in her Lord prevailed and daddy began to recover. He gained his appetite, reclaimed his hammer and was active once again.

Not long after Alliene's death my parents moved the truck house to a site at the edge of a tiny Kansan town called Beeler. It was here that I was enrolled in first grade in the Beeler one room school house that served all eight elementary grades. There were probably no more than twenty-five students enrolled all served by a couple of teachers. I loved being in school but I didn't like going to school. Let me explain. I had to walk several blocks to school. There was a group of older boys, probably third and fourth graders, who accosted me on the way to school. They tried to scare me by threatening to cut off my ears. And they succeeded. I was terrified every time I ran into these boys. Mother tried to calm my fears and assured me the boys were only teasing me. But I wasn't sure she was right. I had seen their pocket knives.

You may wonder how two school teachers in a one room school can teach eight grades. As I remember the two or three first graders were in one front corner of the room. The teacher would spend several minutes teaching us and then would give us an assignment that would keep us busy until she returned. She would then go on to another grade and repeat the cycle. After a while she would come back and answer any questions then teach us again and give us another assignment. My favorite subject (next to recess) was reading. I avidly read everything I could lay hands on including directions on cans, cereal boxes and Sears catalogs.

I was a wiry little guy and thoroughly enjoyed recess activities even though our play- ground was mostly bare dirt. There were three basic pieces of playground equipment, swings, see-saws (teeter totters) and a leg powered merry-go-round, my favorite.

One of my most vivid memories of our final year in Kansas has to do with the horrible dust storms that swept across Kansas, Nebraska, Oklahoma and parts of eastern Colorado. The dust storms were the result of both man-made and natural factors. The man-made factors included over cultivation and failure to farm so as to impede wind erosion. The natural factors included pervasive drought, strong winds and ultra-fine, barren soil. These factors combined to produce monstrous dust storms that swept across the vast plains of western Kansas where we lived.

One afternoon, probably in the early summer of 1934, we were traveling in our Model-T Ford several miles from home when we were overtaken by a huge, swirling black cloud of dust. Although it was mid-afternoon, in moment we were enveloped in gross darkness. It was impossible for one to see his hand in front of his face. Dad could not see to drive but it was imperative that we continue moving until we could find shelter. The fine dust was a killer if subjected to it for too long. Also, there was great concern for my baby brother, Johnny, who was less than a year old. To keep moving dad got out of the car and holding on to the right front fender he walked on the right edge of the road.

With his feet he could feel the edge of the pavement. Mom guided the car as dad instructed. I think my job was to tend to Johnny. There was no panic but real concern. Mother asked me to join her in prayer as we asked God for protection and shelter. Step by step dad guided us down the road. At last we saw a beacon of hope. A dim red glow from a yard light penetrated the murky air. We turned off the road and found shelter and safety in the farm house nearby. Our prayer had been answered.

People find it hard to believe how penetrating the fine, wind-blown dust actually was. It would penetrate houses even though the doors and windows were tightly closed. In order to protect us from this dust inside the house the farmer's wife spread damp bed sheets over our beds to trap the suffocating dust. In the morning the sheets were black signifying they had done their job well. After treating us to a hearty breakfast the farmer and his wife sent us on our way. Although the dust storm had passed on there remained drifts of dust like black snow piled against fences and buildings.

In addition to drought and dust storms there was another plague that afflicted our part of Kansas, jack rabbits. If a crop managed somehow to survive drought and dust these voracious critters would devour whatever vegetation they could find. To reduce the rabbit population the ranchers and farmers would sponsor a "jack rabbit drive". This was an exciting event for a young boy. Here's how it worked. A woven wire fence enclosure with a very wide mouth that narrowed near the enclosure was erected by the farmers. Then by foot and by vehicles the rabbits were flushed out and directed toward the enclosure. Hundreds if not thousands of rabbits were trapped in the enclosure where they were killed . The carcasses were frozen and shipped to large urban areas for food.

Jack rabbit drives were big community events and there were special activities for the children. I remember winning a foot race and receiving a few packs of penny chewing gum as first prize. Yes, you could actually buy a pack of gum for one cent. I gave some sticks away but not to Johnny. He was still a baby and mustn't have chewing gum.

The lush color of this chrysanthemum illustrates the contrast between arid Kansas during the dust bowl years and the colorful foliage of North Carolina.

CHAPTER 2

GOOD-BY DUSTBOWL, HELLO NORTH CAROLINA

After I completed first grade dad and mom began giving serious thought to leaving Kansas. The economic depression was in full swing. The drought and dust storms had devastated farmers and ranchers. Many in Kansas and Oklahoma were leaving, most headed west to California. An itinerant preacher, Mr. Posey King from North Carolina, met my parents in Kansas and strongly urged them to come to North Carolina and help him "pioneer" a Pentecostal church there. After much prayer and discussion with family and friends my folks decided to go east. North Carolina was to be our new home.

The trip from the barren brown plains of drought-ridden Kansas to the lush green fields of North Carolina was an exciting experience for a seven year old boy. It was my first long trip in our motor home and I loved the adventure. The Model-T truck engine that powered our home on wheels did well on level ground but the steep hills of the Missouri Ozarks was another story. On long hills the engine would stall and force us to stop. Dad had an answer to that problem. When we stalled he would set the brake while mom and I got out and blocked the rear wheels. With the wheels blocked to prevent rolling back, dad released the brake, revved up the engine, then released the clutch and lurched forward until we stalled again. This process was repeated until we reached the top of the hill. Mom and I would then get aboard and off we would go once more. It was great fun but I think I enjoyed it more than mama.

It was a treat to see the summer greenery that greeted us as we traveled east. It was peach harvest time in Illinois. Dad got a job picking peaches in one of the orchards so we stayed there until harvest was over. Those peaches were super big, sweet and luscious. We enjoyed them immensely. Even little Johnny, almost two, was big enough to get in on the treat. We stayed in Illinois long enough to make good friends of the people who owned the orchard. Some years later on a trip back to Kansas we were able to visit them again.

WE ARRIVE IN NORTH CAROLINA

Fortunately, there were still some weeks of summer remaining when we arrived in North Carolina. We located near the small city of Reidsville in the tobacco growing, Piedmont region of the state. The balmy weather made it possible for us to live in the motor home until we could locate more permanent housing. We camped in a wooded area near where dad and Mr. King hoped to build a new church. Dad pitched a tent and installed a wooden floor. This served as mom's kitchen where she prepared meals and where we ate. At night we slept in the truck house. We had running water from a nearby natural spring. Actually, I did the running to the spring, returning with a little pail full of water. It took me several trips to replenish our water supply.

Our camp site was quite pleasant for a seven year old boy. There were lots of small critters in the area, particularly birds, squirrels and lizards. The lizards were the only ones I could get close to so I specialized in getting acquainted with these little guys. One thing I learned very quickly was that a lizard's tail is a very fragile part of its anatomy. It was designed to be fragile so that it would break off easily and allow the rest of the lizard to make its escape. But I did manage to catch one now and then. I tried to make pets of them but they were very hard to domesticate. One died and I made a casket from a match box and conducted my first funeral service. It was easy to dig a grave site in the soft sand with a big spoon. I buried the little critter and knelt down for a while, thinking about death. I wondered if there were pets in heaven. I sure hoped so.

Our summer camp-out was mostly a pleasant experience for me and Johnny. I'm sure it was less pleasant for our parents. I remember one night that was definitely unpleasant for them. Their bed was on a raised platform in the front area of the truck house. Johnny and I slept on a mat on the floor beneath them. On this particular night I was awakened by loud shouts and great commotion. It was quite frightening because I didn't know what was happening. As it turned out, hornets had invaded their bed space and stung them severely. When I awakened they were engaged in all-out warfare against any hornets remaining alive. This episode probably hastened their search for a more permanent place to live.

Lack of money was major problem as the folks looked for a place to rent. Dad had found a job working in a lumber mill but it only paid one dollar a day. That was sub-par even in the depth of the great depression but it was better than nothing. Eventually we were able to rent a crude one room log cabin with a loft. Dad, mom and little John slept downstairs. I was assigned to the loft where I slept on a corn shuck mattress. There were no stairs up to the loft. I had to climb up by means of wooden pegs that were driven in the logs. But that was no problem for an athletic seven year old. However, it did take a few attempts before I developed my climbing technique.

The shortage of money necessitated learning to live off the land. One of my chores was to pick wild greens which mother incorporated into our diet. I picked lamb's quarters, poke salad and dandelions. There were also wild berries to harvest. I particularly enjoyed going with mother to pick wild strawberries. They were small but very sweet and tasty. There were also wild blackberries to pick but they came with a price. The price was a multitude of chiggers. If you don't know what chiggers are, count yourself lucky. Chiggers are very, very small red larva of certain mites found in southeastern United States. They bury themselves into your skin in the warm, moist areas of your body – under your arms, between your legs and in back of your knees. They produce a terrible itch that is maddening.

The home remedy for these obnoxious pests was lard mixed with salt liberally spread over the affected areas. In theory, the lard prevented the chiggers getting oxygen and they consequently died. I'm not sure what the salt accomplished except it provided friction for better scratching. Modern research has proved neither effective. Nothing really, except time, eased the itching.

My next challenge was getting enrolled in a new school. Since we didn't live close to the school I got to ride the big yellow school bus. The new school was much larger than the one I attended in Kansas. Each class had its own room and its own teacher. The kids all talked funny and it took me a while to understand the Carolinian dialect. There was grass on the playground and more swings, slides, see-saws and merry-go rounds. The weather was much milder than Kansas which made recess more enjoyable in winter. I breezed through second grade and entered third grade wiser, stronger and fully capable of understanding North Carolina lingo.

Third grade was probably my most memorable in elementary school. What made it memorable was a little blonde by the name of Marjorie Law. I have never forgotten her name for she was my first love. I delighted doing playground exploits just to get her attention. Sometimes I expressed my affection more directly by tossing a paper wad in her direction or gently pulling a braid. What made it even sweeter was Marjorie showed some interest in me. I was overjoyed when I received the hardback book "Hans Brinker and the Silver Skates" as a Christmas present from her. I wanted desperately to buy her a present but mother carefully explained that we had absolutely no money to buy her a present. Not even a dime could be spared. I was devastated and cried but to no avail. For the first time I realized what it meant to be poor. For years I treasured my copy of "Hans Brinker" but I never saw Marjorie again after we left third grade. But the memory of a little blonde sprite who captured my heart remains.

While I was busy with school dad and mom were trying to establish a new congregation. The Pentecostal emphasis on the supernatural ministry of the Holy Spirit was a relatively new phenomena in the religious world. Many of the established churches opposed this emphasis and the folks experienced a great deal of opposition to their evangelistic efforts. But dad and mom persevered and a small body of "Spirit filled" believers was established. During the warm months, services were conducted under "brush arbors", a framework of upright logs or lumber covered on top by leafy branches.

In the meantime, the new believers under dad's leadership began construction of a church building. Volunteer carpenters, cheap lumber and enthusiasm for doing God's work made it possible to get a building erected quickly. One thing I didn't like about the new building, dad made me set up in the front row where he could keep an eye on me. I don't remember much about the church services. On thing I do remember that happened in church at this time. As a second grader I was proud that I could read most of the words in the hymn book. However, I was thoroughly confused trying to follow the verses as they were sung. I thought I should just go down the page like you do when reading a book. But after the first line I was lost because no one else was singing the second line except me. I finally figured out that songs and music were written differently than books and that each line of each verse had to be accompanied by its musical notes. Once I figured this out my singing improved greatly.

Two other events come to mind. It wasn't unusual for itinerant evangelists and preachers to pass through, hoping they would be invited to preach or conduct a series of services. One such preacher came by and spoke in the Sunday service. He used some language that didn't sit well with dad and mom so dad refused his request for further services and sent him on his way. Later they found out that he was an escaped convict posing as a preacher. The other memory involves a much more personal trauma for mom and dad. I was too young and too naïve to know much about birth. I knew more about death. However, one evening I knew something unusual was afoot. Mother was placed carefully in a car and taken away. She looked alright to me but others seemed very concerned. I found out that they had taken her to see a doctor. It was later that I understood she was expecting a baby but had miscarried. I think this occurred before Christmas, 1935.

A little over a year later the disappointment of the miscarriage was replaced by joy for the birth of a baby girl. Dad had never fully recovered from the loss of Alliene. Carol Virginia's arrival helped restore his zest for living. Nine years age difference separated me from the baby so my life wasn't impacted much. She was just someone to admire and occasionally hold on my lap and play my role of big brother.

My first bicycle, a used Sears Elgin. Dad bought it for
two dollars in Marietta, Ohio, across the Ohio river from
Williamstown, WVa. It provided wonderful freedom and
I could carry Johnny on the cross-bar or handlebars.

CHAPTER 3

GOOD-BY NORTH CAROLINA, HELLO WEST VIRGINIA

After the church building was completed and a congregation of believers established, dad and mom apparently considered their Reidsville mission accomplished. Dad was invited to candidate for pastor of a church in Mount Hope, West Virginia. Shortly thereafter he was elected pastor so we "pulled up stakes" and we moved to Mount Hope. At first we stayed in the nearby town of Oak Hill in a house owned by the coal company. But since dad wasn't employed by the coal company we couldn't remain there long. Mount Hope and Oak Hill were in the heart of the West Virginia coal fields. They were both "company towns" which means their economies were controlled by the big coal companies. Many of the workers lived in company owned houses and bought their groceries and clothes at company owned stores. The companies even issued their own money called script which was the medium of exchange at the company stores. The mines were deep underground, not open pit. The miners descended on little rail cars running on narrow gauge track. These same cars carried the coal back to the surface. It was a strange sight for me to see the miners emerge from down below covered all over with black coal dust. The only way you could tell a black man from a white was the ring around the eyes after the goggles were removed.

After we moved from the company house in Oak Hill we relocated in a decrepit little house near the city limits of Mount Hope. Dad and mom, with the little help I could provide, did their best to make it livable. They barely succeeded. There were no indoor toilet facilities but we were used to that. It was while we were living here that my Uncle Arley, mother's seventeen year old brother, hitch-hiked from Colorado to visit us. There was no guest bedroom so the folks put Arley, Johnny and I all in one double bed. They slept on a single bed placed in the living room. Baby Carol, now one year old, had her own crib.

While Arley was visiting a guest gospel musician stayed with us for a while. To accommodate him the folks went back to their bedroom, the singing evangelist got the single bed, Johnny and I had the privilege of sleeping on the floor and uncle Arley elected to sleep in our car. Arley was six feet four inches tall and built like a string bean. I'm not sure how he wrapped his lanky frame into the back seat of an old Chevrolet sedan but somehow he did it and survived the ordeal. I was sorry to see uncle Arley return to Colorado. It sure was nice to have someone else around from the mid-west who spoke like we did. Or at least spoke like dad, mom and I did. Johnny had already started speaking with a southern accent and he could spout colloquialisms like a native. If I told him to do something he didn't want to do do he would say, "I aint studyin' you." That meant, "Get lost, big brother."

Our experiences in this too small house in the summer of 1938 motivated the folks to earnestly look for a larger place to live. The fact that mom was pregnant with Charles David, while unknown to me, may have been an even greater motivating factor. Anyway, dad located an old house situated in rural area about a mile from Mount Hope. It was quite isolated in a wooded area but still close enough to town that I could walk to school. Our life improved after moving to the country. For me there were woods to explore, trees to climb and room to roam. An additional benefit was more and better food to eat. A flock of chickens soon were part of the landscape. More fried chicken resulted. Also, mom became very knowledgeable about edible mushrooms. We would go into the woods together and she would identify which ones to pick. Some were quite large. Mom sautéed these and they were delicious. My mouth still waters at the thought of them.

Homemade doughnuts were another special treat that mom let me help her prepare. I would roll out the dough and then press the doughnut shaped cookie cutter. Carefully, the raw dough was dropped into a deep pot containing hot fat. The dough sank into the hot fat and when it was cooked doughnuts popped to the surface. We would take them out and place them on some absorbent material until they had cooled a little bit. Then a little powdered sugar dusted on them while they were still warm and moist... mmm ...Maybe not the most healthful treat but oh so good.

Much of the land near where we lived was located above coal mine tunnels. Sometimes the underground coal would ignite and could burn for years. Some of the land I would walk across going to school had burning coal beneath it. I could see smoke arising through fissures in the ground.

Much of my social life revolved around activities in the church where dad was pastor. Pentecostals were still not widely accepted by the mainstream religious community so we found our friends within our own faith group. My best friend was the son of a miner who served as one of the church deacons. Most of the Assembly of God churches in the area were small. Once a month the churches of a region would unite in special services called a "fellowship meeting". These meetings were all day affairs with music and preaching in the morning followed by a big "pot luck" meal. In the afternoon there would be more music, testimonies and preaching followed by a smaller meal. The day would conclude with special music, a featured preacher followed by a time of fervent prayer. As a boy I particularly enjoyed the abundant food and the special music.

Each summer there was a camp meeting conducted in a tabernacle constructed on the church grounds at Mount Hope. This was an exciting time for a boy like me. All the Assembly of God churches in a large area (district) were involved in sponsoring the camp meeting. Some people stayed in cabins, others in tents or in homes of local believers. It was a family affair so there were kids my age with whom I could play. And play we did. One night after the last service was over I was running full speed and crashed into a tree stump. There was a sharp edge on the stump which collided with my left knee making a nasty gash. There was lots of blood gushing down my leg but mom soon took care of that with a pressure bandage that stanched the bleeding. I still wear a clearly discerned scar on my knee that is a reminder of that night in Mount Hope when the stump and I got together.

The most memorable event of our sixteen month sojourn in Mount Hope was the birth of another brother, Charles David, on December 24, 1938. The new baby boy was originally named Walter Elmo after dad's youngest brother and mom's youngest brother. I thought it was a weird name and protested loud and long. The name had already been officially registered and the folks were reluctant to initiate a change. But for some reason, I was very emotionally involved in getting the name changed. I had a good friend in school who was named Charles and I thought the combination "Charles David" was a very distinctive name. I cried, begged and persisted in my efforts to get the name changed until finally mother submitted the form that did the job. Later, Walter and Elmo became two of my favorite uncles. It's unfortunate their names were not perpetuated in our family. But I still think Charles David is a more attractive name.

After school was out in the summer of 1939 we pulled up stakes once more. Dad was elected pastor of a church in Williamstown, West Virginia. Of all the places we lived while I was growing up this was undoubtedly my favorite. We had a huge house, at least huge in comparison with other houses we had lived in. But it was very old-fashioned compared to modern standards. There was no indoor plumbing and no electricity. Natural gas provided the energy for light and heat. There were gas lamps on the walls and gas heaters in the rooms. The best thing about the house from the perspective of Johnny and I was its location. The city ball park and the playground were just across the street, our elementary school was two blocks north and the football field was a block south. We were in the heart of the action.

Although Johnny was almost six years younger than I he was now big enough to be a 'tag along'. He loved going to the playground with me. There was good selection of equipment. The big swings and high slides were our favorites. We learned increase the velocity of the slides by sitting on waxed paper. There were also two regulation horseshoe pits with official weight shoes. Pitching horseshoes was a popular pastime for men in the community. Johnny and I learned a lot just observing how the good players tossed their shoes. We developed an interest in the game and to this day enjoy competing when we get together.

I have fond memories of my school days in Williamstown where I began the sixth grade. There was an outstanding music department. There was an elementary school orchestra so mother took advantage of this and arranged for me to take violin lessons. The folks bought me a second-hand violin and I practiced faithfully for the two years we remained in Williamstown. I advanced far enough to have a chair in the orchestra and even played a solo once in church. But my music career ended when we moved again since private lessons were financially impossible. I think dad was relieved that he didn't have to listen to my practice sessions anymore.

There was also a good athletic department and I was introduced to basketball. We would have supervised intramural games. Basketball is a sport I learned to love and played it for many years as an adult. I also learned to swim at Williamstown which was situated on the Ohio river just across from Marietta, Ohio. I actually learned to swim in Muddy creek, a small tributary of the river. The Ohio was a big, deep river with lots of barges and commercial traffic. As I learned to swim better I thought it would be fun to graduate from the Muddy to the Ohio. One time I got out too far in deep water and grew very tired swimming back to shore. I went under a time or two and nearly panicked thinking I might drown. My guardian angel was on duty and I made it safely to shallow water. I never told mom or dad about this near drowning but I learned a lesson and never strayed so far out again.

The summer of 1940 is very significant in my memory. Dad and mom announced that we were going to take a trip back to Kansas and Colorado to see our relatives. It was adventure time. I could hardly wait for the trip to begin. The day finally arrived when the six of us got into our 1934 Chevrolet four door sedan and headed west. I was excited at the prospects of seeing cousins, uncles and aunts and two sets of grandparent I had not seen for five years. It was a long trip, 1400 miles from Williamstown to Boulder. Fortunately, the Chevvy sedan could go a lot faster than the old Model-T truck that had taken us east. But something the truck house had which the sedan didn't have were places to sleep and eat. We actually got to experience a motel and lunch from a roadside diner. Believe it or not, these were exciting new experiences for all of us.

Our arrival in Kansas brought a horde of relatives to see us. We got lots of invitations for meals and visits. There were numerous Kansas cousins to get reacquainted with. Uncle Melvin's youngest boys, Ronnie and Billy, and Aunt Nellie's youngest son Donnie, were near my age. We had fun just talking and going horseback riding across the Kansas plains together. Once my horse was startled by a coiled rattlesnake. Rattlesnakes were common on the plains and I had been warned to watch for them. Dad and some of his brothers competed in horse racing and that was fun to watch. I had forgotten what a good horseman dad was. One of the most enjoyable events for me was to sit and listen as my folks and the relatives shared events that had transpired the last five years. It was good to learn that the long drought was broken and dust storms no longer threatened. But drought, dust storms and plagues of jackrabbits and grasshoppers had taken their toll and many farmers had suffered ruin. My grandpa Brown and my four farmer uncles were determined to stick it out in anticipation of better days ahead.

After a week or so in Kansas we drove to grandpa and grandma Bluhm's home near Boulder, Colorado. Mother's two youngest brothers, Arley and Elmo, still lived at home. Although they were eight and six years older than I we had great fun together. Grandpa Bluhm had constructed a swimming pool on his berry farm and we really had a wonderful time in the pool. He had also built a special ride that used a tire fastened by pulley to a heavy wire. One end of the wire was fastened high in a walnut tree and the other end was secured to a post a few feet above ground, maybe sixty feet from the walnut tree. The tire was secured with a pulley brake at the high end of the incline. You would get in the tire, release the brake and down you would fly. Also, there were lots of berries to pick and eat, and no chiggers to worry about.

All good things must come to an end. Much too soon for me it was time to return home. We got good-bye hugs from the Bluhm relatives and then drove back to Kansas for another farewell with the Brown kin. On the trip back home we stopped in Illinois and visited the friends we had made where we picked peaches five years previously.

Several things stand out in my memory in connection with the year following our great vacation trip. In March 1941 our sister Violet Sharon was born. Her first name was chosen in honor of mother's sister, Violet Bluhm, who at this time was an ordained minister serving as an evangelist. Aunt Vi came to stay with us for some weeks while mother was regaining her strength. She was our link to all the family we had left behind in Kansas and Colorado.

Another vivid memory, I think it happened in the fall of 1941, was Johnny's serious illness with pleurisy. He developed a high fever and as a result he began to hallucinate. He scared me as he began to give graphic descriptions of the devil who apparently was chasing him. We all joined in prayer for his recovery. There was great rejoicing when his fever broke and he returned to normalcy.

Across the street from us lived a rather disreputable family with several children. One of the boys was about Johnny's age and another was close to my age. We spent a lot of time in the neighbor's house but not because we were particularly good friends with the boys. Dad did not permit us to have any comic books in our house. The neighbors had no such scruples and they had an abundant supply of the latest editions. So Johnny and I would sneak across the street to follow the adventures of Superman, Captain Marvel and all the other comic heroes without fear of being caught. We were both grateful for our undisciplined friends.

Williamstown is home to the famous Fenton Art Glass Company founded in 1905. It was a major employer for the community. I was fascinated by the huge furnaces in which sand, the raw material for glass, was melted to the right consistency for the glass blowers magic touch. Sometimes I could watch through open doors as the glass-blowers practiced their artistry. They produced beautiful vases, bowls, figurines and the like. The "seconds" and cracked were discarded in a huge scrap pile outside the plant. We boys would go through the scrap pile and rescue some near perfect treasures. Only a keen and knowing eye could detect why some of them were discarded. We took some of these on our trip to Kansas and Colorado to give us souvenirs. Near the end of our time in Williamstown one of the big furnaces collapsed and killed some of the workers. As a result the plant was closed and the economy of the town was seriously impacted. Many years later Donna and I visited Williamstown and found the glass factory prospering, bigger and better than ever. I looked around for the big scrap pile of rejects. I could not find it. Apparently that was a thing of the distant past existing only in my memory.

In addition to the glass factory catastrophe there were two other disasters that took place while we were in Williamstown. The first was the Ohio river flood. We lived on high ground above the river plain and were not in danger. Many businesses and homes were down near the river and the flood swept through these low lying areas with destructive force. The other disaster had to do with the bridge that connected Williamstown with Marietta, Ohio on the other side of the river. Marietta was a larger town and dad took us there occasionally. It was something we looked forward to with great anticipation. There was a special ice-cream store there which made massive double-dipper cones for five cents. Dad would almost always favor us with this delectable treat. Sometime doing our last year in Williamstown the wooden flooring on this bridge caught fire and was destroyed. The fire apparently weakened some of the steel structural material and the bridge was closed a long time for repairs. The bridge closure didn't really affect us personally...except it removed any hope of getting another one of those super ice-cream cones.

Because money was so scarce we never had many toys and what we did have were mostly homemade. Over the years I made kites, model airplanes and rubber band powered tractors. However, as I entered my teens I desperately wanted something more sophisticated. It was a glad day when dad presented me with my first bicycle. It was used, had big balloon tires, and needed paint badly. But what could you expect for two dollars? Boy, was I proud of that bicycle. The bike hadn't been used for a long time and the tires were badly deteriorated. But they still held air and that was good enough for me.

One day I was speeding down the street, pedaling for all I was worth. Suddenly, there was a loud bang and the bike began to vibrate. I had a vivid imagination and I fantasized that I was going so fast I was breaking the speed limit. I imagined the bang was the result of police shooting at me. I pumped all the harder trying to escape. It was too late. There was another bang and the bicycle vibrated all the more and would barely move. Reality took over and I realized that both tires had blown out. I sadly pushed my wounded bicycle home. But I was eventually able to get new tires and continued to enjoy the glorious freedom my old bike provided.

The horrific historical act of 1941 was the dastardly sneak attack on Pearl Harbor by the Japanese on December 7. I was almost fourteen years old and remember the day clearly. We had just returned from church when we heard the attack announced on the radio. Very shortly thereafter President Roosevelt officially declared war against the Japanese empire. The next four years were lived under the cloud of World War Two. Two cousins plus uncles Arley and Elmo were called to defend their country. Eventually, all returned safely.

On horses in Kansas while visiting relatives here
and in Colorado. Dad holds 2 1/2
Year old Carol and Johnny and I are on the other horse.
I'm 12 and Johnny is nearly 7. Likely July 1940

CHAPTER 4
CEDAR BLUFF, VIRGINIA

To my dismay, in the summer of 1942 dad decided to resign as pastor of the Williamstown church and accept the pastorate of a church in Cedar Bluff, Virginia. Williamstown is situated on the Ohio river in the northwest area of West Virginia. Cedar Bluff is in the southwest part of Virginia, just a few miles from the most southern extension of West Virginia. However, culturally there was a wide separation between the two towns. Williamstown, located on the east side of the broad Ohio river, was quite cosmopolitan for a small town. Cedar Bluff was much more provincial located in the foothills of the Allegheny mountains. These mountain folk were mostly poor but extremely independent. Some lived far back in the hills, totally inaccessible by motor vehicles. I became good friends with one of the boys in church whose family lived way up in the hills. You could only reach their house by walking down the railroad tracks to a trail that led up into the hills. The trail eventually led to a precarious swinging bridge across the Clinch river and then on up to the isolated house where this family lived. It was always an adventure to visit the Lowe family.

The school systems in West Virginia and Virginia were different. Virginia's public school system was based on eleven years, West Virginia's on twelve. As a consequence there was some confusion about which grade I should enter. Eventually it was decided that I should be placed in the eighth grade which was theoretically equivalent to West Virginia's ninth grade. I found the classes quite easy and my home-room teacher wanted to advance me but the principal vetoed her. The one year I had in Cedar Bluff's public school was interesting socially if not challenging academically. I enjoyed a brief infatuation with Nell who responded to my attention by giving me a ring to wear. This was my first infatuation since Marjorie in the third grade. But our socializing was strictly limited to school. There was no dating. I would have been terrified at the prospect of taking a girl on a formal date. Like most Junior High romances this one waned after a few months. My emotional highs once again became linked to sports like football and basketball rather than to girls.

What a difference seventy years have made in our public schools. Two examples come to mind. At Cedar Bluff every Friday morning before lunch there was a chapel service for all the students. Pastors from the local churches were invited to speak. Once when dad was speaking he ran over the allotted time, greatly embarrassing me. In addition to chapel we also had what was called "released time" Bible classes after regular classes were concluded. These Bible classes were not compulsory and parents had to approve a student's attendance. Nevertheless, many students were enrolled.

World War Two was in full swing during our time in Cedar Bluff. Many local men had either been drafted or had enlisted in the armed forces. As a result of the manpower shortage the town fathers asked dad if he would serve as town constable and administrator of the town water system. Dad agreed to do so but with some misgivings about the constable position. He resolved the misgivings by not wearing a pistol. It was a small town with minimal need for law enforcement. The water system job consisted primarily of reading and recording meters and sending out water bills. It became a family endeavor. Johnny helped by jumping down from the town truck as dad drove and reading the meter. Dad would record the reading and drive to the next customer. I just rode my bicycle around town to read and record the meters assigned to me.

In September 1942 I began high school. Cedar Bluff was too small to have a high school. Nearby Richlands was the largest town in the area and Cedar Bluff and other surrounding communities bussed their student there. My freshman year was a time for getting acquainted with other students and the faculty. Gradually I discovered there was a subtle division within the student body. It was nothing overt or clearly defined. It was just a "below the surface" attitude that pervaded the campus. In my sophomore year the division became more obvious as the campaign for class officers developed.

Candidates for the various class officers were nominated and the rivalry became largely a popularity contest between the local students and those bussed in. I was the out of town candidate for class president. I and my boosters waged a spirited campaign with lots of posters proclaiming 'BROWN FOR PRESIDENT'. The 'out of towners' must have outnumbered the 'in towners' since I won the election. The high school principal soon gave me my first official duties as sophomore class president. "Brown, I want those election posters pulled down and this campus cleaned up," he growled.

My primary sports interest at this time was football. I helped organize a town team for Cedar Bluff and we arranged Sunday afternoon games with a team from Richlands. Dad found out I was playing football on Sunday and he forbade me to continue playing. I was our team quarterback and if I didn't play there was no one to take my place. When our next game was scheduled in Richlands I decided to sneak away and play in defiance of dad's order. To my chagrin at half time I spotted dad sitting in his car watching the game. He permitted me to finish the game but afterwards we had a long talk. He explained why he would not give me permission to play Sunday football. His congregation considered it to be sinful and if he let me play it would create serious problems for him with the church. He asked me to promise that I wouldn't play any more on Sunday. Reluctantly, I gave him my word and kept it.

The competitive spirit between Cedar Bluff and Richlands extended beyond school and sports activities. One night some guys from Richlands were attending a party in Cedar Bluff. Several of us from Cedar Bluff were also there. After the party these two groups began hassling one another and a fight was in the making. Someone suggested that rather than a large brawl that each group choose a representative champion to slug it out. Richlands picked its man, a good looking big guy. To my dismay, I was designated to oppose him. I never went looking for a fight but occasionally one was thrust on me. On this occasion I was fighting against a heavier, more compact fellow. My chief advantages were quickness and longer arms. We struggled on even terms for awhile but eventually my longer reach began to take its toll. As I gained the upper hand I preceded to give the Richlands rep a thorough whipping. The boys from Cedar Bluff went home rejoicing in victory. There was an unexpected but good result from this fracas. The fellow I defeated became a friend and supporter. I think he may have advised his friends, "Don't mess with that preacher's boy." Anyway, I never got challenged to another fight.

I experienced several teen-age escapades while we lived in Cedar Bluff but just one of which I am truly ashamed. I had a friend named Melvin who lived several blocks from us. His parents were separated and he lived with his mother. Whenever I wanted more freedom at night I would ask to spend the night with Melvin. His mother was not nearly as strict as my folks. One night Melvin and I were just hanging out together, walking down the railroad tracks. We had nothing in mind nor any particular destination. The tracks led to a railroad trestle that went above the main road through town. We watched the traffic beneath the trestle for awhile and then I got the idea that it would be fun to pepper the cars with gravel as they passed beneath us. There was plenty of ammunition since the railroad ties were anchored in pebble size gravel. The gravel bounced off the first victim as the car slowed but kept going. The lights of another approaching car was the signal to prepare our next salvo. We timed the drop of the gravel so that it intersected the car just as it arrived below the trestle. Again there was the clang of rock on metal and glass. However, this time the driver slammed on his brakes, jumped out of his car, and began to scramble up the embankment in pursuit of us. We took off running as fast as our young legs would carry us. The angry driver never had a chance as we disappeared into the night. We ran all the way to Melvin's house, crawled into bed, and found security under the blankets. Our guilty consciences made us uneasy for a few days, fearful that we may be discovered. However, the nefarious deed remained our secret, a secret I am not proud of. It was a stupid, senseless act that could have led to a bad accident. Unfortunately, teen-agers sometimes do stupid and senseless things, even (or maybe, especially) preacher's kids.

Two momentous events happened during our Cedar Bluff sojourn. In August 1942 sister Barbara Eunice was born. Thirteen months later in September 1943 our sister Faith Lavon greeted us. We were now a family of seven children plus dad and mom.

Nine mouths to feed placed a heavy responsibility on our parents. As a teen and the oldest child, dad began to look to me to provide some financial help. Any kind of jobs for 15 year olds were scarce. Dad decided to become a Fuller Brush representative and I was his designated salesman. I went door to door trying to hawk brushes, brooms, and assorted household items during the summer of 1943. Unfortunately, I was only a mediocre salesman and didn't add much to the family finances. I was glad when the summer sales season was over.

For the summer of 1944 dad had made arrangements with his wheat farmer brothers for me to work for them during harvest. Shortly after school was out dad drove me to the depot to catch a train to Kansas. The war was at its height and the train was crowded with troops. As a result I had to stand for much of the trip. But this could not dim my enthusiasm for the work adventure which I was anticipating. I wasn't sure what to expect but was sure it would be better than trying to sell Fuller Brushes.

Dad's younger brothers, George and Walter, were my new bosses for the summer. They met me at the train station and welcomed me to Kansas. They left me at Grandpa and Grandma Brown's farm house where I was to bunk. As a sixteen year old I had a lot to learn before I could be a productive worker. George and Walt were patient instructors and both had a good sense of humor. I was introduced quickly to the big IHC W40 tractor that I was to drive during wheat harvest. Before trusting me with the task of driving the big tractor in harvest I had to learn how to operate it on less critical turf. I got to pull a disc and plow during the learning process. My uncles gave me free rein to practice and before long I had developed enough skill and confidence to be designated a member of the harvest crew.

Harvest time across the great mid-west wheat belt is an all-out battle to reap the ripened grain before wind, hail or rain destroys or compromises the harvest. And I was a soldier in this battle. My assignment was to drive the big tractor that I had so recently been introduced to. The tractor pulled the combine which harvested the wheat. The harvesting machine was called a "combine" because it combined two vital operations which formerly had required two different machines. The machine my tractor pulled both cut the wheat heads and then threshed out the grain. The threshed grain was then deposited in a large bin attached to the combine. When the bin was full a truck was positioned below the release chute to catch the grain. When the truck bed was full the grain was transported to one of the huge storage complexes that dot the mid-western plains. There the truck is emptied and the grain elevated up into the tall, round storage facility located along the railroad. Eventually, the grain stored in the elevators will be loaded into freight cars and transported to mills to be converted into breakfast cereal, chicken feed or whatever. The wheat farmer is the most important cog in this whole process.

Although I was only a boy I was treated like a man and did a man's work. Seventy years ago tractors did not have enclosed, air-conditioned cabins as they do today. The tractor driver was exposed to blistering sun as well as a cloud of wind-blown dust and chaff. Nevertheless, I loved the work and the comradery of the harvest team. An important part of the team were the women who prepared the meals. At mid-day they served the main meal of the day and it was a veritable banquet. It was not unusual to have two, sometimes three, main course meats. Fried chicken, steak and sometimes augmented by fried pheasant were regularly featured. There were heaping bowls of mashed potatoes and gravy, plenty of homemade bread and butter, various salads and desserts with lots of iced tea and/or lemonade. After such a repast I was fortified for an afternoon of hard, dirty work.

Saturday night was always the night that the harvest crew, men and women, went into town. The town in our case was Ness City, the county seat, with a population of possibly one thousand. The women went shopping primarily for groceries and a chance to visit with other women. The men scattered, some going to the pool hall, some gathering in groups at various sites, discussing the weather, crop production and other pertinent topics. For me it was a time to be with my cousins and hang out with them. There wasn't much going on in Ness City, even on Saturday night. Nevertheless it was a welcome break in the routine and I had lots of fun with cousins Wilma and Jean, daughters of Uncle Jess and Aunt Molly.

Sunday was normally set aside for church and relaxation. Only on rare occasions, such as an impending storm threatening the harvest, would we ever work on Sunday. The home church for grandma Brown (grandpa had not yet become a believer) and for uncles George and Walter was the Assembly of God in McCracken. McCracken was even smaller than Ness City but farmers came from miles around to worship there.

I discovered that summer farm work didn't end when harvest was over. I was put to work disking land for the fall planting of grain. This was not nearly as exciting as harvest. I was on the tractor all day by myself going around and around a huge field. Each round turned over about a twelve foot swath of fertile black soil that was the seed bed for next year's crop. It may not have been the ideal job, but boy, was I glad to have a job. I was paid a princely wage of eight dollars a day and by the end of summer I had a sizeable nest egg to take home. There was never any question but that this would help provide for the whole family.

Upon returning from Kansas I began my junior year of high school. It was a disappointing year in several respects. I loved to play football and was excited about going out for the varsity team. Seniors had the backfield positions locked up. The coach assigned me to play tackle, a position I wasn't familiar with nor wanted to play. However, I gave it my best shot and played enough to win my football letter. But before football season was over dad resigned as pastor of the Cedar

Bluff church. He announced that we would be moving back to North Carolina. Since we moved in November I missed the final games and the awards ceremony. Also, the move ended my dream of playing quarterback on our varsity team. In retrospect, that was probably a good thing. I played recklessly and could easily have been injured.

While in Cedar Bluff I went through a difficult period as I transitioned from a boy into an adolescent. My parents never talked to me about sex and so I was pretty ignorant about the hormonal changes that were taking place in my body as I entered puberty. Of course, I picked up some information from reading and in school. However, I had no one to talk to who could explain about nocturnal emissions (wet dreams) or urges to masturbate, things common to teen-age boys. My brothers were far too young to be taken into my confidence and dad never initiated any "birds and bees" kind of talks. I didn't know a lot about sex but one thing had been made very clear. There were to be no sexual relations outside of marriage. That became so much a part of my understanding that it remained a strong bulwark that protected me from pre-marital sex. I have never talked to my brothers and sisters about their own experience with puberty. I suspect that our mother was a very good teacher and guide for the girls as she prepared them for adulthood. Maybe dad became more open with the younger boys. I'll have to ask Johnny sometime when we are together.

Driving an ancient, steel-wheeled tractor on
Granddad's Kansas wheat farm. 1944

CHAPTER 5

BACK TO NORTH CAROLINA

The move to Harmony, the little town in North Carolina where we initially located, was traumatic for Carol, Johnny and I who had to change schools again. As a junior in high school it was probably hardest on me. I was disappointed that Harmony had no football program. However, it had a basketball team and I wasted no time in going out and making the team as a forward. My athletic ability was a big factor in helping me gain acceptance as a new student. One of Harmony's chief sports rivals was Union Grove high school located in a small community about 15 miles from Harmony.

The move to Harmony must have been traumatic for dad and mom as well. Dad resigned his pastorate with no new church to go to. The plan was for him to minister as an evangelist until a church elected him as pastor. We shared a large house with a young Christian couple who were preparing to be missionaries to the native Americans. This arrangement was only temporary while the folks looked for a more permanent and private place to settle. After about two months they found a small farm near Union Grove so once again we moved. Carol, John and I had to enroll once more in a new school. Union Grove was my third high school I attended as a junior. Basketball helped me make the transition without excessive pain. The BB season was only half over when we moved so I went out for the Union Grove team and soon was on the squad. To play on two different basketball teams in the same year certainly produced some conflicting emotions, especially when we played each other.

The little farm which dad rented helped support the family. We had chickens, pigs and cows to supply eggs, meat and milk. We also had horses and/or mules for plowing and cultivation. One of our milk cows was a temperamental Jersey which had to be restrained with leg irons when milking her. Her persistent, vicious kicking could overturn the milk or cause injury. But she gave plenty of rich milk so dad kept her.

There was a small pond on the farm that was a favorite spot for Johnny and me when the weather warmed. Spring came early in this area of North Carolina so we thought it was warm enough to swim in late March or early April. The pond was dirty and was home to poisonous water moccasins but that didn't deter us from swimming. I was in the pond on a warm spring day in April 1945 when someone came by and said that President Roosevelt had just died. I was saddened by this news. FDR had been elected president when I was four years old and was the nation's leader through most of my life. I sensed it was the end of an era.

A cash crop in this area was cotton so dad decided we should plant cotton. I had a plot designated just for me. Raising cotton was worse than selling Fuller Brushes. I detested picking the stuff. It was hard, back-breaking manual labor. It was November before I finished picking my cotton. By that time the bolls were so weathered and deteriorated that I had to sell at a severely reduced price. But I was greatly relieved to have this farming experience behind me.

More to my liking was the type of farming I had experienced in Kansas. I looked forward to returning to another wheat harvest in the summer of 1945. When I got to Kansas, Uncle George and Uncle Walt informed me I was to be a truck driver rather than a tractor driver during harvest. This was a promotion I wasn't sure I was ready for. I was introduced to the big Ford truck that hauled the wheat from the combine bin to the huge grain elevators. After learning the gear sequence I was given a chance to practice driving down the farm roads. Despite my own uncertainty my uncles expressed confidence in me that increased my own confidence. After all, I was seventeen and lots of Kansan teens younger than I were driving trucks. So I became a truck driver and loved the dashes to the elevators and then back to the combine for another load.

After the 1945 wheat harvest in Kansas I traveled to Eastern Colorado to work for uncle Richard Stephen in his harvest. Uncle Richard was married to aunt Ruby, mom's youngest sister. They had a large farm in northeast Colorado near Sterling. Wheat ripens later as one goes north so I was able to work in both harvests. Since I was now an 'experienced' truck driver, uncle Richard assigned me that job. Aunt Ruby was a good cook so I continued to enjoy lots of rich, high calorie food. Hard work took care of the calories.

After uncle Richard's harvest was over I visited my Bluhm grandparents in Boulder. World War Two was not yet over. Germany had surrendered but Japan continued to fight. Uncle Arley had been transferred from England to Guam. Uncle Elmo was with the Army struggling against the Japanese in the South Pacific. After a short visit I went back to Kansas to continue with plowing and disking for the rest of summer vacation. On a warm day in August we heard the good news that Japan had surrendered and the war was over. President Truman hastened the end of the war by approving the dropping of atomic bombs on Hiroshima and Nagasaki. This persuaded the Emperor to sue for peace. President Truman's drastic decision saved tens of thousands of Japanese and American lives that would have been lost in a conventional invasion.

Returning home from Kansas, I was looking forward to my senior year of high school. At that time in North Carolina the school districts hired qualified high school seniors to drive school busses. I decided to take the test to see if I could qualify. My recent truck driving experience helped me be successful and I was hired as one of Union Grove's school bus drivers. The pay was only thirteen dollars a month, not much, but it went a long way in 1945. After delivering the school kids I could take the bus home so I always had a ride to school and back home.

Union Grove had no football team so I turned my full sports attention to basketball. North Carolinians are great basketball fans and the folks at Union Grove were no exception. Our home games were attended by raucous fans who cheered us mightily. We had a pretty good team and played in several regional tournaments. I was high scorer for our team and won 'honorable mention' at the state tournament in Winston Salem. The girl cheer leaders boosted my ego when they yelled, "Brown, Brown, he's our man! If he can't do it nobody can." However, I was brought back to earth when I heard a girl say, "He would be a good looking guy if his nose wasn't so long." Oh well, some you win and some you lose.

In the fall of 1945 dad was elected pastor of the Assembly of God church in Morganton, N.C. It was a picturesque town about seventy miles from Union Grove. For a while dad commuted back and forth to the Morganton church. In December it was decided the family would move to Morganton during the Christmas break. I think all the family was pleased at the prospects of getting settled in a more permanent location. All except me, that is. I was desperate to persuade the folks to let me stay and finish my senior year in Union Grove. The basketball fans came to my rescue and some parents offered to let me live with their family until the school year ended. The folks finally agreed that I could stay and complete my senior year.

After our family moved from the farm near Union Grove the landlady moved back in. Dad made arrangements with her for me to continue living there until the end of the school year. She was a nice, friendly lady and we got along fine. I missed the family but between basketball and other senior class activities I hardly had time to get homesick. I had one of the lead parts in the senior class play and that occupied lots of my time.

The family came back to Union Grove for my graduation ceremonies. I was pleased they were there as I was one of the senior class speakers. Although I was gradually gaining the independence of adulthood I was very emotionally attached to my family. I adored my sisters. Of course, I loved my brothers but they were just boys. My big brother instincts were focused more on my five little sisters. When I graduated Carol was a pretty nine year old blondie. Sharon was a cute six year old about to enter first grade. The "gold dust twins," Barbara and Faith, cherubic preschoolers, were almost four and three. Norma was just a chubby little baby. They owned my heart.

After graduation I returned to Kansas and Colorado for another summer of wheat harvests and farm work. This time I took along Rylan Weisner, a high school friend and basketball teammate. Rylan was a hard worker and my uncles really liked him. He was one of the few classmates I ever saw again after graduation.

Following another good summer of farm work I rejoined the family in Morganton. I was in a quandary as to what to do at this stage of life. I wanted to go to college but had no funds and could expect no help from my folks. Dad wanted me to find a job and remain in Morganton. The primary industry in this area of North Carolina was the manufacture of high quality furniture Dad arranged work for me at the Morganton Furniture Company. This company had been around for a long time and had an excellent reputation. I was not at all enthused about working in a furniture factory but reluctantly agreed to give it a try. After three days I had my fill of stacking oak lumber for chair parts. I knew this wasn't for me and quit without regret.

I was determined to go to college and figured a G.I. bill scholarship was my best route to get there. This meant I would have to enlist in some branch of the armed forces. Dad and mom weren't very pleased at the prospects of me entering the military. I had talked to them about enlisting when I was seventeen but they rightly refused to sign an age waiver. Now I was eighteen and didn't need parental consent. I was determined to enlist since I saw no other way to achieve my educational goals. All I needed to decide was which branch of service to enter. I chose to join the Army Air Corps, predecessor of the U.S. Air Force. It was a sad and tearful day when I kissed my parents and brothers and sisters good-bye. My bus ride taking me to the huge army base at Fort Bragg, North Carolina was a time of apprehension but also expectancy. The future beckoned and I looked forward to it with optimism. Eighteen year olds are like that.

PFC Brown vaulting over the Lowry Field Photo School
sign. Long closed, my eight weeks in the Army Air Corps
Photography School at the edge of Denver, was great
fun for a kid just turned nineteen, Spring, 1947.

CHAPTER 6
YOU ARE IN THE ARMY NOW

I arrived at Fort Bragg on October 4th but the military bureaucracy didn't get around to swearing me in until October 7th. I was assigned to a holding company while awaiting orders for my basic training assignment. During the day I was part of a clean-up detail that picked up cigarette butts and other trash around the base. I was able to be outside, the work wasn't hard and the chow was plentiful and usually edible. It was nothing like harvest chow but then the work was easier. After a couple of weeks I got orders to proceed to the Army Air Corps Basic Training Center in San Antonio, Texas. Once again I had a long train ride to look forward to. But this time there was no standing in the aisle for me. I was traveling first class on a "sleeper" all the way to San Antonio, thanks to my Uncle.

During World War Two the Basic Training Center was known as SAACC Field, an acronym for San Antonio Air Cadet Center. Although it officially was now named something else it was still popularly called SAACC Field. When I arrived I was quickly assigned to a basic training Flight, the Air Corps' equivalent of an infantry platoon. I was housed with fifty other men in a two story wooden barracks. The next ten weeks were a 'hodge podge' of classes, drills, rifle and pistol qualifications, physical fitness tests, short marches, long marches, parades and KP. The hours were sometimes long and demanding. As a result of high school sports and summer farm work I was in pretty good shape and had no problems with the physical demands.

It's funny the things I remember about basic training. I remember KP (Kitchen Police) duty as my least pleasant experience. It wasn't the work or the hours I minded although the hours could stretch from 4 a.m. until 8 p.m. (0400-2000 hrs.). What griped me was the arrogant attitude of some of the supervisors who treated us like slaves. The officer in charge of the mess hall was a "smart aleck" young Second Lieutenant who belittled and degraded the recruits who worked for him. He was probably a "90 day wonder" who had just graduated from Officer's Candidate School. He was everything I later learned that an officer should not be. Fortunately, we saw him infrequently since he didn't spend much time in the mess hall.

Most of the permanently assigned cooks who gave us ongoing supervision were a disgrace and would not be tolerated in today's army. One morning I watched the cooks as they prepared breakfast. They fired up the huge grills in preparation for scrambled eggs. As the grill got hot, cockroaches that had been hiding in the grill crevices began running wildly across the grill surface. As the roaches scurried about on the grill the cooks poured out the raw scrambled eggs, enveloping the roaches in the mixture. The enmeshed nasty bugs cooked along with the eggs and were then served to the unsuspecting recruits. Needless to say, one recruit had no eggs for breakfast.

A further memory is about the senseless 'horseplay" we sometimes engaged in. One of the favorites took place during the lunch time break. Often we would lounge around in the warm sun after lunch. If someone dozed off, as often happened, he was in danger of getting a "hot foot". It worked like this. Someone would pour lighter fluid on the shoe of the unsuspecting sleeper. Then a lighted match was applied and, presto, instant hotfoot. This had the potential for serious injury but I don't recall anything other than minor burns and embarrassment for the victims.

On January 7, 1947 I celebrated my nineteenth birthday. It nearly coincided with my graduation from basic training and Uncle Sam had a birthday gift for me. The gift was orders to report to the Army Military Police School at Carlisle Barracks, Pennsylvania. This was a very professional facility that provided eight weeks of training in law enforcement theory and practical training. A lawyer instructed us about the military legal system. Judo experts gave us training in this manual arts discipline. We were taught how to exercise mob control. A weapons instructor showed us how to modify twelve gauge shotgun shells so that they would disable a fleeing vehicle. It was interesting stuff for a nineteen year old but not exactly what I had envisioned doing.

About half way through the MP course I realized it had been four months since I had seen any of my family. This was the longest separation I had ever known and I was homesick. One Saturday morning in late January or early February we were released for the week-end. We could be gone until 2 a.m. Monday morning. I decided I would go home for the week-end. I had no car so I was forced to hitch-hike the 500 miles from Carlisle Barracks to Morganton. It was not unusual for soldiers to hitch-hike and people often picked them up. There were no interstate super highways in those days so traffic usually went slower. Even so, I made good time during the day and traveled about three hundred miles. After dark motorists were more reluctant to stop and I got stuck in High Point, N.C. for over an hour. Finally, after hitch hiking for 20 hours I arrived in Morganton about 7:30 Sunday morning.

The folks lived on a farm several miles from town. I knew no one was likely driving on the country road at this time of day so I took a taxi, arriving just as the family was getting up. There were shouts of greeting and I received a warm welcome. We had breakfast together and then it was time for them to go to church. I squeezed in the family car along with two brothers and five sisters. Dad let me out on the main highway, US 64, leading northeast our of town. I bid them good-bye and started hitch-hiking back to Carlisle Barracks.

By 1 a.m. Sunday night (Monday morning)I had gotten as far as Harrisburg, the capitol of Pennsylvania eighteen miles from my destination. But I could not get a ride beyond Harrisburg. It was the dead of winter, bitterly cold, and I was stranded on a lonely stretch of road desperate for a ride. There was nothing to do but shiver, endure and wait. Finally, around three o'clock that morning someone stopped and took me near the main gate of the base. It was past curfew time but I managed to slip into the barracks and into bed without discovery. By the time I had thawed and rested a bit, reveille sounded. It was time to get up and answer roll call. Had my unauthorized absence been detected? Apparently not as the Sergeant called my name without further remarks. I was home free after hitch-hiking a thousand miles for one hour with my family.

As the graduation date from the Military Police school drew near I received orders to my new duty station. I was delighted to discover I was being assigned to Randolph Field, Texas near San Antonio. There was warm weather in my future and this made me happy after a winter in Pennsylvania. My first week of duty as a newly minted Military Policeman was routine jeep patrol around the base checking traffic, illegal parking and other minor infractions. This was too good to last and very soon I was reassigned to guard prisoners. My duties involved guarding work details of prisoners from the stockade with a loaded shotgun. I had to keep them in view at all times and make sure none escaped. Fortunately, my career as a shotgun toting prisoner guard was short lived.

We were required to read the Squadron bulletin board daily. Usually it just contained routine information concerning Squadron activities. But on one particular day there was an announcement that really caught my attention. It said, "There is an opening for orders to Photography School at Lowry Field for a qualified candidate. If interested, see the First Sergeant." I lost no time in making my interest known. To my surprise, in a few days the first Sergeant called me to his office and told me that I had been selected for photo school. I was ordered to check out of the MP section and get ready for the flight to Lowry Field, Colorado. Yipee!

Lowry Field was located in Denver where my Uncle Arley and Aunt Pauline lived. Uncle Elmo, not yet married, also lived there. My Bluhm grandparents lived in Boulder only 40 miles from Denver. I looked forward to being near family once again. It was early March when I left Randolph Field. Previously, Uncle Sam had provided me with rail transportation but this time I was going to fly. I had never flown before and I wasn't sure what to expect. When it came time to leave I boarded the DC-3 which was the standard military transport of this era. We taxied out on the runway and I leaned back, closed my eyes, and tried to act real cool. I didn't want anyone to know that this was my first flight. The engines roared and the fuselage vibrated in sinc with the whirling propellers. After several minutes I cracked my eyes open to check how high we were flying. To my chagrin, we were still warming up on the runway.

We eventually took off and I settled back to enjoy my first airplane ride. The drone of the engines and propellers had a hypnotic effect and soon I was dozing for real. When I awoke some time later I looked out the port hole and saw huge drifts of snow below. After all it was March and snow was normal this time of year in Colorado. As I continued to marvel at the billowing snow drifts below questions began to form. Why weren't there any trees or buildings projecting up through the snow? Finally, it dawned on me that it wasn't snow drifts I saw but the tops of great fleecy clouds. Oh, well, it was my first flight.

I took to photography school like a duck to water. In addition to theory we had lots of practical experience both with cameras and in the dark room. Most of our camera work was done with a professional press camera called a Speed Graphic.

Instead of rolls of film the press camera used 4 X 5 inch sheets of film in a holder that was inserted in an adapter in the back of the camera. The light sensitive emulsion was covered by a hard plastic slide that had to be removed before opening the shutter. If you failed to remove the slide no light could reach the film, hence no picture. I learned this the hard way on more than one occasion.

Although photo school kept me busy during the day I had plenty of free time in the evenings and on week-ends. This gave me an opportunity to visit my relatives, especially on week-ends. Both my uncles attended Central Assembly of God, church with lots of young people. I often went with them and became acquainted with the youth group. Pastor McClure had two attractive daughters whom I admired, mostly from afar. Not long after I arrived at Lowry Field, Pastor McClure resigned and the church elected a young twenty seven year old evangelist named Charles Blair as the new pastor. His wife, Betty, was a gracious, attractive and talented young woman. I did not know it at the time but Charles would continue as pastor of this congregation for more than fifty years. A few years later I would return to Denver and be elected as youth leader of this exciting, growing church. But more about that later.

Upon graduation from Photography School I returned to Randolph Field, Texas for my new duties as an official Army Air Corps photographer. Long before video cameras and VCR's the military used 35 mm film strips as training aids. The official Film Strip Production Center was located at Randolph Field. Most of the employees were civilians skilled in air brush artistry. They would take raw photos and with an air brush eliminate unwanted background or foreground material, leaving only the pertinent item in view. I was assigned to be the photographer that would supply the raw photos for the artists.

Because some assignments required photos of classified material I had to be investigated by the FBI for Top Secret clearance. I heard that some of my acquaintances were curious as to why the FBI was asking them questions about me. Most of my assignments were projects that could be photographed locally. However, one major project had to do with a new 20 mm weapon that was being developed at Wright-Patterson Field near Dayton, Ohio. I was required to spend a couple of weeks at Wright-Patterson to complete this assignment. I enjoyed the change of scenery but it was an inopportune time for me to be gone from San Antonio. But military orders took precedence over other considerations.

To my delight, I discovered that I didn't have to wait until the end of my enlistment to enroll in college. Uncle Sam had an educational program that allowed active duty soldiers to enroll in night classes at local colleges or universities. In addition, there was an educational fund that paid the tuition. What a deal! Trinity University was located in San Antonio and I enrolled for night classes in trigonometry and geometry. I enjoyed math but my background in it was not very strong. However, I did well in both of these classes until I got orders to go to Wright-Patterson for two weeks. When I returned to these classes I was so far behind that I really struggled to catch up. I received a passing grade but I was frustrated, knowing I could have done much better.

The summer of 1947 was an interesting time for me. Quite a few of the recently graduated West Pointers had come to Randolph Field to take flight training. Included were several members of the undefeated West Point football team.

Among them was the famous "All American" fullback, Doc Blanchard, as well as the "All American" West Point quarterback. These famous sports figures were going to play football for Randolph Field. Even though my football experience was limited to a year in high school I decided to try out for the team. The coach assigned me to play end so I got to participate in the pass catching drills, receiving passes thrown by a superb quarterback.

In addition I had the thrill of scrimmaging against and tackling Doc Blanchard, the hard running fullback. However, I didn't have the expertise or experience to match the level of play of the college graduates and other older players. Although I still enjoyed football I made a decision to discontinue football and concentrate on basketball. Doc Blanchard completed his flight training and eventually ended his military career as an Air Force general. But to me he would always remain that hard charging all American fullback that I had tackled in scrimmage.

Randolph Field had a good basketball program. Each squadron had its own team and competed with other squadrons for the Base championship. But the squadron competition, as much fun as it was, was preliminary, like intramural play. After the squadrons completed the early season play the best players were chosen for the team that represented Randolph Field. I was one of the better players on the base and easily made the Base varsity team. We played local Junior College teams and other military bases. I thoroughly enjoyed the comradeship and competition basketball afforded.

Although my new life in the military was proving to be interesting and in many ways better than I expected, I still missed my family and high school friends in North Carolina.

Sometime, I think in the fall of 1947, I got permission to take leave. I was eager to visit my family again. It was actually my first leave, since you could hardly count the brief hour with the family when I hitch-hiked home from Pennsylvania. I didn't have much money since much of my meager pay check was automatically allotted to go home to help the folks. Consequently, I decided to try my luck hitch-hiking again. The first day I made pretty good time, getting as far as Shreveport, Louisiana which is about 400 miles from San Antonio. I remember Shreveport particularly because I was stopped by the police as I thumbed a ride near the edge of town. To my dismay the police ordered me not to hitch-hike inside city limits. I furtively walked through the city, raising my thumb to passing cars when I detected no police cars in the area.

Hitch-hiking in the late 1940's following World War II was quite common, especially among servicemen. There was some risk involved, mainly from reckless drivers, but it was not nearly the dangerous risk it is today. I don't really remember where I slept while on the road, probably in parks or some grassy wayside since the weather was warm. After my miserable experience hitch-hiking from Pennsylvania in January I never again made the mistake of long distance travel in winter.

I made my way across the southeast without further incident until I arrived in Statesville, North Carolina. This small city was the county seat of Iredell county where Union Grove and Harmony are located. Statesville is about eighteen miles from Union Grove where I had graduated from high school the previous year. It is about sixty miles from Morganton where my folks lived. I was debating whether to continue on to Morganton or to take a brief side trip to Union Grove to see some of my high school friends. Suddenly two bedraggled young fellows in an old flat bed Model A Ford drove up to where I was standing. One of them shouted, "Hey, Brown, do you want a ride?" I had no idea who they were but they apparently knew who I was.

It turned out they lived near Union Grove and knew me from basketball. So I decided to accept their offer and first go to Union Grove. The only place to sit was on a junky car seat that sat loosely on the flat bed of the old truck. I climbed aboard and soon discovered that my benefactors were "bootleggers" who were actually delivering some of their "white lightening" to customers in Statesville. I also detected they had been sampling some of their product. To my consternation they got the idea that they were being followed by police. I think they were paranoid as I didn't see any cops behind us. Nevertheless, they began to take evasive action, fleeing down one street and then switching to another. My perch on the loose seat on the flat bed became increasingly perilous as we wove in and out. A sharp turn caused the seat to begin to slide off the edge of the truck bed and I thought I was a goner. Fortunately, one of the fellows realized what was happening. He was able to reach around and grab me just before I went overboard. He could do this because there was nothing between us but air since there was no cab on the truck.

The bootleggers took me to where Rylan Weisner lived. He was my best friend and basketball teammate from high school. As the Weisner's brought me up to date on other classmates I realized that things would never be the same again. I was on a journey that would take me far from Union Grove. I was eager to get back home and see my family.

My first real visit home after enlisting in the Army Air Corps was a refreshing change from military life. I was eager to show off my new skill as a trained professional photographer. I had lots of photogenic subjects, five sisters, two brothers and mom and dad. Norma Jean was the baby and she along with four and five year old Faith and Barbie were my favorite subjects. We called Faith and Barb the "gold dust twins." They both had blond hair, were about the same size and were cute as a "bug's ear." Faith was the shy one, Barbie more outgoing but they were equally adept at stealing their brother's heart. Of course, my five sisters didn't monopolize all my time. There was some roughhousing with brothers John and David. I had to show off my judo training even though they were too young for any real competition.

The leave period passed all too quickly. Hitch-hiking back to San Antonio provided one very frightening experience. I was somewhere in the deep south, Mississippi or Louisiana I'm sure. It was late at night when I caught a ride with some rough-neck guys who had been drinking. They sped away down the narrow, fog shrouded, two lane road, going up to 80 miles per hour. I sat hunched up in the back thoroughly frightened. I had not yet made a commitment to Christ but that didn't prevent me from sending up fervent prayers for a safe escape from the "guided missile" speeding down the foggy, two lane highway. For some unaccountable reason the driver suddenly slowed down and turned off the highway into a farmer's open field near the road. The field was soft and this further slowed the vehicle. The driver decided to have some fun and began to do circles in the soft ground. This was my chance to make my escape. I threw open the back door and tumbled out of the car onto the soft field. I ran back to the highway with the sounds of the circling car still ringing in my ears. I caught another ride and eventually made my way safely back to Randolph Field.

Since my duties at the Film Strip Preparation Center did provide so much free time my supervisor assigned me as a photographer-in-training to the San Antonio Light, one of the daily newspapers in the city. I covered some of the sports events and worked in the dark room lab where the film was developed and printed. It was a good experience for a neophyte photographer. I also continued to take night classes at Trinity University.

Randolph Field was famous as the "West Point of the Air." It was here that fledgling air cadets were transformed into Army Air Corps pilots. (Actually, in 1947 the Army Air Corps ceased to exist and became a separate service, The United States Air Force). I would watch the cadets as they performed their aerial maneuvers and thought that I could do that. I decided to apply for air cadet training. After completing the paperwork I began a series of physical tests. While in this process I was informed that the Air Force had raised the minimum age limit for cadet training to nineteen years and six months. I was too young so had to drop out of the process. By the time I was old enough to reapply I had changed my mind. If I was to become a cadet I would have to extend my enlistment beyond three years. I decided to remain a photographer until my three year enlistment was completed and then leave the military.

In January 1948 I celebrated my twentieth birthday. It was to be the most significant year of my life. With the passing of my teen years I increasingly realized my own mortality and began to do some serious thinking about where I was headed in life.

Although I had been reared in a devout Christian home I had not really experienced a personal encounter with Jesus Christ. In fact, I had left home something of a rebel against the strict, sometimes legalistic, religious expectations I encountered at home. Actually, I wanted to do "my thing" without having to answer to God. Some of the reading I was doing in classes at Trinity University raised the disturbing concept that there was no God. If this were true it brought a certain short term comfort. It meant that I need not fear having to answer to God for my wayward ways since He didn't exist. But on the other hand, it produced long term despair and hopelessness since, if there was no God, there was nothing to look forward to but death. And it meant that my life had no real meaning since I was only an insignificant speck of protoplasm adrift momentarily in time. This was countered by the testimonies of my parents and other Christians who claimed to have had personal encounters with God. Was there really a God who got through to people on a personal level and made himself known to them? I knew many people who answered "Yes" to both questions.

However, one of the books I had been reading, "VARIETIES OF RELIGIOUS EXPERIENCE" by psychiatrist William James, claimed that nearly all religious experiences could be explained as natural psychological phenomena. Was this renowned psychiatrist correct? Was Christian experience all a subjective mirage? But James did admit he had run across an occasional, extremely rare experience that pointed to the intervention of an unnamed spiritual power some called God. As I mulled these things over in my mind I was forced to admit that I was hopelessly confused. I didn't know who or what to trust. I guess I was just an amateur agnostic searching for truth. Where did I find it? I had read the Bible but could it be trusted? Certainly many Christians, including my parents, replied with a resounding "Yes". But what about the critical scholars that argued, "No". Where did I go and to whom did I go to find authentic answers to these questions?

This was a painful time for a young man reared in a Pentecostal preacher's home now alienated from his roots. In many ways I was naïve and unprepared to deal with the arguments of materialists and humanists. I had no mentor or confidant with whom I could discuss my inner struggle. I certainly didn't feel comfortable discussing or sharing my doubts and spiritual battles with dad or even mom. I didn't think they would understand.

One night in March 1948 I returned from classes at Trinity. I often had time to do some serious thinking while waiting for the bus that I rode back to Randolph Field. Sometimes I would look up into the magnificent, star-studded sky and think to myself, "What a majestic, intricate universe swirls around up there. Many scientists say the universe is just a cosmic accident. But how could it happen without a creator God? Even if it is some kind of stupendous materialistic accident, how did the raw materials originate? And if there is a God who designed and put it all together, how can I be sure?"

These kinds of thoughts were filling my mind on this particular night in 1948. I recall returning to the barracks and climbing into the upper bunk where I slept. My body was still but my mind kept racing and sleep eluded me. I was desperate to find answers to the big questions roiling within... answers which would determine the direction of my adult life. As I lay in my bunk I came to a conclusion, very simple, yet so basic and foundational to my search. My conclusion was this: "If there really is a God like the Bible describes then He surely can communicate with me so that I know He exists." I decided to act on that simple thought.

About midnight I crawled out of my bunk and went to my photographic work place. I stood alone in the darkness of the main office and prayed a brief prayer. It went something like this: "God, I don't know if you really exist. If you do exist I don't know if you are interested in an insignificant soldier like me. But if you do exist, if you care for me, if you have a purpose and plans for my life as the Bible says and if you can get through to me so that I know you are for real then I want to know you and live for you."

After quietly praying I waited, not knowing what to expect, if anything. Suddenly the empty room was filled with an awesome presence. I was exhilarated but terribly frightened by this manifestation of a supernatural Being. In my fear I said, or thought, I'm not sure which, "God, don't come on so strong. I am not sure I am ready for this." Immediately the astonishing sense of a Divine Presence began to recede and I was left alone in the dark room, just as when I entered.

But now nothing was the same. God had amazingly responded to a young soldier's earnest cry. I was now convinced that the God described in the Bible really existed. His response to my simple prayer had been overwhelming. I was well aware of William James' efforts to reduce all religious experience to natural psychological explanations. But I knew that I knew that God had communicated his awesome presence to me. There had been no words, no religious hype, no soft music; just an overwhelming, incredible awareness of God's holy love surrounding me. I was sure did exist and that He responded to my sincere search for truth. However, I was still struggling with my promise to commit my life to the Lord. Was I really ready and willing to follow through on this promise? That was the next critical issue I had to resolve.

I wrestled with this question for the next week or so. It all came to a head one Sunday night in March 1948. I had gone to church and at the conclusion of the service I had gone forward to the altar area to pray. I prayed quietly but intensely for I was in a real spiritual struggle. My prayer was no monologue. Instead, I was engaged in a real dialogue with Jesus Christ. He was searching the very hidden places of my heart and bringing them to the surface. He confronted me with attitudes and ambitions that would have to be surrendered to His will. Could I fully trust Jesus Christ with my life? That was the decision He was calling me to make. One by one we dealt with the issues and I deliberately chose to trust the Lord with my life. In military terminology, it was an unconditional surrender on my part.

Actually, it was not totally unconditional. I had tried previously to live as I had been taught a Christian should live and I had always failed to measure up. I knew I could not keep the commitment I had made unless His Spirit provided the power to do so. Having been brought up in a Pentecostal pastor's home I had heard numerous sermons about the activity of the Holy Spirit. The text in Acts 1:8, "You shall receive power when the Holy Spirit comes on you..." was very familiar to me. I was equally well acquainted with the account of Acts 2 that tells the story of the Holy Spirit filling the disciples as they waited in obedience in the upper room in Jerusalem. I knew that after being filled with the Spirit they were charged with new spiritual power and new insight into spiritual truth. But I wasn't sure that God still acted in the same manner as He had done in apostolic times. So I shared my struggle with the Lord. "Jesus, you know I have tried to live as I thought I should but I was never able to fulfill my good intentions. If you still baptize believers in the Holy Spirit as you did in New Testament times then I desperately want to be empowered by your Spirit. I need help. I can't live for you without the power of the Holy Spirit. Please fill me with the Holy Spirit like you did your first disciples."

As I conversed with the Lord I became increasingly aware of His presence. I knew that Jesus was gloriously alive as the Bible describes. I was filled with gratitude for what God was doing in my life. Quietly but fervently I began to thank Him and praise Him. "Thank you, Lord, for caring about people like me. Thank you for loving me and dying for me. Thank you, thank you, thank you!"

By this time all the other people who had been praying had left the altar. Most had gone home and the pastor was waiting to close the church. Because I was praying quietly the pastor had no idea what God was doing in my heart. I became more and more focused upon Jesus Christ and marveled that He was revealing himself to me. I was keenly conscious that Jesus was communicating with me Spirit to spirit. As my sense of wonder and awe increased I was filled with a spirit of praise. I raised my arms in token of thanksgiving and surrender to Christ.

As I expressed my thanks and praise I began to do so in some language other than English. It was a language unknown to me. I instantly recognized that what I was saying was being spoken under the supervision of the Holy Spirit and not directed by my mind. I also was aware that what I was experiencing must be similar if not identical to what the original disciples experienced on the day of Pentecost. There was no babbling. The language was clearly enunciated and had a variety of inflections. It had the quality of a public address. Although my mind was not directing the speech it was active throughout in silent praise and worship of God. I was aware that in some way I did not fully understand, I was experiencing two realms of reality at the same time. Later I realized that the apostle Paul addressed this phenomena in First Corinthians 14:14 Paul stresses that this kind of spiritual expression is primarily to be exercised in private prayer and not in public meetings.

Because my experience was similar to that of the Roman soldiers described in Acts 10:44-47 which was equated to the experience of the disciples at Pentecost I sensed a strong tie to these first century Christians. Jesus Christ was alive and was still baptizing believers in the Holy Spirit. As I returned to work and everyday activities there was a new consciousness of God's presence. I was still the same "me" but there was an added dimension, an awareness of God that pervaded the ordinary.

When the Army's undefeated West Point football team graduated
in the spring of 1947 two all-Americans plus several other first-
string team members came to Randolph Field for flight training.
They would provide the core of Randolph's football team. I
decided to go out for the team. One super-star all-American
was Doc Blanchard. The other was the quarterback shown here
passing to prospective ends. I went out for end and am waiting
for my turn at far right. My claim to fame was that I tackled
Doc Blanchard once in a practice scrimmage. Blanchard went
on to become a General in the newly formed Air Force.

Summer, 1947.

CHAPTER 7
ASSIGNMENT TO PARADISE

It was not long afterwards that I received notice that I was being transferred from Randolph Field to Hickam Field in Hawaii. I applied for leave so I could go home before sailing "overseas". Hawaii had not yet become a state and was still categorized as an "overseas Territory". I don't remember hitchhiking home so I probably caught a bus. I was now a corporal so I had a little more money to spend. The folks were still living on a little farm near Morganton where dad pastored the Assembly of God church. The days at home were spent helping around the farm and just being with the family. It was summer so all the school kids were home. I was able to practice my photography and enjoy my young brothers and sisters.

In 1948 military personnel were not normally flown overseas. Almost all were transported by sea in "troop ships". These were large passenger ships configured to carry several thousand military personnel and dependent families. My orders were board one of these troop ships in San Francisco. But first I had to get to San Francisco from North Carolina, nearly three thousand miles.

I decided to try my luck hitch-hiking across the United States. My orders provided several days for travel so I thought I could reach my destination in plenty of time and save a bundle of money. I decided to first head north toward Washington, D.C. It occurred to me that I should go to one of our Air Force bases and see if I could hitch a ride on a military plane. I don't remember which base I visited but it was probably Andrews AF base near Washington. As it turned out I selected a good base. There was an old PBY Catalina plane scheduled to go all the way to California. They had room for one passenger and I was welcome to go with them. The only drawback was that the PBY, a patrol plane designed to land on land or water, was extremely slow. Its long range cruising speed was only 117 miles per hour. Even so, that was twice as fast as auto travel. I gladly accepted the offer and got aboard with my duffel bag in tow.

It was obvious that the slow patrol plane would require at least three days to fly across the United States. I don't remember where the first stop was. The next stop I clearly recall was at Hill AF base near Ogden, Utah. The crew was scheduled for a rest stop at Hill and gave me the option of laying over with them or trying to get other transportation. Foolishly, I opted to hit the road again rather than wait a day. I was getting tired of being cooped up on the slow moving patrol plane. So I took my duffel bag and made my way to the main highway heading west. It was July and heat waves radiated up from the pavement. I managed to catch a ride out of Salt Lake City, on past the Great Salt Lake, finally being deposited somewhere in the middle of the desert. Traffic was pretty sparse through the hot desert and rides were few and far between. I began to regret my decision to hit the road rather than wait for the airplane.

Between rides I walked along the highway, hoping someone would take pity on me. While walking in a desolate area I noticed a freight train stopped on the tracks some distance ahead of me. I could see a railroad crossing between me and the train but had no idea why it would be halted out in the desert. In a short time I reached the crossing and discovered a tragic scene. The train had just plowed into a car and killed all the occupants. There were no cell phones in those days and neither police nor ambulances had yet arrived. Body parts were strewn along the tracks, an arm here, a leg there. It was a gruesome sight but there was nothing I could do other than breathe a prayer. Fortunately, I soon caught a ride and was relieved to leave the grim site.

I was glad to make it across the desert and appreciated the cooler temperature of northern California. The base where I was to wait for the troop ship was located near Vallejo. I was pleased to learn that I would have to wait two weeks before boarding the troop transport to Hawaii. On Sunday I visited the Vallejo Assembly of God. The pastor announced that volunteers from the church would be bussed to Santa Cruz during the week to help roof the new gymnasium/tabernacle on the Bethany College campus. Since I had no duties while awaiting my sailing date I got permission to join the volunteer workers going to Santa Cruz. The weather was good and I had an enjoyable day pounding nails on the big roof.

When my sailing date arrived all the men sailing to Hawaii were bussed to the pier where the troop ship was docked. I had never been on a ship before but I had gotten advice from men who had experienced troopships. "Make sure you take an upper bunk" was one piece of advice I remembered. The enlisted men all slept in the lower decks where hammocks were hung four or five high, one above the other. I laid claim to a top bunk and soon found out why that was a good idea.

The crossing to Hawaii took five days. After a day or two we hit some rough seas and men began to get sea-sick right and left. Many of those feeling nauseated laid down in their hammocks. If they suddenly got sick and had to throw up, the men below were in danger. The top bunk was the safest place to be. By the time we arrived in Honolulu the lower decks and "heads" were all awash in the filth of sea-sick soldiers. Happily, the rough seas didn't bother me much but the horrid smells and filth sure took my appetite away.

One of my top priorities after arriving in Hickam was to find a church where I could worship and share Christian fellowship. I visited an Assembly of God mission church in Honolulu and enjoyed the worship and friendly atmosphere. However, most of those in attendance were older than I so I decided to keep looking for a church with more young people. Pearl Harbor was the Navy installation located next to Hickam.

Providentially, I met a young Christian sailor by the name of JC Miller who was stationed at Pearl. He was married and lived in a "Quonset hut" furnished by the Navy. Quonsets were semi-circular steel houses much used during and following World War II. JC invited me to his quarters (military term for house) where I met his wife Edith and their two children. Randy was almost three and Glona was not quite one. I felt right at home with these youngsters and before long we became good friends. The Millers were involved with a new church being established in the town of Wahiawa, about 15 miles from Hickam and Pearl. They invited me to attend with them. Since they had a car, a sporty 1941 Buick, I was glad to accept their offer.

In 1948 Wahiawa was small but attractive Hawaiian town located near Schofield Barracks, a large Army base. Harold Hedrick, the missionary pastor, was an enthusiastic church planter and excellent organizer. There was a good mix of young people from the military and civilian communities. The pastor put us to work and we got some experience doing house to house evangelism. The congregation's temporary worship center was provided by two Quonset huts. Construction had begun on a new building but it was not completed until after I had gone home.

Softball was a major sport on many military bases and Hickam Field had an excellent team. Their ace pitcher had numerous no hit games to his credit. The Army, Navy and Air Force bases throughout the Pacific area fielded teams to vie for the Pacific championship. Hickam won the tournament and became the Pacific area entrant to play for the military world championship to be played at the Air Force base in Roswell, New Mexico. The Command provided a large (for 1948) four motor C-54 transport to fly the team to Roswell. To my surprise and delight I was selected to accompany the team as the public relations photographer. There must have been about thirty of us that boarded the C-54. The passenger capacity was forty-nine so there was plenty of room to move about. The cruising speed was 275 MPH, only about half as fast as modern passenger jets but a lot faster than surface travel by ship. The range without refueling was 3900 miles. Since California was only 2500 miles from Hickam we had a good safety margin of fuel. The flight to Roswell was uneventful except I had to endure too much raunchy talk from the macho young athletes.

When we arrived at Roswell Air Force base I was provided with a key to their base photo lab. During the tournament there were numerous hard played, competitive softball games so I was able to get lots of good action pictures. Hickam's superior pitching paid big dividends and our team won the military world championship. At the conclusion of the tournament there was a big banquet. Again I took lots of photos and printed many extra copies so that each member of our team could have a souvenir.

After winning the military championship our team was invited to compete in the national AAU (Amateur Athletic Union) tournament in Los Angeles. Some of the men were ready to return home but the majority wanted to continue to compete. We finished in fourth place in this tournament. The caliber of play was high and our ace pitcher got "high" as well. He had a drinking problem and he had obviously had too many beers shortly before pitching his last game. The loss was not too disappointing since everyone was ready to go home. The team returned to the welcoming cheers of the home base. I enjoyed the break in routine but I was glad to return to my regular schedule.

I had another brief but out of the ordinary assignment that took me out to sea. B-17's, the work-horse heavy bombers of World War II, were being equipped for the peace time job of air-sea rescue. A life boat was attached to the fuselage beneath the bomb bay. The boat could be released from the belly of the plane and dropped into the sea to serve as a rescue boat. The Command decided to simulate a night air-sea rescue operation. A B-17 was supposed to rendezvous at night with a PT boat somewhere in the Molokai channel between the islands of Oahu and Molokai. My assignment was to ride in the PT boat and photographically record the event. The Molokai channel has notoriously rough seas. The high speed PT boat sped across the channel as the waves ferociously struck the hull. After several hours of this battering I was so exhausted that I lay down in the aft section of the boat.

Despite the noisy engine and the pounding waves I was soon sound asleep. As it turned out, the plane and the boat missed the rendezvous point so I was battered in vain. But it did give me an appreciation for the sailors who operated PT boats, the small, swift torpedo boats made famous by John Kennedy.

About a mile from Hickam Field's main gate was the entrance to the military golf course. I had never played golf but decided I would try it. Enlisted men could check out golf clubs at the pro shop for only a token fee. I knew nothing at all about golf but I enjoyed going out by myself and just whacking the ball around the course. I would often play thirty-six or more holes. My worst mistake was not taking any lessons from a professional and getting some basic instruction. As it was, I compounded my ignorance and practiced my mistakes until they became second nature. Although I did get some pointers years later it was too late to overcome all the bad habits I had developed. However, I have always enjoyed the game, especially when I could play with my brother John. I hope I can enjoy some years playing with my grandson, Cody. He has much better form than I did when I started playing. I think he will be much better golfer than I if he plays regularly.

The University of Hawaii in Honolulu provided evening extension classes aboard some of the major military bases. I enrolled as soon as my work schedule permitted, jumping at the chance to accrue some additional college credits. One of my classes was anthropology. The professor had some nutty ideas. Once he seriously predicted that there would be no more blacks remaining in America after fifty years. His basis for this pronouncement was the current interracial marriage statistics. I'm sure he was long dead before the error of his prediction became obvious. But the classes were stimulating and I was able to enroll for a second semester before leaving Hawaii.

The Millers and I became good friends and I spent a lot of free time at their Quonset quarters. We learned together how delicious fully ripe pineapples actually were. After all the pineapples in a commercial field were picked the really ripe fruit was left in the field and could be picked by scavengers. These golden ripe pineapples, when frozen in the Miller's freezer compartment, were just delectable, especially on a hot day. Often, I served as a baby sitter for Randy and Glona. JC and I got an idea for making a few bucks with my photographic experience. We talked Edith into reluctantly allowing us to use her laundry room as our photo lab. Our plan was to make photographic Christmas cards. I produced some samples for our sales talk and we began to take orders. We never made much money but we had fun trying. I'm sure Edie was happy when Christmas was past and she could reclaim her laundry room.

Hawaii undoubtedly is one of the most beautiful and livable places on our planet. However, after a year there I was beginning to feel "fenced in". My enlistment expired In October, 1949 and I was looking forward to a new chapter in my life. I departed Hawaii near the end of September. Once again I was sailing aboard a troop transport but it was better the second time. I had been promoted to Sergeant so my accommodations were better. In addition, I was commissioned to escort a prisoner back to the United States for incarceration. I was armed with a pistol and had to accompany the prisoner from the ship's brig to the mess hall, or galley, as the sailors termed it. This gave me "head of line" privileges. At last, I got some benefit from my Military Police training.

Probably millions of returning U.S. military personnel have been greeted by the spectacular beauty of the Golden Gate bridge scanning San Francisco Bay. I was certainly impressed as we sailed under the graceful bridge and on to the pier. After being relieved of my weapon and prisoner I was directed to board a bus that would take us to Camp Roberts for completion of the discharge process. Camp Roberts had been a major training center during World War II but was now reduced to a skeleton crew for processing discharges. The Officer in Charge offered to discharge me several days early but I refused this offer for two reasons. I wanted to fulfill my enlistment completely so that there would be no chance of being called back to active duty because of some technicality relating to not meeting my full obligation. The second reason was I wanted a full pay check.

I think the officer was surprised that I did not accept an immediate discharge but he granted my request. There was a downside to refusing an immediate discharge. With all the short term transients on base a lot of thievery was going on. Someone stole my duffle bag and I lost most of my uniforms and civilian clothes. I never intended to wear a uniform again so I didn't miss them but I was sorry to lose my civilian clothes.

Hitch-hiking across country again didn't appeal to me. Since I was discharged from the Air Force I no longer qualified for a "hop" on a military plane. I decided to see the heartland of America from the window of a Greyhound bus. I boarded in northern California. We had a rest stop in Las Vegas, Nevada. In 1949 it was small, sprawling desert city with none of its present glitter and glamour. I remember being served by a waitress with blue hair. I suppose she thought it was stylishly modern. I just thought it strange.

I took a lay-over in Denver for a few days while I visited relatives and surveyed the college situation. My uncle Elmo had just married Eloise and they were still on their honeymoon. Uncle Arley and aunt Pauline were settled in Denver and my Bluhm grandparents were still living in Boulder. I was thinking very strongly about going to College in Colorado and the University of Colorado and the University of Denver were the universities I was considering. But before enrolling in a college anywhere I had to continue the trip to North Carolina to see my family. It was back to the bus for the second half of a long trip.

It was great fun getting reacquainted with my family whom I had not seen in more than fifteen months. The girls outnumbered us boys five to three but while I was gone mom made it more even by giving birth to Philip Eugene. So I had a new baby brother to get acquainted with and to practice my photo skills on. Phil was a winsome, intelligent little guy and his eight siblings showered him with lots of attention and affection. He certainly won my heart with his exuberant spirit and ready smile.

In 1951 God began to deal with me concerning my professional goals and training. Perhaps it was the cloud of war that triggered a reassessment. I like very much the world of math and athletics but I had a deep sense that God wanted to point me in another direction. Once again I had to struggle with holding on to my plans and ambitions or to surrender to God's leadership. I sensed that God was asking me to prepare myself for Christian ministry. This was not in my plans. Dad once told me, "Son, never become a preacher if you can do anything else." As I wrestled with God about a career change I came to the conclusion that, unless I wanted to rebel against the Lord, I could do nothing else but prepare for the ministry. So in my junior year I changed my major to "oral communication" and my minor to "religion". The University of Denver is a secular school so I had to sharpen my faith against the iron of materialistic secularism. Fortunately, I was fully involved in a growing, active church led by a dynamic young pastor. Here I could see the power of God at work despite the humanism I encountered at the university.

After I had been attending Central Assembly about a year I was elected president of the youth group. My main responsibility was to plan and lead the Sunday Youth service that preceded the main Sunday evening evangelistic service. By virtue of my office I was also a member of the governing Board of the church.

These college days were an exciting, growing period of my life. I experienced my first serious girl-friend. She was a pretty, gentle, serious minded girl. We went together for about a year before I realized I was not the right person for her. It was hard to break up but it was the right thing to do. She later married a fine Christian man and the two became leaders in their church. After breaking up with Micky I dated a number of different girls but none were steady girl-friends. I was not yet ready for marriage.

The GI bill was a tremendous help to young veterans returning to civilian life. It would have been hard for me to go to college without it. (Although I know God could have helped me find a way). All tuition and books were paid for and I received seventy-five dollars a month for living expenses. Although a dollar went a long way in the fifties I still needed additional funds for living expenses. In the summer of 1950 I worked with my uncles Arley and Elmo in the building trade. Later that year I was hired by Montgomery Ward as a part time sales employee. By working after school and on Saturday I could accrue about 30 hours weekly. Most of my work was in the paint department although occasionally I would be assigned to another department. I received an hourly wage plus a commission on sales.

I bought my first automobile in 1950 while attending Denver
University. It was a 1937 Chevrolet sedan. It can be partially seen in
this family snapshot taken when I visited the family in North Carolina
while I was driving to ROTC summer camp at Ft. Lee, Virginia. This
is the only picture I have with all nine of my siblings plus dad and
mom. Alliene alone is missing and had died almost twenty years
previously.
1951

CHAPTER 8
OFF TO COLLEGE FULL TIME

Mother tried to persuade me to go to a college in North Carolina. In deference to mom I did briefly consider a couple of North Carolina colleges. But in the end I decided to go back to Colorado. It was now the end of October, too late to enroll for the fall term. It would be January, 1950 before I could enroll for winter term. I still had mixed feelings about whether to go to the University of Colorado or the University of Denver. DU was a private school while CU was a state institution and had lower tuition. Finally I settled on DU even before I went back to Colorado.

My decision was based on three practical factors: (1) Tuition was not important because I had the GI bill which paid all tuition. (2) Part time jobs were more available in Denver than in Boulder. (3) Central Assembly, pastored by Charles Blair, had a good youth group and a strong musical program. I was looking forward to getting involved there. Having made my decision I once again said good-bye to the family after Thanksgiving and headed west. I can't remember whether I traveled by train or bus. I didn't hitch-hike.

Newlyweds, Elmo and Eloise, who lived near DU, let me stay in their apartment while I looked for a more permanent residence. In the meantime I took steps to enroll for the winter term. I decided to major in math, a subject I liked. My minor was physical education. My ultimate goal was to become a high school coach. I enjoyed the math classes. The logic and order appealed to my mind. The physical ed classes were of two types. There were classes that had to do with the sciences and theories of physical health, strength, endurance and the like. Other classes involved learning the basics of a given sport.

My swimming class was very demanding. I had to learn and practice the various swimming strokes. I had to pass the water survival and life-saving training. This included jumping off the high diving board, going to the bottom of the pool and simulate saving someone from drowning. We had to practice making a life vest from a pair of dungarees. This involved tying a knot at the end of each leg so that air could not escape. The pant legs were filled with air and then by putting your chest over the waist of the dungarees to keep air from escaping you had a crude life preserver. It actually did work but I'm glad I never had to use one except in the swimming pool. I also took a class in tennis and was introduced to the basic techniques and footwork. However, it was many years before I would play tennis with any regularity.

In June, 1950 the Korean War broke out. My college counselor said it was likely the war would continue for several years and I might very well be called back to active duty. She then suggested I should consider enrolling in the Reserve Officer Training Corps. Because I was a veteran with a blemish free record I would only have to take two years of ROTC to receive a commission as a 2nd Lieutenant. I looked into the program and decided to enroll. If I were to be recalled I preferred to go back as a lieutenant rather than a sergeant. I wanted to enroll in the Air Force ROTC but it was not available on the main campus so my only choice was the Army Quartermaster Corps. Newlyweds, Elmo and Eloise, who lived near DU, let me stay in their apartment while I looked for a more permanent residence. In the meantime I took steps to enroll for the winter term. I decided to major in math, a subject I liked. My minor was physical education. My ultimate goal was to become a high school coach. I enjoyed the math classes. The logic and order appealed to my mind. The physical education classes were of two types. There were classes that had to do with the sciences and theories of physical health, strength, endurance and the like. Other classes involved learning the basics of a given sport.

With the combined money from a steady job plus the GI bill I was able to purchase my first car. It was a 1937 Chevrolet sedan in reasonably good shape. Having my own wheels provided me with a sense of freedom I hadn't experienced since I got my first bike as a twelve year old. I fell in love with the old Chevy. Or maybe I just loved the sense of freedom a car provided. Gasoline cost about twenty cents a gallon, which, factoring in inflation, is about the same as today.

In the summer of 1951 all the Quartermaster ROTC cadets were ordered to Ft. Lee, Virginia for summer camp. I decided to drive my car to Virginia via a stop in North Carolina to see the family. The car ran well and the trip to

North Carolina was uneventful. I was able to spend several wonderful days with dad and mom and my three brothers and five sisters. Gayle had been born in 1950 while I was in Colorado. She was now fifteen months old and a cuddly, happy toddler that was loved and spoiled by everyone. Philip, the baby boy, was a sweet, playful four year old adored by all. Before I left for Virginia all twelve members of the family posed together beside my 1937 Chevrolet. To my knowledge this is the only picture I have with all my siblings. Alliene who had died years before was the only one missing. An enlarged copy of this photo sits proudly on the bureau in our guest bedroom. Every time I look at it I am flooded with good memories of a long time ago. I was proud to be the big brother of my nine siblings.

Ft. Lee was a large training base steeped in tradition and rich American history. It was named of course for General Robert E. Lee, the illustrious military genius who opted to lead the Confederate army during the Civil War. He was stationed at this base as a young captain and the house where he lived is still part of the Ft. Lee landscape. Ft. Lee is located about twenty miles south of Richmond, near Petersburg where the last major battle of the Civil War was fought. Washington, D.C. lies one hundred and twenty-five miles north of Petersburg. The training we cadets received was a combination of classroom instruction and field exercises. I didn't find the training overly demanding. The most onerous condition we faced was the oppressive, stifling, summer climate. Our uniforms would get damp during the day's activities. We would spread them out to dry but in the morning they would be just as damp as when we took them off. The humid climate was in sharp contrast with the drier climate of Colorado. The contrast to what I was now used to made Virginia all the more oppressive.

Many of the cadets did not bring automobiles to summer camp. This made me and my 1937 Chevrolet very popular on week-ends. One week-end five of us jumped into my car and took off for Washington, D.C. We were near the Washington city limits when suddenly the cooling fan came loose on the shaft and spiraled back into the radiator. Before I could stop the engine, the whirling fan gouged many small holes into the front surface of the radiator. We stopped and assessed the damage.

I was able to once again secure the fan on the shaft but the radiator was leaking water like a sieve. We managed to secure some water in a container. We filled the radiator and drove a few miles and then the engine began to overheat and we would stop and pour in more water. We repeated this process until we managed to get into D.C. We tried to find a radiator shop but most were either closed on Saturday or demanded more than we could pay.

An idea came to mind, from where I don't know, perhaps I had read about it somewhere. In desperation I decided to give it a try. All I needed was a toothpick, a cotton rag and a pack of chewing gum. Total cost was five cents. The idea was to force small pieces of rag and chewing gum into each hole with the toothpick. It took probably an hour of meticulous work but finally all the holes were filled. With hope and crossed fingers we started the car and, wonder of wonders, there were no leaks. As the radiator warmed, the chewing gum, adhering to the cotton rag, spread a thin seal around each hole.

We made it back with no further problems and I continued to drive my car during the rest of the time at Ft. Lee.
After summer camp was completed I drove back to North
Carolina for another brief visit with family before continuing
to Colorado. Dad had a friend who had a radiator shop and
the professional repairman removed the radiator, cleaned it,
and then soldered the holes. I drove the old Chevy back to
Colorado, via a stop to see Kansas relatives, with no further
problems.

One of the big problems facing a single college student is
finding a decent place to live at a reasonable price. I finally
located a low-cost basement apartment with a small kitchen
near the University campus. It was dark and unsightly but the
price was right so I decided to rent it. The landlady was an
older, motherly type and we got along fine. My meals were
very utilitarian, just enough to hold body and soul together. I
became an expert preparing cream of tomato soup and ham-
burgers. Amazingly, I still like them both. It's probably the
high salt content in the canned soup.

After putting up with the dingy basement and cooking
my own meals for a year I was ready to look for new accommodations. One of the church families had a well- lighted,
large basement room with bath that became available. As an
added incentive the rent included the evening meal. I was
more than glad to change my domicile. The Bjork home became my home until I graduated from college and went into
the army. Later, when I enrolled in Seminary, I again stayed
with the Bjorks. There were five children in the Bjork family and Annalee and Glen became special friends. Dad Bjork
was a gentle, hard-working Christian gentleman who always
had a friendly word to share. Mom Bjork was an energetic

housewife and social dynamo. Mr. Bjork suffered a sudden, fatal heart while I resided with the family. He was relatively young, still in his fifties, and it was a difficult time for the family. Mrs. Bjork eventually married again, outlived her second husband, and died in 2005 near a hundred years old. Donna and I still maintain contact with Annalee.

Here I am with baby brother Phil and our mother in Denver. Some of the family, including mom and Phil, had come to my graduation and commissioning as a 2nd Lieutenant. I drove them home in my new 1952 Nash Ambassador, again on my way to Ft. Lee for Infantry combat training as well as QM school. The Korean War continued to rage and even Quartermaster officers had to take this training since the casualty rate for lieutenants was high.

August, 1952

CHAPTER 9
YOU ARE IN THE ARMY...
AGAIN

As a result of the credit hours I had accumulated at Trinity University and the University of Hawaii I was able to graduate from Denver University in the summer (August) of 1952. Many friends and relatives were there including my parents who had driven from North Carolina. In addition to my BA degree I received my commission as a second lieutenant in the U.S. Army Reserves with an obligation for two years active duty. The Korean War had now been going on for more than two years. It should have been an easy victory for the United Nations forces spearheaded by the United States. However, when hundreds of thousands of fanatical Chinese Communists streamed across the Yalu River to aid the North Koreans the war was greatly intensified and prolonged.

Because many lieutenants were being lost in Korea, Quartermaster officers were required to take combat infantry training. In September 1952 I was ordered to go to Fort Lee, Virginia for combat training and advanced QM training. This training was much more intensive than the summer camp in 1951 had been. We had to crawl on our bellies under barbed wire with live machine gun bullets firing above us. We practiced throwing hand grenades. We were drilled in the techniques of bayonet combat. We had to qualify with rifles and sub-machine guns on the range. We were sobered by the prospects of actually having to apply our training if the Korean War continued.

While undergoing this combat training at Fort Lee I had one of the most profound spiritual experiences of my life. Ever since my commitment to Christ and the experience with the Holy Spirit in March 1948 I had made a conscious effort to fulfill my commitment. I attended church regularly, read the bible, prayed, and witnessed. Despite doing all the things I thought a Christian was supposed to do I had no sense of intimacy with Jesus as I had known four years previously. The words of Christ to the Christians at Ephesus seemed directed to me, "Yet I hold this against you: you have forsaken your first love...Repent." I took this admonition seriously. I'm sure the war situation and the possibility of being ordered into combat helped focus my thoughts on my relationship with the Lord.

I remembered something I had learned as a result of my San Antonio experience. If you are willing to be honest and open with God you could have real two-way communication. I drove my car (a new car, not the old Chevy) to a secluded wooded area and began to talk to the Lord, "Lord you have told me I should love you with all my heart, all my mind and all my strength. I confess that I don't love you. How is love generated? I want to love you. I want to have a close relationship but I feel estranged and don't know what to do."

After I had poured out my heart to the Lord I waited quietly for His response. His reply soon came. It was brief, direct, tender and very personal. Jesus said to me, "Glenn, I know you don't love me but I still love you." The reality of His love began to radiate in the depths of my being. He actually loved me, despite my faults and failures ! As this truth penetrated my heart, joy, peace and new love began to spring up. I didn't have to earn His love. I just had to accept it and respond to it. I began to understand what St. John meant when he said, "We love because He first loved us."

You may wonder if I heard Jesus speak in an audible voice. No, I didn't. What is an "audible voice"? It is a result of sound waves stimulating the auditory nerves by vibrations in the air. The auditory nerve transmits the vibrations from the inner to the brain. The brain translates the auditory signals into sounds that can be recognized. Now what God normally does is bypass the mechanical process and goes directly to the brain. There is no chance of faulty transmission or misinterpretation. When the Lord communicates directly He leaves no doubt as to His identity. As Jesus said, "My sheep know my voice." I certainly had no doubt that Jesus was communicating directly to me.

When I was ordered to active duty in the army my monthly income increased appreciably. I was single with no prospects of marriage. I decided to buy a new car since I could handle the monthly payments with no difficulty. I sold my faithful 1937 Chevy to my brother Johnny who had moved to Denver after graduation from high school. One of the part time jobs I had while in college was working for a Nash dealership. I decided to buy my first new car from my old boss. It was a 1952 Nash Ambassador and cost me a good portion of a year's salary. After completing the training at Fort Lee I received orders to report to Fort Carson, Colorado. By the time I got back to Colorado the 1953 Ambassadors were in the showroom. I was intrigued by some of the features on this new model, especially the high compression aluminum head engine. I bought into the Nash sales propaganda and made a deal with my former boss to trade in the like-new 1952 model on the new one. Later I had reason to regret my decision. But at the time I was proud of my huge, sparkling cream and burgundy two-tone automobile. I was young and foolish.

My faithful, Army-issued saddle horse was not as sure-footed
as the small-hoofed mules. It was much safer to walk and lead
on a narrow mountain trail with steep drop-off. This was
taken on a hot day in June shortly before I was relieved from
my assignment as Platoon Leader in the Army's last mule pack
Company. Gannet Peak, highest mountain is barely visible in
top left. That's where we established the base camp for the 10th
Mtn. Division troops doing glacier training on Gannet Peak,
site of largest glacier in lower forty-eight states. June, 1953

CHAPTER 10

MOUNTAINS AND MULES

I was pleased to be stationed at Fort Carson, near Colorado Springs. It was only about ninety miles from my "old stomping ground" in Denver. However, I was flabbergasted by the new assignment. I was ordered to be a Platoon Leader in the Army's only QM Mule Pack Pack Company. I didn't even know the Army had a Mule Pack outfit. But it did and I was in it. The Platoon that I was in charge of had about one hundred mules and fifty muleskinners (the soldiers that worked the mules). The ways of the Army are inexplicable. I never had a clue as to why I was chosen for this unique assignment. Surely it was not because I had herded a few cows on a horse when I was a little boy. Nor would it likely have been because I plowed with mules and horses on farms in Virginia and North Carolina. I don't think the Army knew about any of this. But I was glad I had this past experience and was not a total novice.

After meeting the Commanding Officer and getting briefed at headquarters I reported to the corral where the mules were kept. Some of my men and NCO's were awaiting me. One of the men was tending a large, saddled horse. After introductions and small talk one of the non-commissioned officers indicated it was traditional for a new officer to demonstrate his riding skills. I was invited to mount the saddled horse for this traditional ride. Although I was suspicious about getting on the horse I didn't dare refuse.

Once I got in the saddle I began the wildest ride of my life. The horse bolted almost immediately. With ears back and mane flying he sped away at a mad gallop. I tried to restrain him with the reins but it was impossible. I quickly came to the conclusion that this was a familiar routine for the horse. I decided to concentrate on staying in the saddle and just let the horse run his course. Eventually, he did "run out of steam" and I was able to make my way back to our starting point at a trot. The men had their laugh and I had passed the test without disgracing myself. In the next six month I would spend a lot of time in the saddle but never again on that "test" horse. I was issued a beautiful bay mare that was a joy to ride.

I had a lot to learn in order to become a competent officer in my unique assignment. Fortunately, I had some experienced NCOs and trained muleskinners to help me. Our basic equipment was the Phillips military pack saddle. It was heavier than its civilian counterparts but furnished a steadier platform for maximum cargo. I had to learn its complete nomenclature and be able to demonstrate its use. Eventually I had to teach classes to mountain troops concerning correct mule pack techniques and procedures. It wasn't very high tech stuff.

My first three months with the mule pack outfit were in the dead of winter, January, February, and March. Most of the time was spent at Camp Hale, high in the Rockies near Leadville. This camp had been constructed during WWII for training the Tenth Mountain Division for warfare in the Italian Alps. This Division had been deactivated in 1945 at the conclusion of the war. In 1948 it had been reactivated as a mountain training Division and located at Camp Hale.

My mission at Camp Hale was to instruct and demonstrate how to use pack mules in mountain terrain. One such demonstration resulted in the coldest, most miserable night I can ever remember enduring. I was ordered to take a demonstration contingent of my mules and men on an overnight pack exercise. The morning we began the exercise was a typical bright, sunny, winter day in the high Rockies. The sun reflected brilliantly off the snow-covered terrain. Although the temperature was about twenty degrees f. it actually felt warmer because of the sun's reflection. I had elected to walk rather than ride my horse and before long I was warm enough to strip to my shirt.

As we continued our march we entered a wooded area with numerous snow drifts. Because of the mule's small hooves, they quickly broke through the crust on the drifts and were up to their bellies in snow. Once this happened the mules were helpless. The muleskinners had to take off the packs, help extricate the animal, reload the pack and continue the march. By late afternoon, after too many snow-drift episodes, I halted the exercise and we unloaded and tethered the mules. Since we had no tents the senior NCO had the men make preparations for sleeping under the stars. Dry wood was collected and before long fires were started.

The warm temperature of the day soon dissipated as the sun began to set. Quickly the bitter cold of the high mountain night air enveloped us. I had foolishly not brought my arctic sleeping bag, lulled into a false security by the warm morning sun. Instead, I had brought the lighter weight mountain bag which is sufficient for temperatures down to zero. I climbed into the bag with my boots and field uniform intact. Even so, it was impossible to get warm. I located some horse blankets and piled them on top of me and managed to survive a miserable night. We learned that the night temperature had dropped to thirty-two degrees below zero. That would have severely tested even my arctic sleeping bag.

After spending the three months of winter at Fort Carson and Camp Hale I was ordered to the Wind River Mountains region of Wyoming. My task was to establish a base camp near the Wind River Indian Reservation just west of Burris. Burris was not really a town, just a post office. From there I was to move the base camp toward Gannett Peak, the highest mountain in Wyoming. How fast I moved was determined by how fast the melting snow drifts permitted the mules to advance. Gannett peak not only was Wyoming's highest mountain but also the site of the largest glacier in the continental United States.

The Tenth Mountain Division was scheduled to conduct glacier training there as soon as my platoon could establish a base supply camp at the base of the mountain. For the whole month of April it was impossible for us to advance beyond the initial base camp. The snow was still so deep that it was impossible for the mules to navigate further up the trail.

Since we were essentially immobilized for a month while waiting for the snow to melt we looked for ways to pass the time.

During the day the men could practice packing techniques but that soon grew old. After the mules were fed, watered and secured the men were free to explore the countryside by foot or on a mule. All of our food was C-rations or other Army canned rations. We lived in squad tents heated by gasoline which was gravity fed into the stove from five gallon cans elevated outside the tent. The stove was essentially a rectangular steel box. When hot, the side of the stove served as an efficient toaster. The Army issued delicious canned bread. When you opened the can the bread was soft and slightly moist. If you slapped a slice on the side of the hot stove it would stick there until heat dried one side of the bread. When toasted it would fall off and then you could toast the other side. With butter, jam and a cup of hot coffee it was delicious. In my imagination I can still savor it.

Although the Army canned rations were nutritious and palatable they became very monotonous after while. We had no weapons for hunting game. The only authorized firearm was a 45 caliber pistol issued to me. However, this didn't prevent the men from trying to get some fresh meat. One day I wandered back to camp and smelled the wonderful aroma of fresh game being roasted over an open fire. I followed my nose to the camp fire and saw a strange sight. At first I thought they may have captured some large chicken-like fowl because it looked like chicken ribs being roasted. But I was wrong. The squad leader explained that the men had killed a large rattle snake. They skinned the reptile and divided into pieces about the size of a chicken back with the ribs attached. I was offered a piece and gratefully accepted. It was quite tasty, much like chicken, but only a small shred of meat could be nibbled from each piece. A good appetizer but definitely not a main course.

In those days all the C-rations included cigarettes. I didn't smoke in fact, had never smoked or used tobacco in any form. Nevertheless, I had accumulated quite a few cigarettes from my C-rations and didn't know what to do with them. One of the popular pastimes during this waiting period was card games of various kinds. I never gambled but small stakes poker was popular among the men. I watched enough of the poker games to get a good feel for how it should be played. I liked the challenge of skill mixed with luck. I had an idea that would allow me to play without risking any money. I suggested to some of the poker players that we play for cigarettes. They agreed and soon we had evening poker sessions with C-ration cigarettes as the only stakes. To my amazement and amusement I eventually won all the cigarettes in the camp. Maybe I should have thrown them away. Instead, I redistributed them to the smokers and ended my poker career as a champion.

The month of May brought warmer weather that melted some of the snow which was blocking our advance. As the crow flies we were about 25 miles from Gannett Peak but the winding trail we must follow was probably twice that far. Had it not been for the heavy snow in the higher elevations we could reached our destination in less than a week. As it was we had to wait for the snow to melt enough that the mules wouldn't flounder in drifts. In May we were able to advance a few miles and establish another base camp at a higher elevation.

While we were making the transition we were overtaken by a blinding blizzard. The blowing snow made it all but impossible to see the trail or to follow the lead packers. As a result of the confusion I had to halt the march. It was reported that some of the mules had wandered away during the storm and were no longer in the train. I issued orders for an all-out search for the missing animals and joined the effort. Eventually the wind and snow subsided enough so that mule tracks became visible and they could be tracked. By the time they were all rounded up and secured I was exhausted and famished. All I had to eat was a cold can of C-ration baked beans. I can't describe how utterly delicious those beans tasted. Exhaustion and hunger are powerful appetizers and can transform common food into a banquet.

June brought more warm weather and further melting snow in the higher elevations. As a result we were able to make further progress toward our goal. As we ascended into higher elevations we ran across clumsy birds called sage hens. These birds apparently had not had much contact with humans and we were able to capture a few. With great anticipation we prepared the hens for roasting over an open fire. Unfortunately, our disappointment was as great as our anticipation. The meat was so tough and stringy that it was scarcely edible. The sage hens need no longer fear us.

When I was first assigned to the Pack outfit I heard a great deal about the superiority of mules over horses as pack animals. It was alleged that mules were less temperamental, easier to train, better foragers, and stronger than horses of similar size. Mule hooves are smaller and tougher than horse hooves and thus better suited to narrow, rocky trails. Most importantly, mules are more intelligent than horses. Horses will self-destruct. They will eat themselves to death if sufficient food is available and will work themselves to death if goaded.

Mules hardly ever can be tricked into putting themselves at risk. I saw this dramatically illustrated while on the trail in Wyoming. It was late June and we were closing in on our final goal. The snow had melted sufficiently to allow us to advance several miles at a time. As our mule train proceeded up the trail one of the mules suddenly stopped and refused to move. He was goaded, pulled, shouted at and threatened in various ways. He refused to budge. At last, tiring of the abuse, he lay down on the trail pack and all. The muleskinner assigned to him had to take off the pack and lighten the load. It was only when the weight met the mule's criteria would he continue the march.

As June progressed so did the mule train. Near the end of the month we could clearly see Gannett Peak with its great glacier rising above the surrounding terrain. The temperature was pleasant and it was enjoyable just riding my horse in this gorgeous country. There was a stream near the trail called Dinwiddie creek which had its source from the melting glacier. The water had a strange, semi-translucent turquoise color. I had never seen anything like it. I had hoped we might catch some fish from the stream but it seemed barren. I learned the unusual color and texture of the water was caused by the imbedded vegetation released from the melting glacier.

By the end of June we were at the foot of the mountain and ready to set up base camp for the mountain troops doing glacier training. But my journey on this trail was finished. I had received orders to report back to Fort Carson and to prepare for an overseas assignment. I had expected to receive orders to Korea but fortunately the war was winding down. Negotiations were under way for a cease fire, a pact that would be signed in August 1953. Instead of orders to Korea I was going to Germany as part of the occupation Force.

It didn't take me long to complete the check-out procedure at Fort Carson. I bid friends and relatives in Denver good-bye. In a few days my new 1953 Nash Ambassador was loaded with uniforms and personal gear and I was ready to drive across country. My first destination was a brief stop in Kansas to see my grandparents and other relatives. After that it was on to North Carolina to spend some time with the family before sailing to Germany.

It was great to have some time with the family again, especially since it would be over a year before I could see them again. I was not the center of attention, however, when I arrived. All my siblings "oohed" and "aahed" at my new car. It was fun taking them for a spin and seeing how proud they were. Dad's car was a little two-door 1950 Chevrolet sedan, a good car but very small for a large family. As dad saw how much better the Ambassador accommodated the family he came up with an excellent idea. He suggested I consider leaving my car for the family while I took his Chevvy to Germany. As an officer I was entitled to free shipment for my automobile. Dad's suggestion made sense to me. His car was plenty big for my needs and by taking it I would avoid any transit damage to my new car. Much to the delight of my brothers and sisters I agreed to the switch.

I drove the Chevvy to New York and turned it over to the Military Sea Transportation Service for shipment to Germany. I reported to Fort Hamilton in Brooklyn while I awaited passage on the MSTS ship that was to take me to Germany. Since I had about two weeks before my departure date I took in as many New York sights as I could. I visited Yankee Stadium and watched my first major league baseball game. I also attended one of the very popular radio quiz games and actually got called up from the audience.

Here I am with one of my close friends at Camp Baumholder, Germany. I expected to be sent to Korea but fortunately for myself and many others, the Chinese asked for a "cease fire" in Korea and the war halted. I was ordered to Baumholder instead. Much of urban Germany was still in ruins as a result of WWII. Baumholder was located in a rural German countryside near France. The beautiful Moselle river valley was not far away. After being promoted to 1st Lt. I was given command of a Quartermaster Detachment that was responsible for POL, rations and laundry service aboard the Base. I've forgotten my friend's name. Sure wish I had kept closer contact with my Army buddies.

January, 1954

CHAPTER 11
GERMANY

The voyage from Brooklyn to Bremerhaven, Germany was far more pleasant than the voyage from San Francisco to Honolulu that I had taken five years previously. The accommodations were much better and the food was superior. I discovered the truth of the old Army cliché RHIP (rank has its privileges). I'm sure a lot of the young officers aboard the ship who had not served as enlisted men didn't appreciate their favored status as I did. The warm July weather made sailing a pleasure and the five day crossing passed quickly.

My arrival in Germany was my first experience in a foreign country.(Other than the Territory of Hawaii). My car would not arrive for several weeks so the Army was dependent upon the German rail system for transportation. It was only eight years after the end of WWII and there was still much evidence of the destructive power of the Allied bombing. Major cities still had portions that were reduced to rubble. But there were many signs of recovery as well. The Marshall Plan, introduced in 1948 and continuing until 1951, together with German initiative and hard work were in the process of producing an economic miracle. I was looking forward to spending the next fourteen months in the land where many of my ancestors had originated.

My orders were to report to the major Army base at Baumholder. It was a large base but the village of Baumholder was a very small community on the western border of the German state of Rheinland Pfalz. This state borders on Belgium, Luxembourg and France so the Base was situated within easy driving distance of three countries. The old Roman city of Trier, with fascinating remains from the Roman era, was located in Rheinland Falz, not many miles from Baumholder.

The German rail system was largely restored and quite efficient. From Bremerhaven the troops traveled by rail to Frankfurt. We stopped in Frankfurt for several hours before proceeding on to Kaiserslaughtern, the closest major city near Baumholder. While waiting in Frankfurt I decided to visit a nearby historic hotel that the US Army had taken over after the war. The lobby was very grand but I was more interested in finding a restroom. Unfortunately, I had no grasp of the German language and faced a dilemma when I found the restrooms. One was labeled HERREN. I concluded that must be for her or women. The other was labeled DAMEN. I would have felt more sure of myself if it had read HISEN but the fact that it ended in 'MEN' reassured me. that this must be for men. So I barged in the DAMEN door. Too late I realized there were no urinals. An angry German woman muttered something like "dumkopf Americanish". I didn't understand all she said but I got the message and beat a hasty retreat. This was my first lesson in the German language.

Military vehicles met us in Kaiserslaughtern to transport us the remaining sixty kilometers to Baumholder. I was fascinated by the rural countryside that we drove through. It was harvest time for grain and hay. What really caught my eye was that most of the heavy farm work was being done by women. The war had destroyed the men in many households so the women were pitching hay, harvesting crops, and doing whatever else needed to be done on the farms. In typical European fashion most of the farm families lived in a central village with their small farms located in the surrounding countryside. As I walked through the village I was surprised to discover that the farm animals were housed in close proximity to people. Often large animals such as cows or horses were sheltered in a stable below the house. Later I learned there was a practical reason for this. In the winter the warmth from the animals helped heat the house above.

What a contrast there was between my new duty station and the old mule outfit. Instead of isolated duty with only dozens of men I was now part of a large base with several thousand troops. My new assignment was platoon leader in a Quartermaster Company. At the time I reported there was a large field exercise in progress and many units were involved including my new outfit. A jeep had been dispatched to take me to our bivouac area located in the middle of a German forest.

What impressed me about our camp site was the appearance of the forest. It was as neat and orderly as a park. I discovered that this was typical of German forests. The citizens who lived nearby would come to the forest on week-ends and pick up trash. Fallen trees or limbs would be taken away for fuel. It was a national tradition. The field exercise was quite enjoyable. The warm July weather was pleasant and we even had hot food prepared. This new duty wasn't too bad. I had just completed three months of bivouac in the mountains of Wyoming that was much more demanding.

After returning from the field exercise I was given a typical assignment for a new 2nd Lieutenant. It was probably the least coveted job for a young officer but one hard to escape. I was appointed Battalion Mess officer. This meant that I had responsibility for feeding approximately 600 men. Kitchen police were German nationals. Normally lower ranked GI's performed this necessary duty but labor was so cheap that Germans could be hired for only a pittance. The GI's were happy to kick in a small sum each month to cover the labor cost. Actually, the Germans coveted a KP job. They were furnished good meals and the pay was equal to or better than many jobs in the civilian sector.

When I found out my labor force was German nationals I thought, "This will be a good opportunity to learn the German language." I wanted to learn German and thought this would give me an incentive. To my chagrin, this was not to be. The labor agreement with the German workers specified they were to be supervised by an English speaking German national who would take orders from the Mess Officer but the German supervisor would transmit orders to the KP's. I was to have no personal contact with them.

The only real problem I had with the German workers had to do with theft of food. The butcher noticed that meat was disappearing from the locker. The workers were inspected before going home at night. Yet somehow meat was being pilfered undetected. The CID (criminal investigation division) was notified and the mess area was put under surveillance. Shortly thereafter one night one of the workers was arrested with packaged meat in his possession. As it turned out this man was sneaking out meat during the day and placing it in a garbage can. When he departed at night he easily passed inspection. Later he would return to the garbage area and extract the stolen meat. It was while doing this he was detected and arrested. He was fired and I think that was the only punishment he received. To my knowledge there was no further thievery.

I wish I could say the troops ate well under my mess administration. By and large the basic meals were OK but without a doubt we must have had the poorest baker in the army. He was a big-bellied staff sergeant who supposedly had been to baker's school. Whoever gave him a passing grade did the army a disservice. He could take choice ingredients and transform them into an inedible glob. His pies were atrocious with crusts so tough they would have challenged a sharp bayonet. The cakes were no better. I didn't know enough about baking to instruct him so we were stuck. The best I could hope for was that he would get transferred. It didn't happen on my watch.

I survived my tour as Mess Officer and was assigned a new duty as Supply Officer with the additional assignment as Motor Pool Officer. The back-bone of the Army is the non-commissioned officer corps. The senior NCO's were usually career men who had seen a lot of lieutenants come and go. My senior supply NCO was a wily old Tech Sergeant who sometimes was too smart for his own good. The Supply department had to undergo major semi-annual inspections. The inspector would check to see if we had all the gear and equipment we were authorized and evaluate its condition. He would also check to see if there were any overages that had to be accounted for.

The senior Supply NCO had acquired considerable more equipment than was authorized. The NCO had devised a plan to evade the inspector and thus avoid a bad report the extra equipment would bring. The night before the inspection an army truck was loaded with the surplus gear and the driver was instructed to drive around the base the next day until the inspection was completed. Unfortunately, the inspecting officer had heard about this dodge and the Sgt. was ordered to produce the truck and its cargo for inventory. The inspection report duly noted the irregularity and we were reprimanded.

The officers I worked for were an interesting lot. My first commanding officer was a typical "red neck", reserve captain from West Virginia. He was course, vain and extremely racially prejudiced. He was married but had not brought his wife to Germany. I think he was a good friend of a local German fraulein. My Executive Officer was a sharp, well educated, black first lieutenant. He was married to a lovely black woman and they made a very attractive couple. The CO went out of his way to belittle and put down this fine lieutenant who was in every way a superior officer to the CO...except in rank. The lieutenant and his wife were very gracious to me and invited me to their home for dinner shortly after I reported. I felt repulsed by the captain's treatment of this fine man but could do little except give him and his wife my friendship. President Truman had integrated the Armed Forces in 1948 while I was in Hawaii. This had the immediate effect of raising the status of black soldiers. However, racial prejudice was still deeply implanted in elements of our society. It certainly was in my CO from West Virginia.

Approximately a month after my arrival in Germany I was notified that my automobile had arrived at the port city of Bremerhaven. In 1953 Bremerhaven still bore scars from the fire-bombing it received in WWII but the port itself had been restored and was one of the busiest in Germany. I rode the train to Bremerhaven, a distance of more than seven hundred kilometers. After completing the necessary documents to obtain clearance for my car I drove it away. I was delighted and grateful to be mobile again with my own wheels.

It was wonderful having one's own car in Europe at this time. US military personnel were permitted to buy gasoline on bases at fifteen cents per gallon. We were also issued tickets for fuel that permitted us to get gasoline at German service stations at a greatly reduced price. There were numerous cities and picturesque areas that were worthy destinations for a Saturday drive. One of my favorite drives was down the Moselle valley with its ancient castles and world famous vineyards. The Moselle has its origin in the French mountains south of Nancy. It flows north through Metz and on to Luxembourg and Germany where it trisects the borders of these three countries.

Leaving France the Moselle forms the border between Luxembourg and Germany for about twenty-five kilometers and then swings northeast to Trier. It eventually joins the Rhine at Koblenz after winding nearly six hundred kilometers through three countries. The section through Germany was particularly rich in photogenic old castles, picturesque villages and lush vineyards. Trier had been an outpost of the old Roman Empire and still retained remains of the Roman aqueducts and baths. This region was a tourist's paradise and I enjoyed it thoroughly.

There were plenty of opportunities for day trips but some areas required longer periods of time. We were allowed thirty days leave per year so I had plenty of time for extended trips. One of my first longer trips was to Paris. One of my friends was a recently married lieutenant who had brought his wife to

Germany. They wanted to go with me to France so we planned our trip together. We rented rooms in an ideally situated low-budget hotel in Paris. We did the usual touristy things in Paris. We toured the Louvre, Notre Dame, walked down the Champs Elysees, saw the Bastille, visited restaurants, laughed at the quaint sidewalk toilets that left you half exposed,

We strained our necks eyeing the top of the Eiffel Tower and enjoyed a variety of French cafes. My friend and his wife were New Yorkers and much more sophisticated and worldly than I. They wanted to take in some of the Paris night life and asked me to go with them. However, I didn't think this would enhance my Christian testimony so begged off.

Our treatment by the French didn't make me eager to visit Paris again. They could be rude and cold. My theory is that the French were still smarting from their recent ignominious defeat in WWII. As a result they were insecure and compensated in negative ways. I remember well one incident in which I was harassed by a street peddler of pornographic post cards. I let him know I wasn't interested and told him to go away. He immediately responded in English, "You go away! This is my country." So it was and so I did.

Another interesting trip was through the low countries of Holland and Belgium. Somebody went with me I'm sure but I can't remember who. It was early spring in 1954. I had hoped the tulips would be blooming in Holland but it was too early for most of the varieties. Nevertheless, there were lots of interesting sights to see. We visited Marken Island where all the residents dressed in traditional Dutch clothing including wooden shoes. The children were darling and we took lots of pictures. We visited an Edam cheese factory and enjoyed tasty samples. In Amsterdam we stayed at a small hotel on one of the canals and enjoyed a leisurely, delicious continental breakfast. Here too we toured one of the famous diamond cutting houses. In Rotterdam we were engulfed by hordes of bicyclers who rode down the main streets six or eight abreast.

When in High School my first sports love had been football. When we moved from Virginia to North Carolina in my junior year the new school had no football team so I had to concentrate on basketball. But I had always regretted not being able to determine how good a football player I might have been. In the fall of 1953 I learned my battalion in Baumholder was fielding a football team to compete in a Command league with the other battalions in the area. I was asked about trying out for the team and decided I would. The old dream had not completely died.

I quickly learned that eight years away from football could not be made up in a few weeks, especially since I was trying to play quarterback. But I practiced hard ...too hard. While practicing throwing blocks on a dummy blocking tackle I tore the muscles in my rib cage. This resulted in a debilitating, extremely painful injury. My ribs were wrapped in gauze and tape to minimize any movement. But nothing could alleviate the intense pain that sometimes seized me and rolled me out of bed onto the floor. I don't think I have ever endured anything more excruciating. I knew my dream of ever playing football again was over.

In the spring of 1954 I was promoted to First Lieutenant. Following my promotion I was assigned a new job with increased responsibilities. I was transferred to a large QM company which had its headquarters in Kaiserslautern. However, I remained in Baumholder and was given responsibility for major QM responsibilities there. These included the ration dump and the POL (petroleum, oil, lubrications) dump as well as the laundry facility. Essentially, I acted as the Commanding Officer of a large detachment. I conducted inspections and was responsible for discipline within the unit. I took my responsibilities seriously and performed them acceptably, I think. At least, my superiors thought so. However, I knew that I was not suited to be a career Army Officer and looked forward to my release from active duty.

I was very pleased to discover a small but active group of Christians among both the officers and enlisted men. I soon became a leader within the group. Our leadership team provided oversight for a weekly interdenominational service and various social activities. Our senior chaplain was a Southern Baptist with whom I became good friends. He asked me to teach the Sunday morning adult Bible class conducted at the Chapel. I enjoyed all these activities and they helped solidify my conviction that God was leading me to prepare for the ministry.

A day in June, 1954 was the occasion for one of the saddest times of my life. It started when I received a call that I should report to the Red Cross representative's office. When I got the call I knew this had the potential for a very bad day but I had no idea what to expect. The Red Cross rep gave me the message from home that informed me of the death of Philip Eugene, killed by a car in front of our house. I was completely emotionally demolished by this news and could not control my expression of grief. I could not stop crying, to the embarrassment of the Red Cross representative. He remarked that he had never seen anyone take a death notice so hard.

He didn't know that I was weeping for more than my own loss of a beloved baby brother. I knew the terrible impact Phil's death would have on dad and mom and the rest of the family. Dad had envisioned Phillip as his companion and "strong right arm" in his declining years. Mother had shared dad's dream and her sorrow was increased by the knowledge that dad's dream had been shattered. The youngest children in a large family are especially treasured by their siblings. Gayle, our precious baby sister and youngest of eleven was still part of our circle. Phil, our treasured baby brother, was gone. I sensed the collective grief of my parents and brothers and sisters.

Upon learning of Phillip's death I immediately requested emergency leave so that I could fly home for the funeral. To my dismay my local commander said he could not approve emergency leave for the death of a brother. Only the death of a parent or spouse would qualify for emergency leave. I was disappointed and angry and asked who had the power to waive this regulation. I was told that only the Commanding General at Army Headquarters in Heidelberg had that authority. I requested permission to plead my case at Army Headquarters. When this was granted I jumped in my jeep and drove the 150 kilometers to Heidelberg. But the Army would make no exception to the regulation and my request was denied. I relayed this information home via the Red Cross. Months later when I returned home, mother took me privately to where Phil was buried and shared her memories of his funeral service. Her faith and love were so strong and resilient.

Because of my activities within the Base Chapel program I deepened my contact and friendship with the senior Protestant Chaplain. He was an older, pot-bellied Southern Baptist and he and his wife were parental figures for many of the young soldiers. This friendship led to a memorable vacation trip together.

Baumholder's senior Protestant chaplain is the large, bald
gentleman next to me. His wife is on the far right. As I recall,
all the others were involved in some special way with the Chapel
program. I taught the Adult Bible class on Sunday morning.
This affable Southern Baptist chaplain and I toured parts of
the Middle East, Europe, together with bits of N. Africa and
Asia Minor in conjunction with a trip to Israel. July, 1954

CHAPTER 12

MY MEDITERRANEAN TOUR

Knowing that my tour of duty was about over the Chaplain suggested that he and I take a three week leave together, visiting numerous countries in the Mediterranean basin. I thought this was a great idea and began to make plans for one last travel adventure before returning to the USA. I had written home about this proposed trip prior to Phillip's death. When I could not obtain emergency leave to go home for the funeral, mother wrote to urge me to continue with my travel plans.

We planned an itinerary to nine countries: Italy, Libya, Egypt, Lebanon, Syria, Jordan, Israel, Turkey and Greece. At this time the United States still had major air bases in many countries which were holdovers from WWII. By getting rides on military aircraft we figured we could cut our travel expenses considerably.

The first leg of our itinerary was from Germany to Rome. We were able to obtain space on a military transport from

Frankfurt to Rome. As we were processing for the flight at the air base I was suddenly faced with an unforeseen emergency. My shot record indicated that I was lacking a required vaccination and I was not permitted to travel. This was a major problem and threatened to undo all the plans the chaplain and I had made. I was able to resolve it but not in a way that I am proud of. The military employed some German nationals as doctors. I persuaded one of these German doctors to "doctor" my shot record so that it reflected the required shots. I rationalized that it was only my health at risk and I was willing to take the risk. With my new shot record I was able to board the airplane for our flight to Rome.

Rome in July was a hot, steamy city. But, weather aside, I was fascinated by this ancient place. My imagination had free play as I walked the old streets and toured the historical icons. In the coliseum I could visualize the Christian martyrs standing prayerfully as they awaited the charge of hungry beasts of prey that would rip their bodies to shreds. I walked with Paul on the Via Appii, I celebrated communion with believers as they huddled around a candle in the catacombs. More recent significant sites were also viewed with interest. St. Peters with its priceless art treasures was a feast for the eyes. My friend and I stood in the great square along with hundreds of other visitors as the Pope came to the balcony and gave his papal blessing to the assembled throng. We saw the building and the balcony from which the tyrant Mussolini harangued the crowds. We watched tourists as they tossed coins into Trevi Fountain. Our all too brief days in Rome got our travel tour off to an excellent start.

From Rome we caught a military flight to Wheelus Field, a large American air base near Tripoli, Libya. Wheelus had been established as a major US base during WWII and continued in that status until Khaddaffi took over the government of Libya in the late sixties. When we landed, the desert heat must have been near 110 f. But it was much drier than Rome and the nights cooled considerably. We heard about fantastic Roman ruins that were out in the desert within driving distance of Wheelus. We hired a vehicle and driver/guide and took off across the desert. Eventually we came to the ruins. I could scarcely believe my eyes. I had no idea that Roman civilization Had flourished in what was now trackless mounds of shifting sand. I was told that this was once fertile land that produced abundant grain for the Empire.

The ruins were spectacular and marvelously preserved in the dry desert air. I was particularly impressed by the ingenious water and sewage system that had provided fresh water and removed the waste. It was far superior to anything that I had experienced as a boy growing up in rural America. One day in Libya sufficed to see what we wanted to see. The next day we were able to catch a military hop to Egypt.

The streets of Cairo were clogged with humanity, many of them Muslim women dressed in black burkas. We had been warned about taking photos of the women but I did sneak a few furtive shots. The local shop owners, of course, recognized us as tourists and tried to sell us all manner of souvenirs. We looked much but bought very little. The next day we made arrangements to make the traditional camel ride to the great Pyramids. A significant archeological discovery had just been made shortly before we arrived and we were able to see it. A secret underground passageway had been discovered leading from the great Pyramid to a buried boat that was designed to be the means of transporting the soul of the buried Pharaoh to his eternal dwelling place. Stored on the boat were remains of ancient food supplies meant to nourish the Pharaoh during his sojourn. I became intrigued by the ancient Egyptian beliefs and teaching about the dead. They squandered the wealth of an empire to try to assure that at least the Pharaoh would gain eternal life.

As we traveled along the Nile river I observed the Egyptian peasant farmers as they tilled their plots. I was amazed at how primitive their farming implements were and even more amazed by their use of manpower. Some of the plows were no more than sharpened beams of wood and many were propelled through the soil by teams of men. What a contrast to the mechanized farming I had experienced in Kansas and Colorado.

Our last day in Egypt was given to touring the Egyptian Museum. Here were displayed antiquities dating back five thousand years. There were over 100,000 items including huge statues, mummies of various pharaohs and their queens, household furniture, jewels, boats, tools and weapons…far too much to absorb in a day or even a week. I was fascinated by the mummies and spent much of my time observing and comparing these well preserved bodies.

There were no military flights available from Egypt to Lebanon so we had to catch a commercial flight from Cairo to Beirut. On this flight I met a middle age American school teacher who said she was flying around the world. She told me that all the luggage she had was in her purse. When I asked how she could do this she said she wore nylon dresses and undies. Each night she would wash them and by morning they would be dry and ready for another day. I traveled light but not that light.

When we arrived in Lebanon I was pleasantly surprised by the attractiveness of Beirut. I felt much more at home there than in Cairo. There were nice parks and a public beach. As expected, the weather was hot and the Mediterranean looked so inviting. I took advantage of a public change facility and was soon cooling off in the sea. We spent the night in a hotel near the Mediterranean and the next day hired a driver/guide and car to take us across country through Syria and Jordan to the Israeli border near Jerusalem. We went across the mountains of Lebanon, where the famous cedars originated, into Syria. We had been warned that Damascus wasn't particularly friendly to Americans but decided nevertheless to visit this city, so rich in biblical history. We walked its ancient streets, including Straight street where Paul spent several days after his conversion. We visited the wall over which Paul was lowered to escape his would-be assassins. But we didn't like the atmosphere in Damascus and felt we were always under scrutiny. The next day we continued on toward Jerusalem.

Our brief time in Jordan opened my eyes to the rage and hatred that Arabs had for Jews. We spent the night at a small Arab inn operated by a lovely Muslim family. They were warm and gracious hosts who appreciated our business. However, when they knew we were planning to visit Israel they were quick to verbalize their hatred of Jews. Their antagonism was so intense and virulent you could hear it in their voices and see it in their faces. It was beyond my understanding then and still is.

The border between Jordan and Israel in 1954 included a "no man's land" sealed off by barbed wire. At this time Jordan controlled the old city where most of the tourist attractions were located. We visited the traditional site of the crucifixion controlled by the Roman Catholic Church. We also visited the less garish, more realistic site called "Gordon's Calvary" located outside the old city wall. We walked to the wailing wall and followed the traditional path of Jesus to the crucifixion site. It was a short auto ride from Jerusalem to Bethlehem. As we approached the village we viewed the hillsides where shepherds heard "good tidings of great joy". The Church of the Nativity was first constructed by order of Constantine in fourth century. It was largely rebuilt in the sixth century and remodeled again in the twelfth century. It was built over the cave stable that served as the birthplace of Jesus. Like most holy sites controlled by the traditional churches it was decorated garishly. As I heard about the competition between the various church bodies that controlled different sites within the Church of the Nativity I was disappointed with the testimony this portrayed to the world. Leaving the church we visited the souvenir shops that lined the main street. I was surprised to learn that the majority of the citizens of Bethlehem were Christians. The shops were filled with Bibles, New Testaments and various Christian artifacts made from olive wood. I bought several New Testaments with covers of polished olive wood to give as gifts.

Although most of the traditional holy sites were in the Jordan controlled region we still wanted to cross over into Israel and see the progress the new nation was making. Also, we intended to fly out of the Tel Aviv airport. To get into the Israeli side you had to pass through a narrow barbed wire passageway across "no man's land" guarded by men with automatic weapons. It was necessary to cross from Jordan to Israel because neither Jordon nor Egypt would permit anyone who had an Israeli stamp on their passport to enter their country. We entered without incident and spent part of two days in Israel before catching a commercial flight to Istanbul, Turkey.

Although Turkey was predominantly an Islamic society its government in 1954 was strongly secular. We found the Turks very friendly and visibly pro-American. Turkey had been our ally during the Korean War and the Turkish troops had fought fiercely alongside our troops. The Korean truce had only been in effect a year so there was still a large residue of good will towards the United States.

Istanbul was a unique, exotic city with a storied past. It was founded about seven centuries before Christ and was originally known as Byzantium. In the fourth century A.D. Emperor Constantine made it the capital of the Roman Empire and it was renamed Constantinople. When Rome fell to the barbarian invaders in 410 A.D. Constantinople became the center of Roman civilization. For the next 1000 years this strategic city served as the center of western culture. It also became the seat of power for the Orthodox Church which was established as a counter to the power of the Roman Catholic Church. Actually, there was not much difference in doctrine and the rivalry was more political than religious.

In 1453 the Ottoman Turks conquered Constantinople and the Islamic world has controlled it ever since. Many Christian churches were demolished, others were converted to mosques and some were simply used as barns or warehouses. And of course, the city's name was changed from Constantinople to Istanbul. I knew something of the history of Istanbul so my visit there was clouded with the knowledge that some of the great churches founded by Paul and other disciples once flourished in what is now known as Turkey. The sad truth is that both the Western and Eastern Christian church became corrupt and, as John prophesied in Revelation, the "candlesticks" were removed.

Despite the shadow of history we were fascinated by Istanbul. The bazaars, the food, the culture were all interesting. We visited the famous Blue Mosque. After taking off our shoes we were permitted to enter and observe the worshippers and the beautiful architecture. It was impossible to experience the huge city of Istanbul in a couple of days but we absorbed as much as we could before taking the short flight to Athens.

We arrived at the Athens airport in early evening and asked a taxi driver to take us to a recommended hotel. One amusing incident took place at the hotel. It was a hot July day and we both wanted a shower before going to dinner. Fortunately, in keeping with European custom, the hotel served dinner until 11 p.m. so we had plenty of time to clean up and cool off. I invited the chaplain to shower first while I lounged in my shorts. The chaplain stripped and was preparing to step into the shower when suddenly without warning the chambermaid walked into our room. The bare chaplain panicked and hid behind a raised closet door which left his skinny white legs in clear view. I couldn't help laughing. The little maid went about her business of leaving fresh linens and then departed, no doubt chuckling to herself about those strange Americans.

I certainly felt more at home in Athens than in Istanbul. Athens' history actually predates that of Istanbul. I was fascinated by the ancient architectural gems which still remained. Of course, the Parthenon on the summit of Mars Hill is the most famous. Although worn and partially defaced it still retained great beauty and spoke of the grandeur of ancient

Athens. From Athens we took a motor trip to Corinth. The nearly demolished remains of the city's market from the days of Paul stirred my imagination. I could picture the great Apostle as he brought the light of the gospel to the moral darkness of Corinth.

There was more we would like to have seen and experienced but one can only do and see so much in three weeks. It was time to catch our plane to Frankfurt and then back to duty at Baumholder. We returned, thanking God for a safe trip and treasuring a host of unforgettable memories.

It was early August when I got back to the base at Baumholder. My two year active duty commitment to the Army would be completed in late September so I only had a few more weeks in Germany before I would be sailing home. Dad suggested that I try to sell his car in Germany rather than shipping it home. He thought I could get a higher price than he could obtain in North Carolina which was probably correct. It had served me well with no mechanical problems. I sold it easily for a price that Dad was pleased with.

These youngsters are either enrolled in the Sunday School or Vacation Bible School at the church I established in Granby, Colorado in 1955 while in my second year of seminary. An attempt had been made earlier to start an Assembles of God church but that had failed. A shell of a building had been left without siding or roofing and a bare, unfinished interior. I commuted 90 miles from Denver to work on building during summer of 1955 and got it enclosed from the weather. Some of the youth that I had led at Calvary Temple drove up from Denver and helped me canvass the town, enlisting children to come to Sunday School. We started with the children and eventually some of the parents began to come. God helped me and the children get a church started that continues sixty years later. When I graduated from Seminary in 1958 Donna and I got married. The men in the church helped me construct a parsonage which we moved into before Celia was born in August, 1959. We continued ministering in Granby until I was inducted as a Navy Chaplain in 1960.

1959

CHAPTER 13

BACK TO DENVER AND SEMINARY

In mid-September I said good-bye to my friends in Germany and traveled to Bremerhaven to embark on a ship bound for New York. I remember little about the voyage home so it must have been pretty routine. The North Atlantic can be quite docile in September. I stayed for a few days at Ft. Hamilton in Brooklyn while my discharge was processed and then on to North Carolina to see the family and reclaim my car.

I had a poignant homecoming. Mother took me privately to Phil's gravesite and shared details about his death and funeral. The strength of her faith and trust in the Lord Jesus was amazing. She radiated a "peace that passed understanding." Dad's faith sustained him as well but he struggled more with releasing Phil into God's hands. He battled with resentment against the teen-age girl who drove the car that killed his boy. Phil's death was a devastating blow to Dad and it took time for the Lord to bring acceptance and healing. I think Dad was emotionally more fragile than Mom. My week at home got me in touch with my roots again and replenished me emotionally and spiritually.

Upon returning to Denver I contacted the Bjork family to see if I could once again obtain room and board with them. Mrs. Bjork welcomed me back and I settled in to my familiar room. While I was in Europe my brother John had married Bernice Sheveland. She had come to Denver to work and through mutual church activities John had met her. They fell in love and after a short courtship decided to get married. I had never met his new wife and meeting her was one of my top priorities. John's bride was a cute little blond of Norwegian extraction who was born and reared in Wisconsin. When I met her in October she was about seven months pregnant with Phil but despite her advanced pregnancy she was animated, perky and a ball of energy. I could readily see why John had fallen for her.

After moving into the Bjork home I discovered I couldn't enroll in Seminary until after Christmas. The Bjorks owned a mountain cabin southwest of Denver in the rugged Pike National Forest area. Knowing I loved to fish they suggested I take my fishing gear and stay in their cabin for a week or so and explore the fishing sites before I got back into a demanding routine. I jumped at the opportunity and quickly packed my gear and headed for the mountain cabin. The Colorado fall weather was beautiful with lots of golden, shimmering aspen decorating the mountain sides. After studying a terrain map I decided that I would try to walk up to a small lake for my first fishing try. When I started out in the morning it was a lovely sunny day and I was looking forward to an exhilarating walk in the mountain air. I was traveling light with just my fishing tackle and a bag lunch. After walking a couple of hours and not yet arriving at the lake I was suddenly enveloped in the grey world of cloud cover. The low lying clouds had completely obliterated the sun and without sight of the sun I quickly lost my sense of direction. The army had taught me how to navigate at night or in fog with the aid of a compass, which I didn't have. Why hadn't I thought to bring a compass?

I pressed on in the fog hoping I would come to the lake. By noon I had not located it and figured I had better head back to the cabin. As I turned back, going in a direction that I supposed was toward the cabin, I began to see terrain that did not look at all familiar. Finally I was forced to face the fact that I was hopelessly lost. I took stock of my situation and decided my best chance of getting back to safety was angling down until I came across a stream. I could then follow the stream until it led me to a road or some other indication of civilization. By this time I had eaten my lunch and had plenty of energy. I moved quickly downward, following each dry ravine or gorge, hoping it might lead to one with water. Hour after hour I walked through some rugged territory but without finding the stream I was looking for. Occasionally I saw the bones of some large animal, probably a deer. I didn't know if a hunter had left a carcass there because it was too difficult to pack out or if it had died a natural death.

Toward evening the temperature became progressively cooler. As long as I kept moving I was plenty warm but I began to imagine what it might be like if I had to spend the night in the high country. Late in the afternoon I intersected a deep ravine and I could hear water running below. I had found a stream. However, the ravine, more like a gorge, was so steep and rocky that I didn't dare try to make my way down to the stream bed. I was forced to follow the upper edge of the ravine as it wound its way down the mountain. At last the ravine began to widen out and I was able to gingerly make my way to the flowing water. By this time it was growing quite dark as well as much colder.

Throughout the day I don't remember praying any specific prayer but I'm sure I was having some earnest conversations with the Lord. The Lord was with me. As darkness settled in I saw a light gleaming in the distance on the other side of the stream. Without hesitation I waded into the shallow but cold, swift flowing mountain stream and made my way to the opposite side. The water absorbed by my trousers quickly froze as I stepped from the creek. It didn't matter. I had seen a light and I pressed on towards it. The light proceeded from a mountain cabin that seemed to be occupied. I knocked loudly on the door and soon a rough looking fellow answered. I could have hugged him but refrained. I told him my story and he told me to get in his pick-up and he would take me to my cabin. He drove about twelve miles to get me home so I had been way off the mark in my calculations. But, as the old saying goes, "All's well that ends well."

I drove back to Denver determined to enroll in seminary and follow through on my commitment to Christ to enter the ministry. The only seminary I knew anything about in Denver was Iliff, a liberal Methodist school located on the campus of Denver University. I visited Iliff and perused the curriculum. I was surprised to discover that they offered no courses in Hebrew or Greek, the original languages of the Old and New

Testaments. I felt both were important for a good foundation in biblical theology. As I investigated further I discovered that the theology of Iliff was not bibliccally oriented. The school considered the bible simply a product of human imagination. I knew Iliff was not the school for me.

When I explained to the registrar at Iliff that I was looking for a seminary in the Denver area that offered Hebrew and Greek I was informed about a Baptist seminary that had recently been established in Denver. This school was located in the historic Bonfil's mansion. I visited the seminary and was pleased with the classes offered, including biblical Greek and Hebrew. It was too late to get enrolled in the fall quarter so I talked to the registrar about enrolling for the winter quarter. There was just one problem; the seminary was affiliated with the Conservative Baptist denomination which was historically opposed to Pentecostals. I was again Youth Leader at Calvary Temple, one of the largest Evangelical churches in Denver, which just happened to be Pentecostal. No Pentecostal had ever enrolled in the seminary so I was seeking to be a "ground breaker". In addition to being a Pentecostal I also had leanings toward Arminianism and human freedom as opposed to Calvinism and predeterminism. Despite my heretical leanings the Admissions Committee decided to permit me to enroll for the 1954-55 winter term.

While I was waiting for the winter term I visited my old boss who now owned a hardware store in the new University Hills shopping center. I had enjoyed working for Max Struble when he was my department head working at Montgomery Ward while in college. Max was glad to see me and said he could use a part time employee if I wanted to work while in seminary. I was quick to accept his offer. I still had about three academic years of G.I. bill eligibility remaining which paid all my tuition plus about $100.00 a month for living expenses. With a good part time job working about 25 hours per week I could live quite nicely. I had finished paying for my car while serving in the army so I had no indebtedness.

I took to the academic environment of seminary like a duck to water. The president of the seminary was Dr. Thomas, an aged intellectual whom I suspected was there more for the new seminary's accreditation than for leadership. The dean was an exciting young theologian by the name of Vernon Grounds. I sensed that Dr. Grounds was the real leader of the school and this was confirmed the next year. Dr. Thomas stepped down and Dr. Grounds was installed as President.

To my surprise, I discovered that the seminary had a basketball team that competed in the Denver church league. I joined the team and enjoyed playing again. However, I didn't really know the other team members since I had just arrived on campus and they were mostly upper classmen. As a result I felt like an outsider with no sense of comradeship. I completed the season but that was my last basketball until I went into the Navy as chaplain.

The most demanding initial aspect of seminary life was assessing the professors. All of them were academically qualified and had valuable knowledge to share. However, some were dull and uninspiring. One just endured their classes. Others were gifted instructors who made their subject matter interesting and, at times, even exciting. As I think back, my three favorite professors were these: (1) Stuart Hackett, a young philosopher/theologian who enthusiastically expounded on Rational Empiricism, his philosophy of choice. Dr. Hackett was a Greek scholar and theologian par excellence. He asked the right questions and made you think. (2) Vernon Grounds. Dr. Grounds was a warm hearted professor who conveyed personal interest in each student. He had a keen wry wit which permeated his lectures. His classes offered challenging ideas mixed with practical application of Christian truth. (3) Raymond Buker, Sr. Dr. Buker was a veteran missionary who had spent years laboring in Nepal. He was a tough but gentle man whose very life exemplified Christian commitment and faithfulness. Of course, there were other good professors but these three particularly made lasting impressions on my life. Because I had no previous experience with biblical Hebrew or Greek I had to take introductory classes in both during the summer of 1955. I was surprised at how much I enjoyed Hebrew. It was so different from western languages, a different alphabet and reading from right to left, and it fascinated me. I also enjoyed Greek but that was no surprise. I had looked forward to learning this foundational New Testament language.

When I returned to Denver from Germany the Calvary Temple young people once again voted for me to assume the office of Youth Leader. After about eight months the Lord began to deal with me about resigning that position and launching out as a pioneer pastor. I discussed this with the Rocky Mountain District officials of the Assemblies of God and they recommended two communities for me to consider. One was a little town out on the plains of Eastern Colorado called Fleming. The other was a little mountain town about ninety miles northwest of Denver called Granby. After visiting both towns, assessing their potential and considering each one's driving distance from Denver I prayerfully chose to invest my ministry in Granby. I informed the District officials of my decision and they gave me their official approval and blessing.

Granby was picturesquely located in Middle Park near the eight thousand foot elevation level. It was nestled in the valley of the Fraser River which joined the Colorado River a short distance southwest of town. Snow-capped mountains reared their majestic white peaks to the east. The District Home Missions department had designated Granby as a site for a home missions Church. A small, elevated lot had been purchased on which a church building had been started but never finished. The building was framed but lacked a roof. Asbestos shingle siding covered about half the building. Inside, the ceiling lacked sheetrock and there was no trim around the windows, doors or floor. It was a monumental challenge but I was young (27) and used to hard work.

I had decided to take the summer off and devote my time to summer school and church building. My first priority was to get the church roofed. With some help from local men we soon had the job completed. Funds were so limited we were forced to use asphalt composition roll roofing. Not only was it cheaper but went on much faster than individual shingles. And although it wasn't particularly attractive it provided quality protection. My next priority was to get siding on the exterior walls and get the exterior trim on windows and doors. I knew winter weather at Granby's altitude could be extremely severe so it was important to get the outside weatherproofed.

But what is a church building without people? I had been given the names of two families with Assembly of God roots and they were eager to help establish an Assembly of God church. But two families do not make a congregation. Furthermore, neither family lived in Granby. One family lived in Tabernash, a neighboring town to the southeast. The other lived in Hot Sulphur Springs, a neighboring town to the west. I decided that we needed to canvass Granby with a survey to help us ascertain potential candidates for church. I presented this as a missions project for the young people at Calvary Temple. Several carloads of energetic young people drove the ninety miles of mountain road to Granby on a warm Saturday. They fanned out over the town, knocked on doors and personally conducted interviews for the survey. As result the church got a lot of good publicity plus the names of several interested adults. Even more children expressed an interest in Sunday School. By July we were ready to advertise our opening service. There was still a lot of finish work to be done on the interior but we could still conduct worship and Sunday School. The congregation was "blue collar" and didn't mind a few rough edges.

I named the new church "Central Assembly" because we were given a neon sign that originally identified Central Assembly in Denver. When the original Central Assembly congregation outgrew its home they built a new church called Calvary Temple. My uncle Elmo helped install the gift sign above the entry way of the Granby church. At night it could be seen for blocks.

It was nearly 200 miles round trip from Denver to Granby. Much of the road had lots of curves with few passing lanes. Consequently, on a good day you could count on two and a half hours driving time, one way. Time on the road was time I could better spend working on the church building so I looked diligently for a place to live in or near Granby. I found an old, unoccupied cabin not far from town, where I could stay for practically nothing. It was in a wooded area, pretty isolated, but the price was right. Dad came up from Prospect Valley and helped me for several days. He was a good camp cook. I especially remember how tasty his fried potatoes were, generously flavored with bacon and plenty of onions. He liked to fix steak with his potatoes but his potatoes were much better than his overcooked steak.

Summer in the mountains is delightful with warm days and cool nights but it passes all too quickly. Nevertheless, I accomplished a good deal during the summer. I finished the summer classes of introductory Hebrew and Greek and got the exterior of the church building prepared for colder weather. With the coming of fall I had to move back to Denver. I had a full academic schedule at seminary plus a part time job working 25 hours a week. I had to limit my pastoral duties to Sunday. I would drive to Granby early Sunday morning, conduct two Sunday services, a.m. and p.m. and then drive back to Denver Sunday night. Slowly the congregation was growing. We had a Sunday School superintendent and a small but dedicated teaching staff. I was young with no previous pastoral experience but one trait I possessed, perseverance. I believed God had led me to Granby and was determined to stay until He led me away.

When I enrolled for my first fall term in September, 1955 I felt much more at home in the seminary. The class just beginning in September would be the class I would graduate with. Since I already had two terms under my belt I unconsciously had assumed a place of leadership in the class of 1958. Up to this time I was known chiefly as "the new guy from a Pentecostal background." But I began to be known as "the guy who questions the party line and who speaks his mind." I found theology classes immensely stimulating and enjoyed the discussions they often generated.

A new theology professor, Dr. Dick B., was added to the faculty for the 1955-56 academic year. His dad was a well-known and successful Conservative Baptist pastor in Arizona. I took a class under Dr. B. and soon discovered that he was not into theological discussions. I asked a question once relating to the present day activity of the Holy Spirit in the church. He got red in the face and obviously very angry. He turned on me and said, "Don't ever bring up that subject in this class." Dr. B. was an exception and didn't last long at the seminary. At the end of the school year he was gone. I met him many years later and he had mellowed and was very gracious.

One of the things that surprised me was the great amount of criticism the Conservative Baptist seminary took from many of its constituent churches. A large number of the CB churches were conservative separatists, that is, they believed that other churches, particularly main line and Pentecostal churches, were doctrinally unsound and they should separate completely from them. Because Billy Graham cooperated with these "apostate" churches they opposed Graham. Because the seminary strongly supported Graham's ministry approach many of the CB churches opposed and criticized the seminary. Dr. Grounds, as president, took the brunt of the criticism. His gracious response to his narrow minded critics was tremendously impressive to me. I envied his sense of humor and sweet spirit which were in sharp contrast to his opponents. Fortunately, there were many moderate CB churches who supported Dr. Grounds and the seminary as well as Billy Graham's ministry. The seminary depended on these churches for much of its financial support.

My weekly drives to Granby were sometimes real adventures, especially in the winter. Berthoud pass on highway

40 was 11315 feet in elevation and could be quite treacherous when it snowed. Sharp curves and no guard rails on the downhill embankment side were dangerous combinations on a slick road. Sometimes there were avalanches that blocked the road and you had to wait while plows opened the lanes. Most of these were controlled and drivers had plenty of warning. My most vivid memory of a "heart stopping" moment happened on a winter Sunday morning following a snow storm on Berthoud pass. My car began to slide on the slippery downhill surface and headed uncontrolled for the steep embankment. Fortunately, the snowplow had been ahead of me and thrown up a small snow bank that kept me from plunging over the edge. Breathing a sigh of relief and a hearty "Thank you, Lord" I proceeded slowly down the mountain.

After one year the little mountain church in Granby had organization and a small but growing congregation. A committed Christian man served as Sunday School superintendent. Several women taught the children and I taught the adult class. It was during the summer of 1956 that I experienced one of the most dangerous experiences of my life although I only recognized the frightening danger in retrospect. Curiously enough, it began in church.

Following a prayer service one of the participants waited around until the others had left. She was a very attractive young wife and mother who served as one of our Sunday School teachers. She apparently had something on her mind that she wanted to talk about but I had absolutely no idea what it was. I was flabbergasted when she approached me and said, "Glenn, I love you." Surely she was speaking of a healthy affection and regard for her pastor. But as I looked at her I knew that she had something else in mind. My first year in seminary hadn't taught me what to do in this situation. I stuttered something and left in confusion.

I wish I could say I handled this awkward situation with finesse and spiritual maturity. Actually, I didn't do anything but temporize, hoping the situation would resolve itself. I didn't want to take any action that would result in the loss of one of our church families. But the situation didn't resolve itself. The young woman continued to convey signals of her ardent infatuation. Fortunately, although I was pretty naïve for a 28 year old, I had enough sense to not let myself be alone with her. Nevertheless, I was in far more danger than I realized.

I began to fantasize about what it would be like to respond to this woman and go away with her. Actually, the fact that I could fantasize about having an illicit relationship helped bring me to my senses. I realized that my future as an honorable man and as a minister were in the balance. The Holy Spirit let me know there was to be no more temporizing. I quickly made it plain to the young woman that I was not interested in a relationship with her. She knew that I meant it. To my knowledge, no one, including her family, was aware of the woman's infatuation or of her attempt to establish an illicit relationship. Her husband was a fine guy and I prayed their marriage would survive.

Once I acted decisively, as I should have done immediately, a great load was lifted from my spirit and mind. Apparently, the young woman confessed her attempt to initiate an affair to her husband. Sometime later he drove to Denver to talk to me and to confirm what had happened. I gathered that she had told him that nothing at all physical had happened. And that was true. I was so thankful that I could look him in the eyes and reassure him that his wife had not been unfaithful, at least not in any physical sense. His wife came to her senses and dedicated herself to being a good wife and mother. Their marriage apparently was reestablished on a good foundation and lasted until the husband died many years later.

So what did I learn from this experience? I learned that temptation can come at you from totally unexpected sources. I learned that sin can appear in very attractive packages. I learned that as soon as temptation is recognized it must be quickly and firmly resisted. I learned that temptation pits short term gratification against long term values. I learned that temptation to a specific sin, successfully resisted, has a "vaccinating" effect. Never again was I ever tempted to get involved in an illicit relationship. I learned that the Holy Spirit is faithful to "convict of sin, of righteousness and judgment to come."

Later in the summer of 1956 we had a family visit the church from Houston, Texas. They were an enthusiastic evangelical family, Baptist I think, and became regular attendees at our services. They had rented a cabin near Granby and planned to spend several weeks there. The dad was a court recorder in the Houston judicial system. As I recall there were two or three children but I can only really remember the oldest daughter. She was a college student and quite attractive. We became good friends and enjoyed conversing and sharing ideas. They were with us about six weeks before they returned home to Houston. I really missed my new friend and toyed with the idea of visiting her in Texas. However, it wasn't a good time for me to pursue a serious relationship. I still had two years of seminary to complete as well as very limited finances. I decided not to go to Houston.

Alliene and I in Kansas. She is probably three
years old and I four and a half.   1933

This is our family in Cedar Bluff, VA. I am 16, Johnny is 10, Carol is 8,
David is 5, Barbie is 2 and Faith is one. Aunt Vi stands at left.
1944

Because of the windy, cold weather in Iceland athletic events were conducted inside a huge field-house. Our team won the Station volleyball championship in 1965.

Faith Chapel members having fun in the sun and sand. Someone will remember where this is but not I. I guess it is 1984 or 1985

Although I played other sports, for years basketball was my favorite. I played competitively until I retired from the Navy.

1972

Barbara and Faith about 5 and 6 years old. Barbara is the older and more outgoing. Faith is demure and more shy. They were my favorite photographic subjects. We called them the "gold dust" twins because of their blonde hair.

General Olsen presents me with the trophy for the " most improved golfer" in 1972 at the Marine Corps Supply Center in Barstow. That tells you how bad I must have been when the year began. This was the only time in my military service that I ever played golf on a regular basis.

Captain Quinn, the new commanding officer of
NAS Moffett, is congratulating Donna and wishing
her God speed at my retirement ceremony.

How did Jim Wark wrangle his way into the middle of all these lovely ladies? You will notice he is the only one not paying attention. Great Faith Chapel memories.

1985

The Brown siblings at the biennial family reunion in Colorado in 1991. Norma Jean on far left and Charlie on far right. Both of them have gone HOME to be with the Lord and join Faith, Phil and Alliene. There's a great big family reunion ahead for the rest of us, in God's good timing.

1991

Sunday School graduation day at Faith Chapel in Pleasanton,
California. Linda Taylor is the class teacher. Jim Wark, SS
superintendent, observes in background.

1985

Faith Chapel Board members, front to back: Linda Taylor, Melissa Filipowicz, David Grajeda, Glenn Brown, Tim Tooman, Jim Wark.

1986

The Grajeda family, David, Sophia, Jason, Mia and Chris. Later
Vanessa would come along. David and Sophia contributed
immeasurably to the spiritual life of the church. Although David
has gone HOME, Sophia continues to serve as church Secretary.

My six lovely sisters and Dads' and Mom's pride and joy.

1982

A torrid table tennis game while visiting a Vietnamese Naval base near Danang. This was a good "Asian relations ice breaker".

1969

Our wedding took place in beautiful Calvary Temple where I had
served as Youth Leader while attending Denver University and
Seminary. Pastor Charles Blair officiated. My two Bluhm uncles,
Elmo and Arley, were groomsmen. My sister Carol, far left, was a
bridesmaid. Marilyn Horton, close friend of Donna's, was maid of
honor. Pastor Hill's daughter served as flower girl.

June 24, 1958

CHAPTER 14
COURTSHIP AND MARRIAGE

June 24, 1958

A lthough I was only 28 some friends had the idea that it was time for me to get married. One such friend was Fred Harvey, one of the young men in the Calvary Temple youth group. He called me in the fall of 1956 about a young woman he wanted me to meet. He suggested a double date with him and his girl-friend. I agreed to a "blind date" and Fred made all the arrangements. This was the first time I met Donna Wirth, at this time a senior in college. The four of us went to a University of Denver football game. I don't remember much about the game. I think my alma Mater lost decisively which was not unusual. I do remember there were no romantic sparks generated between Donna and me. We both continued our academic pursuits, she in college and I in seminary, with no further contact for almost a year.

My brother Charles David, eleven years younger than I, graduated from high school in 1957. He joined me in Granby to look for work doing the summer. He was able to get a job working with the section gang on the railroad. It was hard work but Charlie was young and used to hard work. During the summer I was living in an old cabin outside of town and Charlie joined me there. I had a terrible time getting Charlie up in the morning to go to work. We had an alarm clock but Charlie would get up and turn it off and go back to sleep. He claimed he never heard the alarm and I began to wonder if he was "sleep walking" when he got up and turned it off. Fortunately for Charlie, I heard the alarm and managed to "hustle and hassle" him out of bed and off to work. I also had a summer job in Granby working as a helper with Johnny Syme, a skilled workman with various floor and counter top coverings. John was such a nice fellow and I learned a lot about his trade just from observing and helping him. His wife and children were members of our church and Sunday school.

Another good friend from Calvary Temple was a talented professional soloist named Ed Searcy. In addition to a superb singing voice he had a great Christian testimony. In the summer of 1957 I invited Ed to come to Granby and present a gospel concert. He came and brought a talented accompanist whom I recognized as my blind date from the previous fall. As I watched her play the piano I noticed that she was not only talented but attractive as well. There was no immediate romantic interest but I did think that Donna Wirth was someone I should get better acquainted with.

By this time Donna had graduated from college with teaching credentials for the Colorado public school system. In the fall of 1957 she had a contract to teach music in the Cherry Creek school district. After spending the 1957 summer in Granby I returned to Denver to begin my last year of seminary. One of the Bjork girls returned home to live so I had to move out and find lodging elsewhere. I was able to rent a room in a large house directly across the street from the seminary. One of the more enjoyable things about living near the seminary was that I was able to join other students who participated in the seminary's food service program. Meal times were great times of camaraderie, pleasant conversation and laughter.

My last year of seminary, especially the first two quarters, was extremely busy. In addition to a full load of pretty heavy subjects I worked at the hardware store twenty-five to thirty hours per week, I pastored the church in Granby and I had started to date Donna. Before long I consolidated two of these activities into the same time slot. My big date of the week with Donna was our Sunday drive to Granby and back. Needless to say, her quality piano artistry was greatly appreciated by the congregation...and the pastor. In the classroom I was enjoying the challenge of Hebrew and Greek. I was doing so well in Hebrew that Professor Kalland actually asked me to be in charge of the class on a couple of days when he could not be present.

My relationship with Donna had progressed to the state that I knew I had to "fish or cut bait". I recognized that Donna was a special girl and I admired what I saw in her life and character. She was attractive, neat, disciplined, intelligent, talented, intuitive and a dedicated Christian. I pictured her as an ideal wife for a minister. There were areas in which we were not particularly compatible. She was neat; I was pretty sloppy. She was generally disciplined; I was task disciplined. I reached conclusions based on logic and evidence; she was more intuitive. Our recreational interests were different. The one all important area which we shared was a common commitment to Jesus Christ.

Before the winter was over I decided to ask Donna to marry me. I had some doubt and fear, not about Donna, but about myself. I knew I was attracted to this special young woman but where were the emotional "fireworks" that should accompany a serious relationship? I was fearful that I was approaching our relationship too much with my head and not enough with my heart. Despite misgivings I kept them to myself except for a brief conversation with Uncle Elmo. I can only say in retrospect that Donna's character and loving actions won my heart as well as my head. She is a wonderful and loving companion with which to grow old.

Once Donna agreed to marry me I suggested we do so before I graduated but Donna would have none of that. She set June 24 1958 as the wedding date. The spring of 1958 was a hectic time for me. In April I was officially ordained by the Rocky Mountain District of the Assemblies of God. In May I graduated from seminary. Graduation ceremonies were conducted in the sanctuary of one of the larger Baptist churches. Many of my friends and family members were there to share this special occasion with me. I was surprised to receive recognition as the graduate with the highest grade point average. A small but welcome monetary prize was awarded for this scholastic achievement.

Our wedding was conducted in the sanctuary of Calvary Temple in Denver. Pastor Charles Blair officiated. His wife Betty played the organ and our friend Ed Searcy was soloist.

The church was decorated with a variety of colorful flowers furnished by Donna's uncle, a wholesale florist. Donna was a lovely, radiant bride dressed in a beautiful white wedding dress. I wore a rented tux. My uncle Elmo served as best man and Uncle Arley also stood up with me. After the evening ceremony, wedding cake and other refreshments were served in the church fellowship hall.

Because of the late hour we spent our wedding night in a local home made available to us. The weather was wild and wet with severe rain showers. Donna's brother Lanny and friends who knew where the house was located, braved the stormy weather to provide us a noisy initiation into married life. The next day the rain was over and we drove to Glenwood Springs, a beautiful area of Colorado, for our poverty enforced short honeymoon.

We started our marriage fully qualified below the poverty line. I had just graduated from seminary with little money and a five year old car. The best we could afford for housing was a rather dismal basement apartment. We had no furniture but relatives and church members provided a selection of used pieces. The living room sofa was pretty bedraggled but Donna camouflaged it with an attractive throw cover and it looked decent enough. Although Donna was able to make our apartment semi-attractive I was determined to provide her with something more livable. I decided to build a parsonage on the back of the church. Uncle Elmo drew up a set of plans for a two bedroom house with kitchen, living room and bath. It also had a full basement which would serve as Sunday School rooms.

I had little experience in carpentry but I was determined to proceed with the building project nevertheless. I borrowed a set of six little books that explained each phase of building a house. I would read a section and then do what it said. Of course, some things had to be done by professionals. Digging the basement required hiring a back-hoe and operator. And the concrete had to be delivered in ready-mix trucks. Since the new parsonage was joined directly to the rear of the church this presented special problems when pouring the concrete basement wall. Normally, the two sides of a concrete form are held securely together by wire ties which keep the forms from spreading beyond the desired width. But when one side of the form is a dirt wall, the result of excavation, then the wooden form has to be secured by angled braces. I had never experienced the enormous pressure that wet concrete exerts against a vertical form. As a result of my ignorance I didn't put sufficient braces against the wooden form. As the wet concrete filled the form the enormous pressure near the top began to bulge the form outward. I saw what was happening and desperately cried for help. If the form collapsed it would be disastrous . Concrete in the mountains was about three times higher than in Denver. Our budget couldn't afford the loss of a yard. My helpers and I frantically reinforced the bulging form with angled braces. We managed to secure the form before it completely collapsed. However, the resulting wall had a "permanent wave." Every time I went downstairs the bulging basement wall reminded me of my close call.

Although the congregation had grown significantly, Central Assembly was still a small church with less than a hundred regular attendees. One Easter I remember our attendance was 146 so we were making an impact in our small mountain town. But realistically we knew we would never have a large congregation. I was praying, trying to determine

God's will for our future ministry. I didn't think we would stay in Granby for a long period of time. My mission to get a church established there had been accomplished and Donna and I were ready for another assignment. Before we were married I had shared with Donna my desire to eventually serve as a military chaplain. She had no objections. Fortunately, she had no idea what she was getting into.

I had thought about entering the military chaplaincy ever since I served in the army during the Korean war era. My time in the military, especially my tour of duty in Germany, opened my eyes to the potential for chaplaincy ministry. I knew seminary training was a prerequisite for the chaplaincy. This motivated me to enroll in seminary as quickly as I could after being discharged in 1954. Pastoral experience was also strongly recommended if not an absolute requirement. With both of these accomplished I sensed it was time to request active duty. An absolute requirement for duty as a chaplain was what the military called "ecclesiastical endorsement." This simply meant that a chaplaincy candidate must be approved and endorsed by a the recognized religious body before the military will accept him or her. When I requested ecclesiastical endorsement from the Assemblies of God I was asked to come to Springfield, Missouri to be interviewed by the Chaplains' Commission. Since Donna was teaching school we arranged for us to meet with the Commission during the Christmas and New Year holiday.

Dad came up from Prospect Valley, it must have been in the fall of 1958, and helped me lay bricks for the chimney of the new house. Actually, I helped him. Dad was a good brick layer and I served as his hod carrier. The parsonage was heated by a coal furnace so we had to have a chimney. With dad's skill the chimney went up quickly. Before winter the roof was on and inside work could be continued during cold weather. And at Granby's elevation of nearly eight thousand feet we had plenty of cold weather in winter. When dad heard we were driving to Springfield, Missouri during the 1958-59 Christmas and New Year break he asked if he could go along. It was the time of the year when the weather could change quickly from good to bad so I was glad to have another experienced driver accompany us. Dad would have a chance to get better acquainted with his new daughter-in-law as well as an opportunity to visit his relatives in Kansas.

Fortunately, the weather presented no problems. I had a chance to introduce my new bride to Kansas relatives during our brief stop there. As I recall, there was some light snow in Springfield and the weather was cold. The Headquarters building at this time was an old converted commercial building. In contrast to the outside temperature, the building was oppressively overheated. Donna began to feel ill, blaming it on the excessive heat.

My meeting with the Chaplains' Commission went very well. I met all the ecclesiastical requirements plus I had five years of active duty military experience under my belt. The major decision seemed to be not if I was qualified to be a military chaplain but which branch of the armed forces should I be assigned to. When asked which branch I would prefer I replied, "I served three years as an enlisted man in the Air Force and two years active plus three years inactive as an officer in the Army. Either one of these would be acceptable to me. I have never served in the Navy and prefer not to be considered for Navy duty." My ugly experiences aboard the troopship from San Francisco to Honolulu were still fresh in my memory. Dr. Thomas Zimmerman, chairman of the Commission, assured me that I met all the Assembly of God requirements. He was pleased that I would be one of their candidates for active duty. I would be notified when an opening became available.

The drive home was uneventful except Donna became quite nauseated on the trip. She thought it was the continuing effects of being overheated in the headquarters building. Dad was the only one who actually recognized what was going on but he kept his opinion to himself. Actually, Donna was two months pregnant and this was the cause of her queasiness.

Now that a baby was on the way it was all the more urgent to complete the new parsonage. With the chimney completed, the roof on and the furnace operating it was now possible to do the inside finish work in reasonable comfort. As result of the local timber industry, lumber was quite reasonable. For this reason I decided to finish the basement in knotty pine paneling. This was not plywood with a knotty pine veneer but individual knotty pine boards. It not only looked attractive but was very practical. The ¾ inch thick wood provided some insulation and was an ideal surface on which to tack Sunday School teaching aids or posters.

I don't remember the exact date in 1959 in which the construction of the new parsonage was completed. I think it was in the spring or early summer. I know it was before Celia was born in August. Donna and I made numerous trips to Denver to select tile, paint, lights and other finish items not available in Granby. Uncles Elmo and Arley came up and did the electrical work. Finally, the finish work was completed and we had a bare house that needed to be furnished. Grandma Bluhm donated an old but serviceable refrigerator. Elmo and

Eloise gave us an attractive kitchen table and chair set. From some source we managed to obtain beds for both bedrooms and a sofa for the living room. At last, we had a furnished new house to move into. I know it was a happy day when we were able to move out of the gloomy basement apartment into the sunny, light-filled parsonage. The new house was a very modest two bedroom dwelling but it seemed luxurious compared to where we had previously lived. And, best of all, we had a clean, new house in which to welcome baby Celia Dawn.

In the summer Granby came alive with hundreds of tourists. It was a fisherman's paradise. Lake Granby, a huge man made reservoir, was stocked with varieties of trout and fresh water salmon. The headwaters of the Colorado river were just a few miles away. The Frazier and Colorado rivers merged near the town. Ten miles north lay Grand Lake, a deep, cold, natural lake which offered plenty of sailing and fishing opportunities. There were several motels in town designed to serve the summer influx.

These motels provided welcome jobs for high school and college youth. My sister Barbara decided she would like to come to Granby during the summer of 1959 and work for one of the motels. She was a lovely little blonde teen-ager but plenty used to hard work and had no difficulty landing a job. We were now living in the new parsonage so we had a place where Barbi could stay. Even though her work kept her very busy it was fun just having her around for the summer. She was in Granby when Celia was born and was able to welcome her first niece into the family.

As the due date for our baby approached Donna's mother came to lend her support. We moved her into the guest bedroom and Barb was consigned to the lumpy sofa bed in the living room. Growing up with five sisters this was not Barb's first experience with an uncomfortable bed. She adjusted with her usual grace and carried on like the trooper she was.

Very early on Tuesday morning, August 4 1959 Donna told me that we had better go to the hospital. There was no hospital in Granby so we had to drive to Kremmling, about 30 miles west of us. We checked Donna into the small hospital and settled in for what proved to be a long wait. The day dragged slowly on. Mother Wirth and I took separate lunch breaks at a nearby restaurant. Donna had a long labor but, according to her, not particularly difficult. Before giving birth she was administered some kind of gas that left her conscious but feeling giddy. About 7 p.m. I was summoned to the delivery room to witness the birth of our baby. The birth process was pretty messy, requiring the use of instruments, and I felt pretty giddy myself before it was over. But the result was a beautiful baby girl whom I held for a moment before the medical staff took her in tow. In those days mothers and babies were not released from the hospital as quickly as they are today. Donna and Celia Dawn were not released until Saturday, four days after birth.

Everything was ready for Celia Dawn's arrival home. Someone had loaned us a bassinet which we located in our bedroom so we could hear the baby at night. During the day Celia lay in a little crib which was usually kept in the living room. She was a pleasant, easy-going baby and brought a lot of joy into our lives as we watched her develop.

Unfortunately, Donna received erroneous post-natal advice that resulted in a serious infection. She was quite ill for several weeks. We don't know but Donna has wondered if the consequences of the infection may have hindered future pregnancies. Be that as it may, we had our treasured daughter. God was good.

Cody and Zoe, have you ever wondered how your mother got her name? I'll tell you the true story of the origin of Celia Dawn. For years I had liked the name "Dawn". The pastor's daughter of the church I attended in Denver in 1947 was named Dawn. I thought it had a nice sound. But more than that, it spoke of future expectations and promise of good things ahead. But what name should go with Dawn? I had read in Readers' Digest that specialists in the English language had determined that the most melodious, euphonious sound in English vocabulary was a combination of the two words "cellar door". I didn't make that up. That's what the language experts had proclaimed. I wasn't about to name our baby "cellar door" but I figured "Dawn" was fairly close to "door" so what went well with "Dawn" to produce a melodious sound. Lo and behold, "Celia" just fit the bill. So that is the true story of how your mother got her melodious, euphonious name.

When I had visited the Chaplains' Commission in Springfield I had been quite specific about the military branches I preferred to serve in. I had definitely asked not to be considered for the Navy. Sometime later in 1959 the Lord began to specifically deal with me about considering serving in the the Navy. I tacitly agreed that if the Lord wanted me to enter the Navy I would agree to do so. However, I procrastinated about informing the Chaplains' Commission of my change of mind. To my surprise, sometime late in 1959 I received a letter from the Commission stating that there was an opening for an Assembly of God chaplain in the U.S. Navy.

They would like very much for me to fill this opening. Would I reconsider my decision to serve only in the Army or Air Force.? The Lord had already prepared me for this decision and I was glad to affirm my willingness to serve in the Navy.

Soon after I indicated my willingness to serve in the Navy I was asked to report to the Navy Recruiting Office in Denver to be interviewed and undergo a physical exam by a Navy doctor. Both went well and I was cleared to be called to active duty as a Navy chaplain. With the prospects of soon being called to active duty one of my primary concerns was helping the church find a new pastor to further the church's growth and influence in the community. I approached a young minister friend who possessed the qualities I thought would bless the church. My friend, Darrell Madsen, agreed to come to Granby as a pastoral candidate.

The church responded positively to the Madsen's and to Darrell's ministry and he was elected to be the new pastor. Unfortunately for the church, shortly after being elected pastor, Darrell was chosen to be the Rocky Mountain District youth leader. As a result he chose to assume the District office and resigned the pastorate. But another pastor was elected and the church went on. When the Brown family reunion was held near Granby in 1991 Donna and I visited the Granby church for the first time in more than thirty years. We were delighted to discover that the church had survived and was still impacting the community with the gospel. The old property had been sold and there was an attractive new sanctuary and new parsonage. On a visit to the church in 1991 we saw only one person who was there in 1960, one of our teens, now a grandmother.

It took me awhile to find my way in the Navy chaplaincy. My first assignment was at Camp Lejeune as a battalion chaplain with the Sixth Marine Regiment. Fortunately, my time as a platoon leader in the Army gave me some orientation to the structure of the Marine Corps and I was able to find my place in it. The structure of the chaplaincy was a little harder for me to figure out because of the tremendous variety of theological stances represented. But my relationship to Christ was secure and I navigated through the theological maze with confidence that He was at the helm.

1960

CHAPTER 15
GETTING STARTED AS A NAVY CHAPLAIN

I had received orders from the Navy to report to the Navy Chaplains' School in Newport, RI by April 1, 1960. We made plans to depart Granby in early March. The Navy sent a commercial moving van to Granby to pack our furniture and belongings which were to remain in storage until we received orders to a duty station after I had completed the two month Chaplains' School. Actually, all of our belongings could have been put in a pick-up truck. Much of our furniture would remain in the parsonage. We left the new washer and dryer that we had purchased after the church agreed to reimburse us.

We made arrangements for Donna and Celia Dawn to stay with her parents in Denver while I completed Chaplains' School in Rhode Island. We decided to buy another car so that each of us would have transportation during our separation.

We had no money but my dad offered to loan us the needed amount. We had decided to get an American motors small station wagon. Dad volunteered to drive me to Kenosha, Wisconsin to pick the car up at the factory. Thanks to dad, I was able to pay cash for the car. I think it cost about twelve hundred dollars. After helping me obtain the new car dad returned to Colorado and I proceeded to Newport, Rhode Island. The new station wagon served me well at Chaplains' School. After completing the school I drove back to Colorado to get Donna and Celia. I had received orders to report in June to the huge Marine Base at Camp Lejeune, North Carolina. We decided to leave the Ambassador parked at Denver in the Wirth's backyard while we were in North Carolina. The first introductory assignment was traditionally quite short so we didn't expect to be at Camp Lejeune very long. As it turned out we were there six months.

My first assignment was battalion chaplain of the first battalion, Sixth Marines. In Marine shorthand the 1/6 was a storied, historic unit which traced its history back to World War One. It was first activated in 1917, sent to Europe where it performed valiantly in several major engagements. During World War Two 1/6 took the brunt, fighting the entrenched Japanese in island after island, slowly but surely wresting control from the Emperor's fanatic forces.

I recognized the importance of being physically fit if I were to have rapport with the approximately one thousand young marines and sailors in my battalion. Consequently, I determined to join the troops when they fell out for calisthenics each morning. I thought I was in pretty good shape but a few mornings with the troops showed me just how flabby I really was. Trying to do the demanding exercises actually made me physically ill during the first week or so. I would throw-up and then continue exercising as long as I was able. But I persisted and gradually my old body was whipped into shape. I would go on marches with the troops but I carried no weapon or ammo or pack so it was easier for me. At times I would spot a young trooper who was having difficulty keeping up and I would offer to carry his weapon for awhile. This won me a few points with the troopers if not with the officers.

I soon discovered that not many marines or sailors stayed aboard the base on week-ends. I had Sunday services in the Battalion area but never more than a handful were present. Most of my ministry consisted of counseling sessions during the work week rather than on Sunday. The Chief of Navy Chaplains at this time was a no-nonsense Catholic priest. You can imagine my surprise when I discovered there were four or five Catholic chaplains at Camp Lejeune who were confined to quarters while awaiting discharge. It turned out they were all alcoholics and the Chief was cracking down and purging the Corps of addicted priests. As I discovered later this was an ongoing problem within the Navy including chaplains. But alcoholism was especially prevalent among Catholic priests. I once felt compelled to confront a Catholic chaplain about his excessive drinking. His reply was, "I took a vow to give up women but I never took a vow to give up bourbon". This is not to say that I didn't know and serve with some wonderful, dedicated Catholic priests. Some of the Catholic chaplains were participants in the charismatic renewal that pervaded mainline churches in the 1960's. They exercised the gifts of the Spirit with grace and power.

The military controlled housing was not immediately available so we had to rent a small house in the civilian market while awaiting allotted quarters. After a month or so we were assigned a nondescript two bedroom bungalow in a military bedroom housing area located outside Camp Lejeune. Coming from the cool mountain air of Colorado the hot, humid climate of coastal North Carolina was particularly oppressive. Of course, there was no air conditioning in house or auto. We didn't even have the presence of mind to buy a fan. Yet, I must say, we seemed to adjust extremely well. As best we could tell Celia endured the heat with no adverse effects. She was an active, healthy baby eager to develop her walking and talking skills. We looked on with pride.

Some unexpected excitement entered our lives in September 1960. I had been invited to speak at a church in a little town an hour or so from Camp Lejeune. We had heard reports that hurricane Donna was sweeping up the east coast but it seemed calm enough as we drove to our destination. While I was preaching Celia added a little comic relief. She escaped from Donna and toddled up the center aisle calling for her daddy. This was undoubtedly the most memorable part of the sermon.

As we started the drive home we noticed that there were no other cars on the road. As we proceeded the wind kept getting stronger but not bad enough to impede driving. But the longer we drove the higher the wind velocity became. As we approached Camp Lejeune we were well aware that we were in a hurricane. By the time we reached our house we wondered if we dared try to get inside. I drove the car as close as I could to the front door and we managed to escape inside. The storm had still not reached its maximum force and we listened in awe as the hurricane whirled and howled about us. By morning Donna had swept north up the east coast finally going as far as New England leaving a path of devastation in its wake.

We counted our blessings thinking we had escaped with only minor damage. Only later did we discover that the terrific wind had forced a flood of water into a storeroom on the back porch. We had prized photos and color slides stored there, including wedding photos, which were destroyed by the water.

The six months spent at Camp Lejeune provided an excellent introduction to the Marine Corps culture. This was likely providential since I spent much of my time in the chaplaincy serving with Marines. Marines stress team-work, self-sacrifice, obedience to lawful orders, competence, devotion to God and country. The chaplain is the recognized expert in religious matters and I never experienced any effort to influence or stifle my preaching or teaching. Of course, there are many ungodly individuals serving in the Marines, who view religion as a "crutch" for the weak. But the majority of Marine Corps leaders recognize the importance of the spiritual dimension and strongly support the ministry of chaplains.

I stayed very busy with my chaplaincy ministry and Donna had her hands full with an active toddler. Sometime in the fall I received orders to my next duty station. I was to be relieved from duty at Camp Lejeune in early December and was to report in early January to the Commander of the Military Sea Transportation Service in Brooklyn, New York. We had approximately a month of leave and travel time between stations. Since there would not be military housing available in New York until February we planned for Donna and Celia to stay in Denver until then. After Christmas celebrations with our families in Colorado I drove the Ambassador across country to New York. Donna and Celia were to fly to join me when housing became available. We decided to leave the new Nash in Denver for Donna's folks to sell.

Providentially, my ship, the USNS Upshur, happened to be in
Guantanamo Bay when the Cuban crisis erupted. While JFK and
Kruschev were still dickering all the wives and dependents of military
personnel were ordered to grab their pre-packed emergency luggage
and immediately board the Upshur for evacuation to the United
States. Some came off the golf course in shorts; everyone wore some
kind of tropical clothes. Once the order was given we were soon
embarking hundreds of women and children; many babes in arms
as you can see from this photo I took. This is an "abandon ship" drill
with everyone wearing a life preserver. I was assigned the task of
finding a place for all the women and children to sleep. It was a tense
few days until Kruschev withdrew his nuclear missiles. The photos I
had taken covered two full pages in the New York Daily News after we
arrived in NYC.

Oct, 1962

CHAPTER 16
SAILING, SAILING O'ER THE BONNIE BLUE

Today overseas deployment of military personnel and their dependents is almost entirely done by air. That was not true in the 1960's. Then almost all were transported by ships. Some of the transport ships were old relics left over from World War II. However, new ships had been added to the transport fleet including two American President Line passenger ships that had been requisitioned by the Navy while they were under construction during the Korean War. These two ships, the USNS GEIGER and the USNS UPSHUR, were both air-conditioned and were the preferred ships for sailing into hot or tropical climate areas. I sailed only on these two ships.

I was surprised to discover that MSTS ships were operated by the Merchant Marine Service. The ship's captain (called

"The Master") and all the officers as well as the crew were part of the U.S. Merchant Marines. In wartime they could be placed under Navy command. Otherwise, they were operating essentially as civilians under Navy contract. There was a small Navy detachment of about thirty personnel assigned to each passenger vessel. There was a Commanding Officer of the detachment and his Executive Officer. The only other Naval officers were a Chaplain and a Navy Nurse. The remainder of the Navy detachment consisted of enlisted men serving as operators of a small Navy Exchange, the "gee dunk" (refreshment stand, ice cream, candy, sodas) and barber shop.

Upon reporting for duty after New Year I was given a briefing and assigned my first voyage aboard the USNS Geiger bound for Bremerhaven, Germany. All subsequent voyages were on the USNS Upshur. I was excited and a little apprehensive about going to sea. Would I get sea-sick? Would I be able to perform all the duties expected of me? Would I be able to relate well to high ranking officers as well as to young enlisted men? I was determined to do my best and trust the Lord with results.

It was fascinating watching the passengers come aboard. The upper deck cabin passengers consisted of officers and senior non-commissioned officers and dependent wives and children. The lower ranking enlisted men were assigned below decks in tiered bunking compartments. I had to design religious and social programs that would reach out to all of them. We would be at sea approximately a week before arriving at our destination port of Bremerhaven, Germany. I conducted daily gospel services on the promenade deck for the enlisted personnel. I had prepared a series of seven evangelistic services, one for each day of the voyage. When the sea was rough attendance increased noticeably. Fear is a great motivator. After the gospel service for the troops I conducted a children's activity hour for the dependent children on board. Some of the troops would assist me. We played games; I did a few simple magic tricks that would fool nobody but young kids; we sang some songs; I shared a story and more or less managed to keep them entertained for an hour. The mothers were appreciative.

I was the designated entertainment officer for the cabin passengers. In the afternoons and evenings I organized various tournaments, mainly around card games. There were pinochle tournaments, cribbage tournaments and, especially, bridge tournaments. We had an entertainment fund that provided prizes for the various winners. Bridge was played mainly in the evening after dinner. I learned to play bridge and enjoyed it immensely. I won so many bridge tournaments that the Commander asked me to refrain from accepting any of the prizes. I just enjoyed the competition and matching wits with the other players. Some had played bridge for years and I learned a lot from their expertise.

Although we carried military personnel and dependents the ship was operated just like a civilian passenger liner. Midmorning between breakfast and lunch, carts with fresh coffee and sweet rolls came through the lounge. Between lunch and dinner more refreshments were offered. Again before bedtime more refreshments were provided. Also, prior to arrival at any port where passengers were to be discharged a special Captain's dinner was served. This usually consisted of prime steak with a selection of side dishes. Dessert was invariably baked Alaska. The civilian cooks and bakers were real professionals and provided excellent service. When sailing to and from Bremerhaven we normally had only two Captain's dinners, one prior to arrival at the German port and the other prior to arrival back in New York. When we sailed to the Caribbean we had six Captain's dinners. No wonder I gained weight with MSTS.

On one of the voyages to Bremerhaven in the summer of 1962 I was presented with an opportunity to visit Soviet controlled East Berlin. We were going to be in port long enough so I could take an overnight train to Berlin and spend two days in this divided city. I quickly took advantage of this opportunity and signed up to board a sleeper train going to Berlin. Shortly after boarding the train I had to surrender my passport to Soviet guards on board the train since much of our journey was through Soviet controlled East Germany. I was hesitant to surrender my passport to the Soviets but I was assured this was the normal procedure and my passport would be returned when we arrived in Berlin. In 1961 the Berlin Wall was constructed which was designed to prevent East Germans from fleeing to the West. Our treaty rights guaranteed access to East Berlin for accredited U.S. military personnel. However, all traffic after "the wall" was channeled through what was designated "Checkpoint Charlie".

When I arrived in Berlin I made arrangements to join a tour into East Berlin. A U.S. Army bus was our transportation. We passed through "Checkpoint Charlie" with no problems and soon were in the heart of Soviet culture. I can scarcely describe the dark pessimism that pervaded the very atmosphere. There was a spirit of hopelessness that was reflected in the dull eyes of the people. I had never experienced anything like it and could scarcely believe the contrast between an oppressed, downtrodden society and a free society. One high-light of our tour for me was visiting a famous cathedral that had been severely damaged during the war. The Soviets refused to allow it to be repaired but you could still see remnants of its former grandeur. It served as a testimony to the godless stance of Soviet communism. After touring East Berlin I wandered around West Berlin trying to decide where to eat dinner. I settled on a Chinese restaurant. Eating Chinese food in the heart of Germany may seem idiotic but when I am undecided about where to eat I often choose Chinese. I returned to the ship with a better appreciation for the freedoms we enjoy.

During my two years assigned to MSTS I made twenty-four round trips from New York. Twelve were to Europe and twelve were to the Caribbean. Each trip was interesting and some were quite memorable. I'll try to describe the ones that stand out in my mind as being special. But before I do that I should tell you that in February after I had completed my first voyage to Europe I was told that government housing was available for my family. Donna and little Celia flew to New York City and I met them at the airport. I took them to our apartment which was in a lovely part of Brooklyn between Sheepshead Bay and Manhattan Beach. The military had one block of housing that accommodated maybe a hundred families. Our assigned quarters had one large bedroom and one bath. The kitchen was sub-standard but Donna made it work. The street was enclosed in a gated chain-link fence for security and Military Police made periodic runs through the area. I felt pretty good about leaving Donna and Celia there while I was at sea. And I was at sea most of the time.

We only had a day or so to get situated in the apartment before I had to go to sea again. New York was experiencing some bad winter weather in 1961 and it was important to have plenty of food on hand. I took Donna to the commissary at Fort Hamilton and we stocked up on a good supply of food. After shopping Donna dropped me off at the ship and she started back to the apartment. I had explained how she was to get back on the beltway but it was all new to her and she took the wrong exit. Before long she realized she was heading to Manhattan rather than south Brooklyn. Finally she was able to exit on an off-ramp but couldn't find her way to the on-ramp. She had plenty of gumption and after making a couple of enquiries she was directed to a main street that took her back to the Sheepshead Bay area where we lived. I didn't know about her adventure until I returned from sea.

I promised I would describe some of my more interesting voyages. Here goes. Winter storms at sea in the North Atlantic could be frightening. One day the wind was howling and the waves were getting larger and more ferocious. Our big ship was being tossed around, wallowing like a fat pig in the bottom of a swale and then shuddering as the power of the mountainous wave threw it upward. Imagine being in the dining room trying to eat in one of these storms. What I wasn't prepared for in my first experience was the steep angles of the ship's rolling and pitching. When the angle became so steep that food and utensils began to slide off the tables and slither across the deck I knew we were in a serious storm. As the ship reached the zenith of its pitch or roll I could feel it hesitate as if it were deciding whether to continue its roll or whether to right itself. Was it possible for this big ship to be overturned by the fury of wind and wave? I didn't know but I wondered. Fortunately, the ship did always right itself. And when it did it began to pitch or roll in the opposite direction. The food and utensils that had disappeared in one direction now came sweeping back across the slanted deck. All the passengers could do was hold on for dear life or they would join the slithering refuse. In two years sailing the North Atlantic I can only remember two such violent storms.

One never to be forgotten trip took us to southern Europe. We sailed from New York across the mid-Atlantic to the big Naval Base at Rota, Spain. Rota is located on the southwest coast of Spain near Gibraltar. This is a region of vast vineyards and it was harvest time for the grapes. I organized a tour for some of the Navy detachment in conjunction with one of the major vineyards. We followed the workers as they loaded the grapes on donkey carts. The grapes were unloaded in a large stone wine-press. Workers inside the press crushed the grapes with their feet (they wore wooden clogs) and the juice ran into the exit drain and was collected in large barrels. It was all very labor intensive and followed a procedure that was no doubt centuries old. Later we were taken into the warehouse where Sandeman sherry was aged and stored. Small drinks of sherry were offered to those who wanted to sample Sandeman's famous product.

After two or three days at Rota we sailed through the strait of Gibraltar into the fabled Mediterranean Sea. We skirted North Africa and made our way to Naples, Italy where we unloaded the remainder of our military passengers. Three days in Naples gave me opportunity to organize a tour to Pompeii, the ancient city near Naples that had been buried by volcanic ash that poured from Mt. Vesuvius when it erupted on 24 August, 79 A.D. The catastrophic eruption covered the twenty thousand residents of Pompeii in a moment of time and few if any escaped. For nearly sixteen hundred years it remained buried in its grave until it was accidentally rediscovered in

1748. Excavation and restoration has gradually continued ever since. As I stood at the site of this ancient catastrophe my imagination took me back to what it must have been like as the sky darkened and hot ash began to inundate the city. Parents vainly trying to protect their children, young men and women trying to flee until the burning, noxious gas choked life from their lungs. Old men and women huddled in despair waiting for death to overtake them.

I was fascinated by the cobblestone streets in Pompeii. I don't know how long the streets had been in place, Pompeii was founded about 800 B.C., but you could tell they were ancient. Ruts formed by chariot wheels were plainly visible in the stone. I wonder how many decades or centuries it had taken to form those ruts. Bordering the streets were dwellings and shops. The dwellings were often two stories high with balconies extending from the second floor. The discoveries associated with uncovering Pompeii in the mid eighteenth century gave rise to interest in neoclassical art and architecture. In this sense some of the architecture in Washington, D.C. can be traced to Pompeii. On the return trip from Naples we stopped briefly again in Rota and then on to New York. It was a delightful thirty day cruise.

There was nothing much more pleasant than sailing from Brooklyn in mid-winter dressed in winter blues and then three days later approaching San Juan decked out in tropical whites. The Caribbean cruises were always quite pleasant with warm weather and placid seas. But they were particularly pleasurable when you were escaping the frigid north Atlantic. One of the benefits that came with my assignment was the privilege of having my family join me aboard my ship while I was on leave. Donna and I decided it would be fun to take the Caribbean cruise as far as San Juan, Puerto Rico and then vacation there while the ship sailed on to Cuba and Panama. This would allow us eleven full days to enjoy the sun and beaches in Puerto Rico.

Another chaplain was assigned to serve in my place and Donna, Celia and I assumed the roles of pampered passengers. Unfortunately, the ship had scarcely left the dock before Donna was overcome with sea-sickness. She spent all three days between

New York and San Juan confined to the bed in our cabin. Celia, about two and a half years old, took to sea like a veteran sailor. She would walk the deck with me and take in all the sights. Once we were watching the wake of the ship with all the bubbles produced by the ship's propeller. "Look, daddy!" Celia cried excitedly. "Lottsa soap."

As soon as we were back on land Donna felt fine. We were able to stay in officer's housing for a nominal fee. We rented a car and drove to some of the recommended tourist areas including the beautiful El Yunqua rain forest with its lush vegetation and water falls. Celia preferred the water and sand to sight-seeing so we spent a lot of time at the beach. Our tropical vacation passed quickly and all too soon we were headed back to Brooklyn. Again, Donna confined herself to the cabin and Celia and I walked the decks. I doubt if Donna will ever agree to another vacation cruise.

In mid-October, 1962 we prepared for another trip to Panama via Puerto Rico and Cuba. Already it was getting cool and I was looking forward to soaking up some sun as we cruised the Caribbean. The USNS Upshur, my assigned ship for the past eighteen months, had a fine professional crew and a close-knit Navy detachment. We were about to have our skills tested in a totally unexpected way. We had dropped off passengers in San Juan and proceeded on to Guantanamo Bay, Cuba, arriving, I think 19 October. Normally we had but a one day layover at "Gitmo" as it was called in military shorthand. But this time the commander called the Navy detachment together and stated that we were having engine trouble and would have to stay another day while repairs were made. The next morning we were told repairs were taking longer than expected and that we would be delayed another day. But first thing the next morning the C.O. called all the officers together and told us the real reason for our delay. We were facing an international crisis. On October 14 one of our U-2 photographic spy planes had discovered that the Soviet Union was installing nuclear missiles in Cuba. President Kennedy was preparing to issue an ultimatum to the Soviets later that day to persuade them to remove the missiles (October 22, 1962).

The Navy and Marines had been put on standby alert. The UPSHUR was to prepare to receive dependents and non-combatants aboard our ship later that morning. Our mission was to evacuate them and return them to the United States. The CO tasked me specifically with the responsibility of finding spaces to accommodate 1703 wives and children in addition to the other passengers already aboard. I searched out spaces below decks that I never knew existed. By 11 a.m., eight hours before the president was to make his speech, the base commander dispatched officers to alert dependents at base housing that they were to be evacuated.

The base had a standing order that dependents must have an emergency bag packed that would enable them to be ready to be evacuated within an half hour. By noon the dependents were streaming aboard. Some of the women had come from the golf course, still in their shorts, taking time only to grab their children and packed bags. The Chief of Naval Operations sent the following message which was broadcast over the ship's loudspeakers: "The calm and serene manner in which you have accepted the threat of possible personal danger while living in Guantanamo has been viewed with admiration and respect. Now our judgment indicates that you should leave the scene of an increasing danger to your own safety...Rest assured we will do all possible to provide for your welfare in the days ahead." The CNO had opportunity to follow through on his promise even before we arrived back in port.

The first priority was to get the passengers aboard the UPSHUR and out to sea. We would worry about finding sleeping spaces later. By mid-afternoon the passengers were aboard and we were well out to sea when President Kennedy broadcast his declaration of quarantine of the water surrounding Cuba. This was diplomatic language for a sea blockade. American warships had been ordered to interdict any Soviet ships approaching Cuba and to remove any offensive weapons. No one knew what the Soviet response would be to the gauntlet laid down by the USA.

But in the meantime I had a more pressing problem. Where was I going to find sleeping quarters for all our emergency passengers? Fortunately, crew members suggested spaces that I hadn't thought of and eventually we were able to find everyone a place to sleep. Meals were another problem. Long lines, crying, complaining children added to the stress. One little frustrated boy, tugging at his mother's hand, gave up and began to urinate. Space was quickly provided for him to relieve himself.

In addition, as we sailed toward New York the temperature became noticeably cooler. Women and children dressed in tropical garb were feeling increasingly uncomfortable. Anticipating this, the Navy had already started collecting donated clothing in the Norfolk area. Huge amounts of warm clothing were collected and shipped to the UPSHUR while we were still out at sea. After making the transfer we spread the clothing out on tables and deck chairs so the passengers could determine sizes and colors. It was like a bargain basement sale in a department store except everything was free.

While sailing back to the USA we, along with the rest of the world, were waiting to see the response of the Soviet Union to President Kennedy's demands. There was a report that the Soviet military had cancelled all leaves and discharges. However, there were no reports of further aggressive action by the Soviet Union or its satellites.

On October 24 the good news was reported that Soviet ships bound for Cuba were turning around and returning home. This made headlines around the world. A nuclear holocaust had been averted.

When the USNS UPSHUR arrived in New York a large crowd of people welcomed us. Many were relatives of families that we had returned to the United States. Also, the press came aboard seeking interviews and photographs. I had taken quite a few photos during the course of the voyage and I was besieged with requests for pictures. Of course, I had no prints, just the exposed film in my camera. This presented no problem to the press as they had their own photo labs. I explained I would have to get approval from the Navy Public Relations officer before I could release the film. To my surprise this was readily given and I released the film to a reporter from the New York Daily News. This tabloid advertised itself as having the largest circulation of any newspaper in the United States. They developed the film and ran a huge center spread of the pictures with my credit line. As an added bonus they paid me. I think it was a hundred dollars which was a sizeable sum in those days.

Normally we only remained in home port three or four days before we sailed again. However, when we returned from the Cuban evacuation the UPSHUR was put on 'standby alert' and remained in port. I had to report in by telephone and remain within the immediate area during this standby period. I never knew for sure why we were being held in port but supposed it had to do with contingency plans in case the Cuban crisis erupted and we needed to transport troops to that area. As it turned out, it was a nice vacation for Donna and me. We couldn't go far but there was plenty to see and keep us occupied in the New York area. Sometimes we could get free USO tickets to Broadway productions. My brother, Charles David, was stationed nearby in New Jersey and he would visit periodically. In December my tour of sea duty was up. I had orders back to the Marines, this time at Parris Island, South Carolina.

I had compiled an excellent record and had been selected for a Regular Navy commission. This was the same kind of commission that Annapolis graduates received and meant that I was perceived as a chaplain with a bright future in the Navy. At the time I was too inexperienced in the way of the Navy to realize the significance of my selection.

These are the chaplains I served with during my two years at the Marine Corps Recruit Depot in Parris Island, S.C. Captain M. O. Stevenson was our senior chaplain and a fine supervisory chaplain. My first year I was assigned as chaplain of Headquarters Battalion. In that capacity I served as Brig Chaplain and Chaplain for Women Marine Recruits. I was assigned a male recruit battalion for my second year. I have fond memories of ministering to these young recruits and their leaders.

March, 1965

CHAPTER 17
MARINE GREEN AT PARRIS ISLAND

I had become emotionally attached to the crew and Navy Detachment that was assigned to the UPSHUR after serving together for over eighteen months. Apparently this was mutual as the crew had a farewell ceremony for me and I was presented with a valuable souvenir watch. It had an inscription on the back that greatly increased its sentimental value. But I can't say I was sorry to get relieved from sea duty. Donna and I were both ready to have a more conventional life.

Our 1953 Nash Ambassador "bit the dust" shortly before we were scheduled to leave New York. The highly advertised "aluminum head" that I had so ardently wanted had welded itself to the engine and could not be detached for repairs. Its life span was concluded at slightly over one-hundred thousand miles. At the garage where I had the Ambassador serviced there was a rather decrepit looking 1957 Ford V-8 for sale. The garage owner said it ran good and since the price was right we decided to buy it. In early December the movers came to load our household goods which would be shipped to Beaufort, South Carolina to be stored until we procured housing in South Carolina. We departed New York near mid-December bound for Oshkosh, Wisconsin to visit my brother John and family before going on to Colorado for Christmas. By this time John and Bernie had two children. Phil was eight years old and Suzie must have been about two.

To our pleasant surprise the Ford bought in Brooklyn proved to be a good, dependable car. We did have to replace a generator on the trip but other than that it was trouble free. I remember very little about this particular Christmas season in Colorado except, like all leave periods, it passed too quickly. All too soon it was time to drive to our new duty station at Parris Island, South Carolina. Once again the trusty Ford got us to our destination without mishap.

The Parris Island Marine Corps Recruit Depot was notorious for its hard-nosed training of recruits. However, a training tragedy in 1956 resulted in public outcry for closer supervision of recruit training. In April 1956 an experienced drill instructor led his platoon on a night disciplinary march through a swampy area intersected by Ribbon Creek. The Sgt. led his seventy-four recruits into the creek bed. As they entered deeper water, panic ensued and six of the recruits drowned. The investigation that followed resulted in more stringent oversight of training procedures.

Four events or activities stand out in my recollection of our two years at Parris Island. The first event involves a "shake-up" in the Depot brig that I initiated. My assignment was chaplain of the Headquarters Battalion. This was the administrative battalion for the Depot and the CO had oversight of the brig. "Brig" is Navy and Marine Corps terminology for prison or jail. As brig chaplain I had unrestricted access to the prisoners. I always met with new prisoners just to get acquainted and to establish rapport for future ministry. There were two categories of prisoners. One category was prisoners from the recruit population and the other was from the assigned active duty Marine or Navy personnel. As I continued to interview new arrivals I noticed many of the recruit prisoners were complaining about watches, money and other valuables being stolen from them. As long as I talked to them inside the brig they were reluctant to go into detail for fear of reprisals from brig personnel.

I got the Commanding Officer's approval to interview recruit prisoners in a secure room in the headquarters building. I brought them in for group counseling with no guards or brig personnel present. I explained that I had a tape recorder and I wanted volunteers who would truthfully and completely recount the thefts they had experienced in the brig. Several agreed to testify on tape. They all accused brig personnel of extorting money and other valuables from them while they were confined. They were quite specific, naming names, giving descriptions of valuables or amounts of money, times, etc.

After I had recorded the accusations I gave the tape to the Headquarter's Battalion commanding officer, Colonel Stewart. He wasted no time in taking action. Very soon there was a complete turnover of brig personnel. A professionally trained brig officer was assigned as well as new guards and supervisory non-commissioned officers. These new personnel brought a new atmosphere to the brig. The old personnel had viewed the chaplain as a threat to their abuse of the prisoners. Events proved them right. The new personnel accepted the chaplain as a team member who could help get the erring marines back on the right track. It made my job more enjoyable and rewarding.

The second event was the purchase of our first house. When we reported to Parris Island we had to rent for a few months. We discovered that the price of homes in this area was very reasonable so we decided to look around for a place that we could afford. A near new little three bedroom brick house near where we were living caught our eye. We dickered with the developer and agreed on a price of eleven thousand dollars. I think we paid a thousand dollars down and financed ten thousand dollars. It had a large lot with live oak trees. There was an attached car port and utility room. On one end was a large screened porch. I later enclosed the porch and added a bathroom. This little house served us well during our tour at Parris Island.

The third event devastated the nation. It was the assassination of President John Kennedy which occurred on 22 November 1963. I remember I first heard the news while visiting the Division chaplain's office. President Kennedy's untimely death plunged the nation into mourning. Flags aboard Parris Island were quickly lowered to half-staff. The subsequent shooting of Harvey Oswald, the alleged assassin, as he was in police custody in the basement of the Dallas police department, was caught by TV cameras. The brazen public murder fueled all sorts of conspiracy theories.

I was assigned as chaplain of the Second Recruit Battalion for my last year at Parris Island. There were approximately seven hundred men in the battalion. The memorable thing about a recruit battalion as far as a chaplain was concerned was the fact that almost all of the recruits attended chapel services on Sunday. Chapel service was not mandatory but those Marines who did not attend were required to clean their spaces, polish brass, clean the "head" or some other house-keeping chore. Consequently, chapel attendance was near one hundred percent. My task was to have the kind of worship service that made them glad they came. Our services featured lively music, a recruit choir, and a short but pointed sermon. I looked forward each week to minister to hundreds of young men during a critical time in their lives. This is the fourth significant memory.

There are other events that make for some good, some bad, memories. Johnny and Bernie visited us in the summer of 1963. Phil and Suzie were their only children at that time. We enjoyed the beach and warm ocean water of the South Carolina coast. A good memory. I started playing basketball consistently again with the Marines at P.I. The games got pretty rough and I got my nose septum lacerated severely enough that it required some stitches to reattach it. But even more painful was the theft of the watch given to me by the crew of the USNS UPSHUR. I had foolishly left it with my clothes in an unlocked locker in the gym while playing ball.

This stark scene is on the far north coast of Iceland only a few miles from the Arctic Circle. It is a massive radar center for tracking Soviet aircraft in the area. There were two such tracking stations in different coastal regions of Iceland. I visited one of these on a monthly basis and stayed a few days each time. They were reached by air only. DC-3's were the ancient aerial work-horses that transported us around the island.

1966

CHAPTER 18

OUR ICELAND EXPERIENCE

In the summer of 1964 I got orders to go to the Naval Station in Keflavik, Iceland. I was detached from Parris Island in September and drove Donna and Celia to Denver. They were permitted to join me in Iceland but they had to wait until military quarters became available, another three months. They settled in with Donna's parents during the interim. Celia was enrolled in a nearby kindergarten

In December housing became available so Donna and Celia made the long flight to Iceland from Denver to Maguire Air Force Base in New Jersey. From there they flew to our base in Newfoundland and then on to Keflavik. This time of year Iceland is in darkness for twenty hours. From ten in the morning until two in the afternoon the sun is barely visible low on the horizon. It's quite depressing and takes some getting used to. We enrolled Celia in kindergarten and it was dark when we took her to class and dark when she returned but it didn't seem to bother her at all. At least we were all together again.

A lot of images come together when I think of Iceland. The Icelandic government did not want intermarriage between Americans and Icelandics therefore did not permit our enlisted sailors and marines to go off base. This led to a lot of depression and excessive drinking. The suicide rate was one of the worst among service personnel anywhere. However, married officers were permitted off base and some even lived on the Icelandic economy, including our senior chaplain.

Iceland had no indigenous population but was first settled in the ninth century by Vikings who brought Irish slaves with them. There is some historic evidence that Irish monks may have come in the eighth century and at least spent summers there. Because of its location, for centuries Iceland had little contact with the rest of the world. As a result of its isolation its original Nordic language was never corrupted. They speak the same dialect today that they did when Eric the Red first landed there. The ancient Viking sagas, penned in the twelfth century, can still be read with complete understanding today. In order to keep their language from being corrupted the government did not permit citizens to have television sets. Eventually, they were not able to resist the lure of TV but that happened after we left.

When Donna and Celia arrived we moved into the Navy officers' quarters that had been assigned us. The housing, except for the Admiral and a few senior officers, was essentially two-story row housing. We were assigned a ground floor apartment and when our furniture was installed it was quite livable. Many of the bedroom windows throughout the housing were covered with reflective foil. This was to prevent twenty hour days of summer sun from invading the sleeping area.

There were three Protestant chaplains and a Catholic chaplain assigned to Kevlavik. The senior chaplain was a Commander and was on the staff of the Admiral. In addition to being a Naval Air Station, Keflavik also was designated a NATO base and our Admiral was the senior NATO representative. I was assigned to the staff of Captain Sparks, the Station Commanding Officer. In addition to the usual week-day counseling and Sunday morning preaching I was the chaplain chosen to make monthly visits to one of the communication sites on the northern coast of Iceland.

These sites featured a large radar dome and other sophisticated, state of the art communication equipment. They were manned by Navy, Air Force, and civilian specialists. Their mission was to track the Soviet aircraft that flew over from the north. Soviet "Bears", a large bomber, flew regularly over the airspace between Iceland and mainland Europe. As soon as Soviet aircraft were detected the Air Force fighter squadron stationed at Keflavik was notified and fighters were launched to ride herd on the bombers until they were out of our zone of responsibility.

There was another communication site even further north, just six miles from the artic circle, that I visited only once. It was designated H-2 Site. The one I visited regularly was H-3 Site. The only way to get to these sites was by air. We flew in old DC-3's, a reliable twin engine transport plane. The take-off and landing site was a gravel run-way near the beach. The flight to H-2 provided one of the most frightening experiences I have had in an airplane. We flew across the full length of

Iceland over rugged glaciers and mountains. The outside temperature was bitterly cold but we were reasonably comfortable inside the plane.

The old DC-3 had a crude passenger heating system. A small one quarter inch fuel line was attached to the exterior of the fuselage. The line entered the interior of the fuselage near the rear where it fueled a gasoline heater. Somehow the line became severed forward of where it entered the fuselage and the raw fuel became ignited. How that happened I don't know unless hot exhaust gases ignited it. Anyway, after catching fire it soon burned a hole through the aluminum fuselage and acrid smoke began to fill the interior. We had parachutes available but I didn't want to even think about jumping into the glaciers below. Fortunately, we were only about ten minutes away from H-2. The lone fire truck was waiting beside the gravel runway as the pilot quickly set us down. The few passengers and crew members swiftly deplaned, coughing and teary eyed but very grateful the fire had not erupted fifteen minutes earlier.

There were no paved highways in Iceland when we first went there. Before we left in 1966 the road between Keflavik and Reykavik, approximately thirty miles long, became the first and only paved road in the country. All the other roads were dirt or gravel. Not that the roads were a major concern for us when we first came since we brought no car. However, our government had an agreement with the Icelandic government whereby we could buy duty-free European manufactured cars. We decided to buy a new Volkswagen. The price delivered to Iceland was thirteen hundred dollars plus an additional one-hundred dollars for shipping fees to the United

States, which we paid in advance. Our new 1965 VW was well suited for the gravel and dirt roads of Iceland.

When we got our new car we decided to do some exploring. There were some interesting sites within fifty miles of Keflavik that had been recommended to us. On a warm summer day (fifty degrees is warm) we went inland on a dusty dirt road towards Geyser. Geyser is an Icelandic word which the rest of the world has borrowed to describe a geothermal gush of hot water or steam. I don't remember Geyser as being particularly spectacular but certainly historically interesting. We continued on to the high point of our trip, Gullfoss. Gullfoss is Icelandic for "gold falls", an awesome waterfall that radiates beautiful rainbows when the sun is shining. Although likely the most popular of Iceland's many waterfalls, Gullfoss is not the largest. This honor belongs to Dettifoss, a huge but muddy waterfall, in northeast Iceland. It is the largest waterfall in all of Europe but too far from Keflavik to rate a visit from us. We also took a short side trip to one of the banana growing regions. This was a large enclosed greenhouse that actually produced tropical fruit in this artificial environment.

Once a month I was transported by jeep to the Marine detachment located at Whale Bay. This site was about sixty miles from Keflavik, north of Reykavik. It was called Whale Bay because it was here that the Icelanders landed and butchered the whales they had caught. The drive was quite scenic and I drove Donna and Celia to the site. We were able to see a huge whale in the process of being cut up. Not a pretty sight but an important part of the Icelandic economy.

Because of the wind, rain, snow and generally miserable Icelandic weather during much of the year there were no outside sports to engage in. As a consequence I took up the new (for me) indoor sport of badminton which was quite popular on base. It took me a few months to get the hang of it but eventually I got rather good at it. My partner and I won the doubles championship for the base. I won my bracket in the singles championship but lost in the finals. It was lots of fun and probably the most physically demanding sport I ever played.

One of the benefits of being stationed in Iceland was every six months we were provided free flights to mainland Europe on the Admiral's plane. We took advantage of each opportunity and made three different trips. On our first vacation trip we flew to Frankfurt. We then took a train to the U.S. Army Retreat Center at Bertchesgaden in the heart of the Bavarian Alps where the Assemblies of God sponsored an annual servicemen's retreat. This was the site of Hitler's "Eagle's Nest", the favorite vacation and retreat spot for Hitler and his henchmen. We were housed in the commodious General Walker hotel. The retreat was lots of fun for Donna and I. And there were enough children present to keep Celia from getting bored. We enjoyed fellowship with other chaplain families, missionaries and Christian service personnel from all across Western Europe. We were able to spend a day in nearby Salzburg which Donna particularly enjoyed. She opted out of the tour of the underground salt mines which I enjoyed. On our return flight the pilot flew us over Surtsey, a small island off the coast of Iceland that was in the process of being formed by volcanic action. We could see the fiery red lava as it flowed down toward the sea. It was quite a sight to see a new land mass being formed out of the ocean. Before we left Iceland, Surtsey was big enough for small planes to land on it.

One of the major spring events after returning to Iceland was Celia's graduation from kindergarten. The school really made a big deal of this. For some reason Donna was not able to go (possibly ill) so I was the parental cheering section. Celia was darling in her cap and gown and missing two front teeth.

Our second trip on the Admiral's plane was spent in England and Scotland. The American forces had a nice hotel located near Hyde Park in London in which we stayed. It was October and the weather was very pleasant, at least at the beginning. We enjoyed walking in the parks, watching the changing of the royal guards at Buckingham Palace, reading names of famous people buried in Westminster Abbey, viewing the crown jewels in the Tower of London, admiring the classic beauty of St. Paul's Cathedral, wandering about in Trafalgar Square... There was so much to see that was steeped in Anglo-Saxon history. We spent much of a rainy day immersed in the British Museum.

For our last few days in Britain we rented a car and drove north to Scotland. Since the British drive on the left side of the road their cars have the steering wheel on the right side of the car. Whenever I got out of the car to obtain petrol I would invariably start to get back in the car on the wrong side. It was easier for me to adapt to the left side of the road than to the right side of the car. As we proceeded north into Scotland the terrain became more rugged and more sparsely populated. We had some difficulty locating a place to spend our first night in Scotland. We finally found a delightful rural "manor" that welcomed guests. The October nights were quite cool and our hostess brought hot water bottles to place at the foot of our beds. These were quite welcome since there was no central heating. In the morning we were served hot oatmeal with thick cream, rolls and butter. Thus fortified, we continued on to Edinburgh and Glasgow. Although these cities were historically interesting we just skimmed the surface of what they had to offer. As our leave time expired, we proceeded to the air base at Prestwick just north of Glasgow. We turned in our rented car and caught the aircraft back to Iceland.

I didn't realize how thoroughly my brain had been oriented to British driving until I found myself facing headlights directly in my lane as I drove home from the Keflavik airport. I was berating the stupid driver whose headlights approached squarely in my lane. Suddenly I realized I was the stupid driver in the wrong lane and very quickly whipped to the other side. This experience accelerated my reorientation to right lane driving.

Our third trip to Europe's mainland in March of 1966 was great fun. The Hewett family joined us as well as the Base librarian and a single Marine. With the two Hewett children, Anita and Duane, there were nine of us. Anita was two years older than Celia and Duane was a year or two younger. But at least Celia had some other children to associate with and talk to. We landed in Frankfurt and rented a VW bus that would accommodate us. Our plan was to drive to the Italian Riviera so we carefully checked the road map and plotted our route. We did fine until we reached the mountains in Switzerland. As we climbed higher in the Alps our road suddenly ended in an unpassable field of snow that stretched ahead as far as we could see. We had to turn around and ended up putting our vehicle and ourselves on a train that went through a huge tunnel underneath the snow covered mountain passes.

Once we arrived through the tunnel into northern Italy the landscape changed remarkably. Above us were snow covered peaks but below us the road was clear and wound around toward verdant valleys. We stopped at an attractive inn in a small mountain village and were warmly welcomed. We were assured there was plenty of room for our party. Brawny mountain women grabbed our luggage and carried it to the assigned rooms. We were served a delicious dinner and the next morning enjoyed a sun-draped continental breakfast before continuing down the scenic highway. The spring-like weather was utterly delightful after the harsh weather of Iceland. We were looking forward to the even warmer weather of the Italian Riviera. The Italian Riviera is a narrow coastal region bordering the Ligurian Sea. At the extreme southwest of this region near the French Riviera lies the town of Ventimiglia. I'm not sure how or why we chose to go to Ventimiglia but it was an excellent choice. Hotel rates were inexpensive and it was a lovely time of the year to be there. Tangerine trees lined the streets and the fruit was ripe and for sale in the markets. I love tangerines and ate to my heart's (and stomach's) content.

After spending a few days in Ventimiglia we left and drove to Monaco. The beautiful lavish homes here were in contrast to the more modest dwellings in Ventimiglia. We enjoyed the views of water, yachts, and spectacular homes but we had felt much more at home in Ventimiglia. We drove past the royal palace of Prince Rainier and Princess Grace and watched the royal guards go through their paces. The weather was delightful and we loved it.

From Monaco we drove back to Italy and up the coast to Genoa. From Genoa we visited Pisa and climbed the famous leaning tower. From there we drove inland to Florence and were overwhelmed with the sculpture and other works of art. From Florence we drove north to Venice and spent a day there. From Venice we drove north across the Alps into Austria. What a contrast we experienced in the weather. As we climbed higher in the Italian Alps it began to snow very hard. A snow plow was attempting to clear the highway so I fell in behind the plow and followed it to the top of the pass where the Italian border guards and custom agents cleared us to continue.

It was snowing hard enough to distract me from seeing the Austrian border guards and custom's station and I passed merrily on by. Unfortunately, the snow didn't prevent them from seeing me. Soon a flashing blue light drove up behind me and a border guard ordered me to come back up the mountain to the guard station that I had bypassed. There was not enough room to turn around so I had to go in reverse up the treacherous, snow covered road. My driving experience in the mountains of Colorado stood me in good stead as I backed up to the Austrian border crossing. After being cleared by customs we proceeded on to Berchestgaden, Germany to the Assembly of God Servicemen's Retreat. There was lots of snow at the Retreat Center but it was cozy in the General Walker Hotel where the Retreat was conducted. This was our second retreat and we had a delightful time renewing friendships from the previous year and making new friends.

One of the benefits of being stationed in Iceland was being able
to fly periodically to the mainland of Europe aboard the Admirals
plane. We made three trips as a family. On the first trip we rented
a car and toured in Germany and Austria. The highlight of the trip
was participating in the annual Assemblies of God Servicemen's
Retreat in the Black Forest near Adolf Hitler's old haunts.

1965

CHAPTER 19

BACK TO THE MARINES AND THEN TO PRINCETON SEMINARY

Sometime during my second year in Iceland I was promoted to Lieutenant Commander. This brought a welcome pay increase as well as potential for increased responsibility. I also received orders to my next duty station. I was to be the senior chaplain at The Marine Corps Air Station in Beaufort, South Carolina.

In June, 1966 we departed Iceland after a memorable time of ministry in a unique little country. We had shipped our VW earlier so it was awaiting us at the port in New York. After flying to New York and retrieving our car we headed across country to visit family and friends before reporting to our new duty station. Retha and Wes Holmes were pastors in Columbus,

Indiana. We surprised them by attending their Sunday service as we drove by Columbus. Retha had been part of our youth group in Denver and was a close friend. After a pleasant visit with the Holmes we drove to Indianapolis where we bought a camper called a Scamper. It was a light weight fold-down camper easily pulled by our VW. When fully erected it had four beds, an ice box, stove and water tank. It was inexpensive and much better than sleeping in a tent on an air mattress. We used it for twelve or more years in camping trips from the east coast to the west coast.

Leaving Indiana we proceeded to Oshkosh, Wisconsin to visit Johnny and Bernie and their three children. From Oshkosh we drove to Kansas for a short visit with Uncle George and Aunt Dora. Celia got a chance to ride one of Uncle George's Shetland ponies but I don't think she was overly thrilled with the experience. But she was a cute little cow girl. From Kansas we proceeded to Colorado where we made the rounds of visiting relatives on both sides of the family. After being gone for nearly two years there was a lot of catching up to do.

My new duty station, the Marine Corps Air Station at Beaufort, South Carolina, took us back to familiar territory. It was only a few miles from the Parris Island Recruit Depot where I had been stationed prior to Iceland. We still owned the house we had bought when I was ordered to Parris Island. It was rented to another chaplain who had left his wife and daughters there while he was at sea. We decided live in government housing. This worked well for us. Celia's school was in the housing area and it was only a short drive to my office. But the ministry at the Air Station was a lot different from Parris Island. It was smaller and the assigned personnel were present much longer than the recruits were.

As senior station chaplain I was the pastor for the protestant congregation. I introduced a popular innovation to the Sunday worship service which I called "Dialogue Sunday". After a short sermon around a basic Christian truth I then solicited questions or comments from the congregation that related to the sermon topic. The Marines seemed to enjoy this feature and I certainly enjoyed the interaction with members of the congregation. We rarely got visits from our extended family since my duty stations were never close to our relatives. It was a special treat when my brother Johnny and his family visited us at Beaufort in the summer of 1967.

As senior chaplain I served on the staff of the Air Station Commanding Officer, a popular and respected colonel. The entire area was saddened when he drowned in a boating accident in coastal waters near the Base. To add to the trauma of the Marine Air Station and especially the Colonel's family, his body was never recovered. I spent time with the family and shared their grief.

While at the Beaufort MCAS the Chaplain's Corps notified me that I had been selected for an academic year of postgraduate study. The academic year began in September 1967. I had the responsibility of determining a major and choosing a graduate school. I first thought of pursuing a degree in family counseling and met with a committee at Duke University. Before I made a decision I was asked to come to Washington and meet with the senior chaplain who monitored the postgraduate program. He said to me, "Glenn, the Navy has a surplus of counselors. What we need are effective, trained preachers. I strongly recommend that you choose a school that has a history of producing strong preachers." The homiletics department at Princeton Seminary had such a history.

After only a year at Marine Corps Air Station Beaufort I was reassigned to Princeton Seminary under the administrative purview of the ROTC unit at Princeton University. Donna and I scurried around looking for a furnished house to rent close to the Seminary but out of the "high rent area". We found a suitable cottage in the little village of Kingston, about four miles north of Princeton. While I got enrolled in the Seminary, Donna enrolled eight year old Celia in third grade at the Kingston elementary school.

The Princeton experience was invigorating and challenging. In seminary language, my major area of theological study was called "Homiletics and Liturgics" or, more simply, preaching and worship. The homiletics professor was a no nonsense Scotch Presbyterian who took preaching seriously. His theory classes contained much helpful information gleaned from his years of experience in the pulpit. His practical application classes were real nail-biters. The students had to preach before the assembled department heads (Christian Ed, Theology, Homiletics, etc) of Princeton Seminary. Each department representative would provide a written critique of the sermon from the perspective of his discipline. I admit I was nervous preaching before such an august group of judges. But it was good discipline and I profited from it.

Apparently, the pulpit committee didn't think I did too badly. I was asked to preach in Princeton's historic Miller Chapel before the assembled seminarians and professors. In keeping with Presbyterian tradition I was limited to twenty minutes. I prayed earnestly about my subject and settled on a sermon that focused on the activity of the Holy Spirit in the history of God's people. After the service, Dr. McCord the

Seminary president, said to me, "Chaplain, we need more sermons like that."

During my four years at Denver Seminary I had studied the Greek language in which the New Testament was written. In the intervening nine years since graduation I had not made much progress in Greek. It so happened that Dr. Bruce Metzger, one of the leading Greek New testament scholars in the world, was teaching New Testament Greek at Princeton. When I saw that he was offering a class in Greek on Galatians I decided to sign up for the class. On the first day in class Professor Metzger told us in his urbane, gentle way that this particular class was not for beginners in Greek. He expected each student to have a good grasp of the language of the New Testament. He further stated that in order to determine if we were good candidates for this class he was going to give a test that would reveal our level of proficiency in New Testament Greek. Students that did not measure up would be excused from the class. He then assigned a portion of Galatians to be translated.

I labored through the exam, guessing at answers more times than not. At the conclusion of the next class period Dr. Metzger motioned me aside as the students filed out. Quietly he said, "Mr. Brown, I suggest that you not continue in our study of Galatians. It is early in the quarter and I am sure you can enroll in a more suitable class." I was disappointed and somewhat humiliated but not yet ready to admit defeat. I replied, "Dr. Metzger, I have been out of seminary for nine years and I haven't been as diligent keeping up with Greek as I should have been. But I want to remedy that. If you would please let me take one more test before excusing me from this class I would really appreciate it." Reluctantly, against his better judgment I'm sure, he agreed to give me another test. By now the good professor had my full attention. I immersed myself in Galatians to prepare for the next exam. I am happy to report I passed it with flying colors. I continued in the class and received a grade of A- for the quarter. I learned a good lesson from this. If you really want to achieve a worthwhile goal there is no substitute for perseverance and hard work.

An interesting phenomenon aboard the Princeton campus was the presence of several Charismatic prayer groups that met usually at noon or in the evening. These were the result of the testimony and ministry of Peter Marshall, Jr. who had graduated a year before I attended. Peter Marshall, Jr. was the son of Peter Marshall, the famous Scottish preacher who became chaplain of the U.S. Senate. His mother, Catherine Marshall, was a renowned author and a leader in the Charismatic renewal movement in the Presbyterian church. As a result of his testimony other students were motivated to earnestly pray for the Holy Spirit to fill them with power and spiritual gifts for service. These dedicated young seminarians gathering to seek an outpouring of the Holy Spirit were inspiring for some on campus and threatening to others. Some of the faculty were threatened because what God was doing was contrary to their theology. But the students persisted despite opposition. I discovered that God was alive and active on the Princeton Seminary campus.

One of the courses I took (at the Navy's request) was a study of the religions of Vietnam. The title of the course was a good indicator of where my next duty assignment was likely to be. The professor was an eminent scholar of oriental religions.

I paid attention and tried to learn as much as I could about a people and culture far removed from my own. A great deal of what I was taught has faded from memory. I do remember a couple of things. Much of the religion of the Vietnamese peasants was animistic. They believed that spirits, some good but mostly evil, inhabited natural objects such as rocks, trees, water, wind, etc. To placate the spirits, offerings of food and drink were left in designated places. The second thing I recall is the important place shamans played in Vietnam's animism. Shamans were religious figures, like wizards, who alone could influence the behavior of benign or evil spirits. For a price they would work their spells.

My dad came to visit us in 1968 while we were in Kingston. He came by bus from Beaver City, Nebraska. He wanted to buy the 1965 VW which we had purchased in Iceland. I was glad to sell it since we had bought a new 1967 American Rambler (a mistake). I remember thinking that dad was too old to be driving by himself across country. He was only sixty-six and would be driving cross-country for a good many more years. How ironic that when I was forty I considered sixty-six too old for long distance driving.

Princeton Seminary is the oldest theological graduate school in the United States. It was founded in 1812 by the Presbyterian Church (USA). For the first century of its history Princeton was a bulwark for orthodox Christianity. About 1930 there was a shift toward more liberal theology. One of the leading conservative professors at Princeton protested this shift and when his protests were disallowed he resigned. He and other conservative leaders in the Presbyterian church pulled away and formed a new denomination, eventually called the Orthodox Presbyterian Church. They formed a new seminary in Philadelphia called Westminster. Thirty years later I found there was still a residue of conservative professors at Princeton but liberal and modernist theology was in the ascendancy. The conservatives accepted the Bible as the true revelation of God's provision for conduct on earth and future salvation. The liberals emphasized what man could accomplish rather than what God had done through Christ. Liberals discounted miracles and the supernatural. I had professors from both camps.

One of my liberal professors was Dr. Paul Scherer, an erudite elderly gentleman who had had a long career at Union Seminary in New York before coming to Princeton. He specialized in New Testament exposition. In one of his courses he assigned me a book to read and critique. The book was a liberal author's attempt to rationalize away the literal resurrection of Jesus. I could scarcely believe the authors failure to deal with all the objective historical support for the reality of the resurrection. His argument essentially boiled down to this: miracles are impossible; the resurrection demands a miracle therefore the resurrection is impossible. I pointed out the obvious weaknesses of the book to the dismay of the good professor. He expressed surprise that I actually accepted the reality of Jesus' bodily resurrection. I learned he was suffering from terminal cancer and had died not long after I graduated. How sad that he had not encountered the resurrected Christ.

Dad and Donna have joined me on the deck of the USS Okinawa as we are tied up. San Diego is faintly visible in the background. I'll be forever grateful for the gracious manner in which the Skipper, Captain H.D. Williams, treated my family when they came to visit.

1968

CHAPTER 20
TO VIETNAM VIA CALIFORNIA

Before graduation I received orders to proceed to San Diego and report for duty to the USS Okinawa (LPH-3) at the conclusion of the school year. Celia completed third grade at Kingston elementary school near the same time I graduated. I was granted leave plus travel time so we had over a month before reporting to my ship. We piled into our new Rambler (The last new car we ever purchased up to this point) and took off for the west coast pulling our camper van behind us.

We visited family and friends on our drive west. We arrived in the San Diego area in mid-June and had the immediate task of locating a house to buy. The weather at this time of year was warm and dry so we camped out while we searched for a suitable house. Our first Sunday in the area we visited the Assembly of God church in Chula Vista. There we providentially met Ken and Ruth Glass who told us of a house for sale in their area. It had been a parsonage for a nearby Wesleyan Methodist church that had closed. We liked the area and the house was an attractive three bed-room, two bath ranch with garage and large covered attached patio. If the price was right we were prepared to buy.

It is hard to imagine from the perspective of today how reasonable California house prices were in 1968. We agreed on a purchase price of nineteen thousand dollars and easily qualified for the necessary loan. Our furniture was still in Navy storage in South Carolina so we had it shipped to our new home on Dory drive in the little community of Sunnyside. Donna supervised our purchase of new carpets and room decoration. We had a large backyard terraced into three levels. Later, I installed an eighteen foot diameter above ground swimming pool on the second level that provided a lot of enjoyment.

In July I reported to the USS Okinawa for sea duty. I had not been to sea since October 1962, nearly six years. My previous ship had been a passenger ship with a civilian (Merchant Marine) crew and small Navy contingent which transported military personnel and families to Europe and to the Caribbean. The Oki -3 (as it was called by the crew) was a helicopter carrier designed to fly marines straight from its deck into combat. When operating in combat the Oki-3 had a reinforced battalion of marines aboard plus a helicopter squadron plus a combat surgical team. These personnel plus the ship's crew made a total of more than two thousand aboard the ship during combat operations.

When I went aboard Oki-3 in July 1968 she had just returned from a nine month cruise operating off Vietnam. She was scheduled to return to Vietnam in November. The intervening months in home port were to be filled with training, maintenance and restocking supplies. I was grateful that I didn't have to go to sea immediately. San Diego is a lovely city and we enjoyed getting acquainted with the area. It was particularly enjoyable to visit the huge one thousand acre Balboa Park. The famous San Diego Zoo is situated in the Park and Celia always enjoyed seeing the animals. Donna and I enjoyed watching Celia get up close and personable with the animals in the children's petting zoo.

I wanted to get Donna and Celia involved with a good church family before I sailed. I would be gone for eight months so it was important they have someone to turn to for support and help if needed. We visited the large First Assembly of God in downtown San Diego and enjoyed the music and preaching very much. However, for several reasons we decided to attend the church we had first visited. First Assembly in Chula Vista was much closer to where we lived. It was smaller and we could more quickly get acquainted. Members there had already got involved helping us locate a house to buy. Pastor Howard Ryan eagerly welcomed us. (He was particularly pleased that Donna was a skilled pianist and that I enjoyed playing golf.) Furthermore, members Ken and Ruth Glass, who lived nearby, had girls with whom Celia could play.

I had a very short orientation by the chaplain I was replacing. He was eager to take leave and be on his way to his new duty station. And I was ready to settle into my new ministry opportunity. Many of the officers shared staterooms but the ship's chaplain was allocated a small private stateroom. The rationale for this was the chaplain needed privacy for counseling and study. Of course, while we were in home port I spent nights at home in a "stateroom" I shared with my lovely Donna.

By summer's end we were all settled in and enjoying our new home in the picturesque San Diego area. Donna got Celia enrolled in the Sunnyside elementary school. She turned nine in August and was entering the fourth grade. She was a pretty little blond with a sharp mind and a warm heart. She loved pets and soon was the proud caretaker of a cuddly kitten.

Donna and I decided to put different colored carpets in each of the three bedrooms. Doing it this way we were able to install them ourselves and save some money by buying remnants. The kitchen needed some work to bring it up to Donna's standard. A little paint and elbow grease helped a lot.

After we made the inside of the house more livable I turned my attention to the yard. The yard had a lower level with a few small citrus trees near the patio. Some grape vines grew along the west fence. There was a level middle terraced area upon which I decided to install an above ground swimming pool. Above the level terraced area was a hillside covered with ice plant. The swimming pool was eighteen feet in diameter and four feet deep so it was big enough to swim in if you went in circles. We lived far enough from the ocean to experience some hot weather. It was quite pleasant to jump in the pool after coming home from work on a hot day. John and Bernie came to visit us either in the summer of 1968 or more likely 1969. Celia and her cousins enjoyed the pool along with John and I.

The late summer and early fall months of 1968 were busy days for the officers and crew of the USS Okinawa. The ship had to be thoroughly inspected and reconditioned as needed. New crew members had to learn the ship's SOP (standard operating procedures) and how to get along with their shipmates. Short "shakedown" cruises off the coast of California helped get everyone familiar with the ship and with one another. By the end of September the ship and crew were ready to sail to whatever awaited off the coast of Vietnam.

Navy ship departures were emotional times both for those departing and the family members left behind. This was particularly so when the ship was scheduled to be gone for nine months. On the San Diego pier was an assortment of sailors and their loved ones bidding each other good-bye. The mournful "all aboard" horn hastened the farewell kisses and hugs. With the crew all aboard the gangway was lifted, the hawsers were released and the tugboats began easing the USS Okinawa away from the pier. I found a place topside where I could wave to Donna and Celia as they receded in the distance. Despite an aura of sadness I believed we were where God had called us to be.

Once the ship was out in the open Pacific under her own power we began cruising at approximately eighteen knots per hour. (About 21 MPH) Her maximum speed was 23 knots but we seldom ever went at top speed. It taxed the boilers and used excessive fuel. At regular cruising speed we covered about five hundred miles every twenty-four hours. It took five days from San Diego to Pearl Harbor where we stopped briefly to take on more fuel and supplies. From Pearl to Subic Bay in the Philippines was another fifty-two hundred miles or ten days cruising time. We had three or four days in the Philippines taking on more fuel and supplies. The weather was hot and humid but not so hot that it kept me from stretching my legs walking around the golf course. I enjoyed watching monkeys cavort in the trees near the golf course. On a Sunday evening before our departure I visited the Philippine Assembly of God church in Olongopo, the nearby port city. The pastor and his wife spoke English and we had a good time of fellowship. Some years later this pastor immigrated to San Diego and ministered to the large Philippine community there.

After our short replenishment and refueling break in the Philippines we sailed for Vietnam. We anchored in the harbor outside Danang where we were to embark our combat troops, our helicopters and crews and the surgical team. The first to come aboard was a reinforced battalion of Marines from the 3rd Marine Division, just relieved from a combat operation. They were tired, dirty and ready for warm showers, clean bunks and hot chow. My experience with Marines made me know that after a few days cooped up aboard the ship they would be "chomping at the bit" to get back on dry ground regardless of danger or dirt. Soon after the Marines arrived a skilled surgical team embarked. The lead surgeon was an experienced commander who was qualified to perform all kinds of operations except delicate brain surgery.

We had a hospital ward with about one-hundred beds to take care of the wounded. The final part of the Okinawa's combat team was the Helicopter Transport Squadron that carried the Marines from the deck of the Okinawa into the battle zone.

I'll try to describe just what it was like to be chaplain aboard the USS Okinawa when it was operating in a battle zone. Without its embarked combat units the number of personnel on the ship was approximately 700. With all the units aboard the population increased to more than 2,400. With this dramatic increase in personnel, space was at a premium. The troops were stacked in bunks four or more high row after row. Mess lines were crowded and long. There was a suppressed air of expectancy as the Marines waited for their orders to engage the enemy.

When battle orders were received for Special Landing Force Alfa to engage the enemy, organized chaos quickly developed on the decks of USS Okinawa. A Marine designated as the Combat Cargo Officer was responsible for getting each squad aboard the proper helicopter in the right sequence. When the CC Officer announced over the ship's public address that a specific unit should prepare to load up everyone knew where to go and what to do.

While the loading process was going on I wandered about on the hanger deck where I could be found if someone wanted to talk to the chaplain. It was on such a maneuver that I met a young man whom I will never forget. Let me tell you about him. He was a Navy Corpsman, perhaps 21 years old, attached to Battalion Landing Team 2/26. He wasn't a big man, maybe five feet nine inches tall, but he exuded a gentle strength and toughness. There were a few freckles scattered about on a face that was topped by close-cropped sandy hair. He spoke with the soft, slow drawl of the deep south, possibly derived from a boyhood in Alabama or maybe Louisiana or Mississippi. His Christian faith ran deep with no hint of self-righteousness.

Somehow, amidst the organized confusion of milling troops and noisy machines, he found me. Respectfully but urgently he asked me, "Sir, can we have a few moments together alone?" "Sure, Doc," I said, "Follow me." I led him to an area of the ship where the noise was less intense and waited for him to speak. "Chaplain, we are going into combat in just a few minutes. Some of my men are going to be wounded. Sir, they are going to call for me to help them and I've got to get there. Please pray and ask God to help me to get to them in time."

I received numerous prayer requests – for safety and protection, for family members, for sweethearts – but Doc was unique in his selflessness. At a time of great personal danger and crisis in an environment of kill or be killed he earnestly prayed that he might be a messenger of life. That was it. His only request was that he might not fail a wounded man who needed his life-saving skill. I led in a short prayer: "Our Father, giver of life, Doc wants to serve you by saving and preserving lives. Use him as your agent of mercy amidst the dangers of battle, in Christ's name, amen." With an easy smile Doc thanked me, shook my hand and left to board a chopper.

The very nature of the war against the Viet Cong necessitated repeated sweeps through the same terrain. Our forces would drive them out of a region and then depart. Soon the Viet Cong would infiltrate the area again and we would again drive them out. It was this sort of deadly cycle that in which our Marines were engaged. After several days of rest from a previous engagement the Marines were always aware that another combat operation would soon take place. Each time before boarding one of the lumbering helicopters, Doc sought me out and requested a moment of prayer together. Always, his earnest request was the same. "Chaplain, some of my men are going to need me. Pray that I'll be able to get to them and help them when they call for me." And always I was moved by Doc's selfless devotion to the men he cared about so deeply."

Our six months on station off the coast of Vietnam was broken into three segments of approximately two months each.

After seven or eight weeks on station the ship was ordered to go to Subic Bay, P.I. for maintenance and a few days rest and relaxation for the crew. We were near the end of our second period on station when Doc came to me after Sunday chapel service with a welcome announcement: "Chaplain, I see you have an electric organ secured above the hanger deck." Then matter of factly he said, "I'm an organist. When we get back from this next operation I'll play for the chapel services." I had no idea that Doc was a musician and I was excited at the prospect of having "live" organ music to enhance our worship services. "Doc," I said, "that's super. I can't wait for you to get back from this next operation."

Just before our ship left for Subic Bay in early 1969 the Marines went ashore for a major engagement. I had my usual special moment of prayer with Doc. "Don't forget," he reminded me, "when you get back from Subic and we come back aboard, I'm going to play the organ for our chapel services." "Doc," I replied, "not only will I not forget but I'll make sure you don't forget either." We said our good-byes in anticipation of being together again soon. I watched him with admiration as he walked resolutely to get aboard his helicopter.

We had an extended stay in Subic Bay while extensive repairs were made on the Okinawa. I contacted Paul and Violet Pipkin in Manila, long time missionaries in the Philippines. They warmly welcomed me and shared what God was doing through their ministry. A new church had just been completed and they were involved in planning the dedication ceremony. They wanted to have a celebration meal following the dedication service but didn't have sufficient funds to purchase the food. I knew that we had great deal of packaged food products aboard the Okinawa for distribution through our

"Operation Handclasp" program. "Operation Handclasp" was a Navy sanctioned program for distribution of goods and materials to third world countries. I told the Pipkins of the food products we had and they said they could use them as the base of their celebration meal. With a few phone calls I made arrangements for our helicopter to land on the pad at the American Embassy with a load of Handclasp prepared meals. Paul Pipkin met us with a pick-up truck and soon the food was loaded and hauled away. This food was truly a blessing and served as the main course for the meal after the dedication service.

There were some fine young Christian men on the Okinawa. Since we had so many free days in Subic I decided to organize a Christian retreat for them. The Captain gave his approval so I passed the word aboard ship. About eighteen men registered for the retreat. I had procured the facilities at the U.S. military Recreation and Retreat Center in Baggio for our retreat site. It was a lovely area, high in the mountains, where cool breezes brought welcome relief from the oppressive heat of the coastal region. Everything was in place except a Retreat leader and the Lord had a good one just waiting for us.

The Pipkins got me in touch with Ernie Reb, a friend of pastor Charles Blair, my former pastor in Denver. I had seen Ernie in Denver some years before and it was great to see him again. He was an inspirational missionary evangelist and had planted numerous churches throughout the Philippines. I believed he would be an effective retreat leader and was delighted when he agreed to serve.

The winding mountain road to Baggio took the better part of a day to navigate. Fortunately, being chaplain on a helicopter carrier came in handy sometimes. Ernie and I and some of the senior men were flown to Baggio by "holy helo". The flight was breathtakingly beautiful. The pilot flew quite low, following the contours of valleys as we made our way up into the high country. The variegated rice paddies in the terraced plots below us and to our sides were like picturesque checkerboards. As we climbed higher the rice paddies disappeared and were replaced with other vegetation and forests.

We arrived at the R & R Center well before the bus. Ernie retired to his room to do further preparation for the first evening session. I reveled in the cool atmosphere while waiting for the guys to arrive in the bus. When all were assembled we had dinner together in the mess hall and then gathered for the evening session. Ernie Reb was a man's man and quickly established rapport with the sailors and marines. God blessed our four days together and we came down from the mountains refreshed in body and spirit. I was so thankful to have such dedicated young men who wanted to keep growing in their Christian faith. They could touch lives with the gospel that I could never reach. I was glad for their presence as we headed back to the war zone.

When the Okinawa returned from Subic Bay we took on board a somber, battle weary force of Marines. The operation they had been engaged in while we were in Subic Bay had resulted in heavy casualties. I looked for Doc among the hundreds of troops that were milling about the ship but failed to see him. When he didn't show up for chapel service I knew something was seriously wrong. As I made inquiries I was able to piece together the account of Doc's final hours. His unit had come under devastating artillery fire. Some Marines had been hit with shrapnel and Doc had run to help them. While he was tending their wounds an artillery shell scored a direct hit, killing Doc and the men he was with. I was stunned by the news and filled with a deep sense of loss. Even after forty-five years, his example of manly Christian love, service and sacrifice in the midst of a hellish war continues to haunt and inspire me. Jesus must have had someone like him in mind when he said, "Greater love has no one than this, that he lay down his life for his friends."

Most of our combat engagements were near the coast north and south of Danang. The wounded warriors were quickly flown back to the ship where a skilled surgical team awaited them. My battle station was on the flight deck waiting with the medical team to receive the wounded. Most of the wounds suffered were the result of booby-traps. The Viet Cong were masters of camouflage. Their cleverly hidden explosive charges were triggered by unsuspecting marines as they walked along. As a consequence, there were many young men who were horribly maimed by a loss of a foot or leg. Unlike the powerful hidden explosive devices used in Iraq and Afghanistan that can claim many victims, most of the booby traps used by Viet Cong were designed to maim or kill an individual.

Since most of my chaplain duties were aboard the helicopter carrier where I ministered to the crew and incoming wounded, I sometimes felt guilty about not sharing the danger of the young men facing enemy fire. I welcomed occasions when there was an opportunity for me to go ashore on some mission or another. Over the course of our tour several such times occurred. Once the chaplain assigned with the marine combat battalion was on leave and I was asked to cover for him. Fortunately, we did not come under enemy fire. I thanked the

Lord for that. Nevertheless, I was grateful that I was able to be in-country for a short time with "grunts", as the combat marines were affectionately called.

Once I was asked to lead a small party of sailors into a residential area of Danang to erect a playground for the children. The sailors had constructed a portable playground which could be assembled on shore. As the sailors assembled the swings and teeter-totters a curious crowd began to gather. It didn't take the children long to figure out what was happening. Soon they were laughing and shouting as they tried out the new playground equipment. This brought smiles to all of us from the OKI-3. American service personnel delight in helping children.

One of the most interesting requests I received involved a twelve-year old Vietnamese girl who had lost her right leg just above the knee after being trapped in a cross-fire between American and Vietcong forces. Our surgical team wanted to sponsor her for a prosthesis and asked me to go to her village and seek her parent's permission for the procedure. The marine assigned to fly me into the village was a veteran combat helicopter pilot. I put on the protective armor usually worn when going in-country and carried my only weapon—an 8 mm movie camera. After clearing the deck of the OKI-3 the pilot headed for the jungle that lay beyond the urban area. He flew high enough to be out of range of small arms fire from bad guys below. When we were over the landing zone he spiraled down swiftly so as not to present an easy target.

The girl's parents listened intently as my interpreter and I carefully explained what we wished to do. After a brief conference, they smiled and said they would gladly grant permission. While they made the necessary preparations for their daughter to leave, the native residents gave me a tour of their village. They were especially eager to show off their school. The facilities were crude and primitive but the children were precious, like children everywhere.

We were on the ground perhaps half an hour. The chopper crews remained with their bird as the pilot let the engine idle. With the aid of a single crutch and village friends, the crippled girl made her way to the entry hatch of the chopper. I saw the makings of a great human interest story so I paused to record the scene with my movie camera. This incensed the marine pilot who chewed me out in very salty language, emphasizing that every second on the ground was a very dangerous second, particularly after parked in one place so long. The angry major growled that even a short delay could jeopardize lives if mortars or artillery had a chance to "zero in" on us. It was a sobering lesson for me and I took it to heart.

Smaller ships such as destroyers do not have enough crew members to warrant a chaplain. The USS Frank Evans, a destroyer operating with a nearby battle group, requested a chaplain to come aboard to conduct Sunday services. When I was asked to do this I was quite excited. It would involve a "holy helo" ride to where the destroyer was stationed. I would then be lowered by cable from the hovering helo to the heaving destroyer deck. It was a pretty simple operation as long as you timed your harness release to the rising deck. I made two such visits to this destroyer.

Shortly after my last "holy helo" flight to the Frank Evans she was transferred from her fire support mission off the coast of South Vietnam to participate in a SEATO (South East Asia Treaty Organization) exercise called Sea Spirit. Some weeks later I was shocked to learn that in a tragic night accident this same ship had been rammed amidships by an Australian aircraft carrier. The Frank E. Evans was cut in two. The forward half sunk almost immediately with the loss of more than seventy men. The stern section remained afloat and was towed to Subic Bay.

This terrible naval accident was inexplicable. The weather was clear; the sea was calm and both ships had excellent radar capabilities. The American Navy had already experienced some embarrassing incidents at sea and was quick to point the finger of blame at the Aussies. The captain of the Australian carrier was court-martialed but as the facts emerged he was completely exonerated. The cause of the accident was a wrong order given by a young, inexperienced American officer on the bridge. His faulty order resulted in the Evans turning directly broadside into the path of the oncoming carrier. It was like a freight train hitting an automobile with even more horrendous results…seventy-four lives lost.

Our hospital bay gradually filled as we continued combat operations. I visited the wounded on a regular basis and was pleased at the positive attitude that pervaded the bay. Even though wounded, the men were happy just to be alive with hopes of going home soon.

One of the most moving and sacred moments I experienced occurred shortly before we sailed from Vietnam. I received a report one day that the eviscerated, naked body of a young marine had been placed in the ship's morgue. He had thrown his body on top of a live grenade tossed by the enemy into his defensive position. Two things resulted: his buddies were spared death or wounds from the grenade and he was instantly ushered into eternity. No dog tags (metal ID tags) were found so his name and religion were unknown. He may have been Protestant, Catholic, Jewish or other. I was requested to go and deliver the appropriate prayers since there was no priest or rabbi.

Numerous thoughts went through my mind as I stood alone in the cold morgue viewing the body. Who was he? What prompted his heroics? What kind of family did he come from? Where was he now? Could I have done what he had done?

I had been requested to deliver an "appropriate prayer"? My understanding of Scripture did not include prayers for the dead. They were eternally in the hands of a just and loving God. I knew my prayer must be focused on the unknown family members who would be devastated when they were informed of this young marine's death. Humbly I prayed for these unknown loved ones, leaving the young man and all my questions in the hands of God. Subdued in spirit I slipped out of the morgue.

Captain H.D.Williams, my skipper on this cruise, was a great commanding officer and tremendously supportive of my ministry. I approached him once about converting some space into a small chapel. He approved the conversion and the USS Okinawa ended up with a lovely little chapel down in the troop compartment area. It was actually against Navy regulations to convert space without official approval so I am sure Oki-3 was the only helicopter carrier that had a chapel. I have often regretted that I did not keep in touch with Captain Williams and his lovely wife, Jerri. God bless them, wherever they are.

During the time we were operating off the coast of Vietnam we had several VIP's come see us. At Christmas in 1968 Rear Admiral Jim Kelley, Navy Chief of Chaplains, paid us a visit.

He wasn't a particularly personable man but, according to Navy scuttlebutt, he was a good politician. I thought he was a little pompous but kept this opinion to myself.

Thanks to the USO we had a troupe of entertainers, men and women, come aboard for a few days. I don't remember who the women were, probably singers. The men were mostly professional sport stars. Joe Namath of the New York Jets was the headliner and very popular with the crew and troops.

Just before we left Vietnam in the spring of 1969 Admiral John S. McCain Jr., Commander-in-chief of the Pacific Command, came aboard our ship. He was the father of the present Senator John McCain III from Arizona. Senator McCain, of course, was a Navy pilot shot down by the North Vietnamese in 1967 and endured years of torture before he was released in 1973.

As the time for our departure from Vietnam neared we were excited at the prospects of returning home. Our return schedule included a port call in Hong Kong. The crew looked forward to this as a good chance to shop and unwind a little before getting home. I enjoyed the Hong Kong respite and managed to shop a little as well as take a tour to the border of the Chinese mainland. Hong Kong was still under British control in 1969. I think this was the time I bought the set of bronze ware for Donna. She brings it out on rare occasions. I also bought a small oriental rug and a set of carved mahogany nesting tables. Donna has kept all of them so I guess I shopped OK. When we left Victoria Harbor in Hong Kong our whole squadron assembled in formation. It was the first time I had seen all our ships in formation and it was quite an impressive sight. We steamed in formation from the harbor and shortly thereafter went our separate ways.

We had left San Diego on 2 November 1968. Our due date to return was 26 June 1969. Since it took three weeks of continuous sailing to transverse the Pacific we left the Vietnam waters around the end of May. After leaving Hong Kong there was nothing but twenty days of endless water between us and San Diego. In the evenings we would gather in the hanger deck and sing. We had a veteran warrant officer who played the guitar and led us in old ballads, patriotic favorites and some country and western classics. It created a warm, fuzzy atmosphere. The crew loved it and it helped the hours speed by.

Our arrival back in San Diego was a happy, wonderful day. As we neared the dock crew members lined the rails looking for a familiar face in the sea of people awaiting our arrival. I spotted Donna and Celia, helped immensely by a huge WELCOME HOME, CHAPLAIN BROWN sign that had been prepared by the Chula Vista Assembly of God church. Making my way down the gangway I quickly located them and took them in my arms. It was good to be home.

Donna was a good Navy wife and had adapted well to our long separation. She and Celia attended the Assembly of God in Chula Vista where Donna was soon involved as a church pianist. Howard Ryan, the pastor, worked hard to assure that we stayed part of his congregation. I'm sure he was primarily concerned about retaining Donna's musical artistry. Neither of us was particularly edified by his ministry style and we had considered attending the larger First Assembly in downtown San Diego. However, that required a much longer commute so we decided to continue at Chula Vista. Pastor Ryan showed genuine pastoral concern for Donna and Celia while I was gone and that was important. Also, Howard was an avid golfer and I enjoyed competing with him on one of the many golf courses in the San Diego area.

The Oki-3, now eight years old, had taken a beating during the WesPac cruise. She was ordered to undergo a major overhaul at the dry dock in Long Beach over a six month period. Except for the single sailors who were berthed aboard ship, the ship's crew had homes in the San Diego area. To get from our home to the ship at Long Beach required a two-hundred mile round trip commute. Since I needed to be aboard ship on Sunday to conduct worship I worked out a convenient schedule with the skipper. I commuted to the ship on Saturday and stayed aboard through Tuesday. This allowed me to have Tuesday night through Friday at home. My sister Barbara who lived in the San Fernando Valley, helped make my commute less expensive and more enjoyable. She loaned me her little Datsun convertible. Thanks, Barb.

My schedule gave me big chunks of time in the middle of the week which allowed me to work on various projects around our house. Attached to the back of the house was a roofed patio approximately 12 X 20 feet. We decided that it would serve us better as a closed in family room. I went to the local building department for a permit and they told me I must submit plans drawn to scale. I got a piece of graph paper and carefully drew plans to scale for my project. I took it back to the building department and I was told my plans needed to be more professional before the project could be approved.

I was disappointed and wasn't sure what to do. If I got a professional draftsman to draw up the plans it would take time and cost money. I wanted to get the room enclosed while my ship was in dry dock. Since time was of the essence I rationalized that it was more important to go ahead and complete the project rather than worry about a bureaucratic hassle. So that's what I did. I built a chimney for a Ben Franklin stove, installed windows and doors and laid an indoor/outdoor carpet on the concrete floor. We enjoyed this "add on" family room for the rest of our time in San Diego. The building inspector that inspected the house before we sold it remarked that the add on room was much better quality work than he usually saw on such projects. He never asked if a building permit had been issued.

Arriving back home at the beginning of summer gave me a chance to get better acquainted with Celia. As I look back I could have and should have been a lot more creative in devising ways to spend special time with her. Being separated as much as we were left a void in both our lives. But I knew enough about her to be very proud to be her father. She was an excellent student with an enquiring mind and a solid work ethic. She had a strong will and was able to verbalize her desires. We moved a great deal while she was growing up but she was always able to adapt to new locations and new people. She made friends quickly wherever we moved but it must have been difficult when she had to leave old friends. It helped that all Navy families were all in the same boat regarding frequent moves.

While the ship was in dry dock, demands were greatly reduced. Many took leave since only a skeleton crew was needed. We had welcome visits from family this summer. Uncle George, aunt Dora, uncle Herbert and aunt Stella were great fun. Johnny and Bernie and their four children (Sandi was a baby) livened up our lives. We had a great time and I hated to see them leave. Dad and mom also came to see us and we had a special time together. It was especially enjoyable for me to take our guests aboard the

Okinawa. If Captain Williams was aboard he was always a cordial, gracious host to my visitors. He was particularly gracious to my parents and his kind words were greatly appreciated.

As we neared the end of our dry dock overhaul in December I faced one of the most critical decisions of my life as a minister and as a chaplain. Every military chaplain is required to be endorsed by a recognized religious body or denomination. Although I had theological degrees from Baptist and Presbyterian seminaries, I was ordained and endorsed by the Assemblies of God. Each year A/G ministers are required to submit a form in which they are asked if they fully subscribe to the Statement of Fundamental Truths contained in article V of the A/G constitution. For eleven years I had answered in the affirmative but for the past year I had been wrestling with affirming one of the doctrines.

While in Vietnam facing the uncertainties of life I reached the decision that I must disclose this doctrine with which I took exception. I knew this might have serious repercussions but my conscience compelled me to take this step. Because of the critical nature of this decision I will describe briefly what happened. I include this account for two reasons (1) It reveals something important about who I am. (2) It may encourage others, possibly my own grandchildren, not to compromise their conscience for the sake of temporary gain or pleasure.

As I have already recounted, Jesus Christ wonderfully baptized me in the Holy Spirit in 1948 when I was a young soldier stationed in San Antonio, Texas. My experience mirrored that of the disciples in Acts 2 and the Roman soldiers in Acts 10. Like them I, too, was surprised with the gift of speaking in a language provided by the Holy Spirit. Now the Assemblies of God teach that there is no valid baptism in the Holy Spirit unless evidenced by the gift of tongues. According to this doctrine, if one does not speak in a language provided by the Holy Spirit he cannot have been baptized in the Holy Spirit. To quote from Article V (8): "The baptism of believers in the Holy Ghost is witnessed by the initial physical sign of speaking in other tongues as the Spirit of God gives them utterance (Acts 2:4)." It was this doctrinal statement that I disagreed with. Although I had spoken in an unknown supernaturally provided language I knew there was no Scripture that states this must be the experience of all who are baptized with God's Spirit. It was built on false assumptions and on a valid religious experience that had been assigned an invalid purpose. The tongues of Pentecost had a far superior purpose than that given by the Assemblies of God. They symbolized all the languages, all the nations, races and people groups to which the gospel must be taken, even to the ends of the earth.

Donna and I were both aware that my ministerial career as a Navy chaplain was in jeopardy. I was sure God had called me into this ministry. I was also sure that I needed to officially declare my doctrinal position to the Assemblies of God. My conscience was clear and now my career path was in the hands of the ecclesiastical powers. Actually, it was in the capable hands of my heavenly Father. The conviction that God was in control enabled Donna and me to maintain some emotional balance throughout this ordeal. Even so, there were times of anxiety. How God intervened and protected my family and my career is fully covered in these books: **PENTECOST REVISITED and PENTECOST REKINDLED.** Both available at Amazon or from me personally at: rglennb@olypen.com.

When the overhaul was completed near the end of 1969 the Okinawa returned to San Diego to prepare for her next

WestPac cruise. The days of ease were behind us and we began a hectic schedule of preparation for our cruise departure on May 1. After major repairs the Navy requires a "shakedown" cruise. The ship is put through its paces testing all systems but within easy distance of port. If anything proves unsatisfactory it is only a short distance to port where corrections can be made.

While going through these maneuvers we experienced a dreaded misfortune. Somehow a fire got started in a mattress storage locker and heavy smoke quickly spread through the ventilation system. The ship of course had a plan to deal with such an emergency and men rushed to join their fire-fighting teams. The fire was finally extinguished without major damage to the ship. However, smoke inhalation caused a number of injuries. One sailor spent weeks in the hospital fighting for his life. It was rumored that the fire may have prevented Captain Williams from being promoted to Admiral. Competition for flag rank is so tough that the slightest blemish may prevent advancement. In Navy tradition the Captain is responsible for all that happens on his ship, good or bad. Probably some sailor sneaking a smoke caused the fire but the Captain took the hit.

The second WesPac cruise was much easier for Donna and me to face than the first one. My two year sea duty assignment would be completed in June 1970 so I would be gone only about two months or so. Furthermore, our first destination after leaving San Diego was New Zealand and I was looking forward to seeing this country. However, I was not particularly looking forward to more than three weeks sailing across thousands of miles of open ocean. Fortunately, it would prove more interesting and exciting than I had anticipated. Even though I anticipated being home again in a couple of months it was still a poignant moment as I bid Donna and Celia good-bye. Many unexpected things could happen while we were separated but we knew we were securely in God's hands.

Our purpose for going to New Zealand was to deliver fighter planes to their government. By the time we were ready to sail our flight deck was decorated with neat rows of combat planes destined for our close ally. Several things stand out in my mind about this trans-Pacific crossing. It was fun. Shortly after getting underway a beard growing contest was approved by the captain for both officers and enlisted men. I was designated as chairman of the beard judging committee. This was high level stuff and I enjoyed it immensely. When we crossed the equator all of us who had never crossed before (polliwogs) had to undergo an elaborate initiation ceremony overseen by king Neptune. We had to crawl through tube tunnels filled with fish entrails and other disgusting articles. We became covered with filth from head to toe. At last king Neptune said enough was enough. We were all hosed down and those who hadn't lost their appetites participated in a tasty picnic. The equatorial weather was ideal for a party on the flight deck.

Pacific means "peaceful" but the Pacific ocean is not always as its name implies. Shortly after crossing the equator we were overtaken by a fierce typhoon that tossed the ship like a rowboat. It persisted all day long and howled throughout the night. Sleep was difficult if not impossible. On the second day we exited the storm and were able to go on deck to assess the results. We sustained considerable damage on the flight deck and superstructure but all the planes anchored there had come through without damage. We proceeded to our destination.

We spent an eventful week in New Zealand. I visited Aukland on Sunday and the city was closed down. I never saw one store that was open for business. I had the address of an Assembly of God church so went there and was able to meet some fine people and enjoy their Christian fellowship. One of my collateral duties was to serve as tour officer and I arranged a couple of tours on the north island. The New Zealand Navy went out of its way to welcome us. They had a formal dinner in our honor that was something to experience. Their Navy is rich with British naval tradition and they displayed all the pomp and ceremony that British tradition embodies. For example, the roast beef that was to be eaten was presented to the commanding officer. He then called for a designated junior officer to come forward and sample the meat. The CO then took his sword from its scabbard and sliced off a small piece off beef. The junior officer carefully tasted it and then announced officiously, "The meat is fit for consumption, sir" after which we all proceeded to enjoy a delicious meal and get acquainted with our sea-going friends.

There was another formal dinner for the Okinawa officers sponsored by the civilian powers that be. New Zealand is a small country and many of her leading citizens were present. I enjoyed my visit to this delightful country very much. Years later I tried to take Donna and Celia there on a "space A" military flight. Unfortunately, we were bumped off in Hawaii. Oh, well, it could have been worse.

From New Zealand we proceeded to the high tech repair facility at the U.S. Naval Base in Sasebo, Japan. There the ship could be thoroughly examined and typhoon damage repaired before she continued to Vietnam. This would take several days.

Next door to our Naval Base was a Japanese shipyard where huge oil tankers were being constructed. These mammoth ships were certainly impressive when one viewed their

bare bottoms as they lay in dry dock. The Japanese had pio-
neered the construction of these massive petroleum carriers.

I was happy to learn that my replacement would join the
Okinawa while we were in Sasebo. My orders to fly home from
Yokota Air Base allowed me a few free days in Japan. Expo '70,
the Osaka World's Fair and Japan's first, was in full swing and I
decided to spend a day taking in this famous Exposition. I bid
my friends aboard the Okinawa good-bye and caught a train
from Sasebo to Osaka. Fortunately, there were enough signs
in English and enough helpful people who spoke English that
I was able to navigate reasonably well. The Expo grounds
were very colorful and swarming with international visitors
although most were Japanese. It was later reported that more
than sixty-four million visitors from eighty-four countries
came to Osaka. There were numerous pavilions, many of
them sponsored by countries. The United States pavilion was
housed in a large inflated structure. One of the most popular
U.S. exhibits was a sizeable rock carried back from the moon
walk in 1969. I crammed in as many sights as possible before
calling Expo '70 a day and boarding a train to Yokota Air
Force Base near Tokyo. With a couple of free days remaining I
played tourist in Tokyo. The July weather was hot, the streets
crowded, the sights interesting and the food tasty. But my
mind and heart were not in Japan. I was ready to go home.

The flight from Yokota Air Force Base to March Air Force
Base was in sharp contrast to the previous slow crossing by
ship... five hundred miles an hour versus five hundred miles
a day. There was no big welcoming committee at the airport,
just Donna and Celia, but they were all that counted. Donna
had driven about one hundred miles to pick me up at March

AFB. After our joyous "meet and greet" time at the airport we were eager to start the drive home. There was lots to do.

We had known for months that my new duty station was the Marine Corps Supply Center in Barstow, California. In early April we had driven to Barstow and met Chaplain Olsen whom I would be relieving in July. He and his wife were enthusiastic, Spirit filled, charismatic Lutherans. They were delighted that an Assemblies of God chaplain and family would follow them.

Donna and I are all dressed up for the Marine Corps ball to celebrate the 196th anniversary of the U.S. Marine Corps. Our three years in the desert on the staff of two different Generals were good years. We served with some great Christian Marines that honored God with their integrity and Christian testimony.

1973

CHAPTER 21

OUR DESERT YEARS

Donna and I were eager to say our good-byes and be on our way to another chapter in our lives. We had made good friends during our sojourn in San Diego and we loved the area. But it was time to move on. God had called me to be a Navy Chaplain and I accepted my Navy orders as being God's will for me at a particular place and time. That was true even if it meant three years parked in the Mojave Desert.

We (Donna, mainly) supervised the professional movers who came to pack our household goods to be shipped to Barstow. Our house was quickly rented to another chaplain moving into the area. We completed our "good-byes" and headed for Colorado to spend some time with our parents and friends in that state. We had deep roots in Colorado and loved to visit there.

We certainly received a warm welcome to the Marine Corps Supply Center in Barstow. August daytime temperatures usually ranged between 110-120 degrees f., quite a contrast to San Diego's moderate climate. The joke going around was that when a bad Indian died and arrived in hell the first thing he asked for was a blanket. We adapted quickly, learning to adjust our schedules to the temperature ranges. Fortunately, the desert cooled considerably at night. The long summer evenings were delightful.

It was not long after arriving in Barstow that my endorsement by the Assemblies of God bubbled to the surface again. I received a request from Ted Gannon, chairman of the A/G Chaplain's Commission, to meet with him and the Rocky Mountain District officials at the Denver airport. He would fly in from Springfield, Missouri and I would fly in from Las Vegas. On the designated day Donna drove me to the Las Vegas airport and I flew to Denver and met with the august assemblage. I had prepared a statement which reiterated my position. I explained, "In the note which I appended to the annual questionnaire I was trying to articulate a protest against denying God His sovereignty or clothing an inference with the sanctity of infallibility."

After reading my statement it was plain that it did not sit well with the Colorado officials. Their negative comments and body language was discomfiting. At this point Rev. Gannon entered the discussion. His interpretation of my comments made me hopeful that an accommodation could be found. In fact, he recommended that my credentials be provisionally renewed for another year while I reconsidered my position. However, the battle wasn't over. The Rocky Mountain District officials were not pleased with the decision from Springfield and I recognized that as long as I was affiliated with that District my credentials would be in jeopardy. Therefore, I requested a transfer to the Northern California-Nevada District. I had become acquainted with Joe Gerhart, the Superintendent of that District. He had served as an Army chaplain during WWII and was still a chaplain in the Reserves. He knew my position, had no problem with it and invited me to transfer to his District.

I submitted an official request to have my credentials transferred to the N. Cal/Nev District. The officials in Colorado were reluctant to honor my request since my credentials renewal was provisionally granted for one year. They wanted to keep me in their jurisdiction so they could continue to apply pressure for an acceptable doctrinal statement. At least, that was the way I interpreted their refusal to grant my request. Bartlett Peterson, the National General Secretary, concurred that I should not be granted a transfer. His reason, however, was that Barstow was in southern California. I shouldn't be permitted to transfer to northern California since one's locale of ministry determines which district has credential jurisdiction.

I quickly saw the fallacy in Secretary Peterson's response. Part of my reply to him went as follows: "In all of my ministry in the Chaplaincy I have never been stationed in Colorado, so obviously an exception to the general rule is made for military chaplains. Otherwise, I would have had to transfer my credentials many times...Having established that a general rule has been waived...I desire to petition for waiver to transfer to the Northern California-Nevada District Council even though I am temporarily stationed in Southern California." I then listed several pertinent reasons why the waiver should be granted. Apparently, my reasoning carried some weight since my request was in fact approved. I was warmly welcomed into the Northern California-Nevada District Council in 1971.

My chaplaincy ministry and integrity was preserved. At last I could breathe a sigh of relief and offer heart-felt thanks to God.

When I arrived at the Marine Corps Supply Depot the senior chaplain was a Roman Catholic. Unfortunately, he had a serious drinking problem and had to be relieved from duty. His replacement was a young priest junior to me so I became the senior chaplain. This had little impact upon my regular duties other than I now answered directly to the Commanding General. The General in command when I first went to MCSD was a rather officious, uninspiring officer. I don't remember ever seeing him in chapel. However, he had a gracious wife who was a regular member of our Protestant congregation.

The chapel program was very similar to that of an evangelical church in a small civilian community. We had an active choir and a graded Sunday School. The congregation of about one hundred was a cross section of Marine officers and non-commissioned officers with a few young marines and retirees. One young Marine officer and his wife, who were active members of our chapel family, became close friends and remain so today. Ron and Earline Johnson and their children are very special people and have enriched our lives. Although Ron has gone to be with his Lord whom he served so valiantly, we still maintain contact with Earline.

The early 1970's were tempestuous days of cultural fermentation. The Vietnam war, distrust of government, rampant drug use and unbridled, illicit sex had all impacted our society in negative ways. Young people particularly reacted with confusion and rebellion. Barstow was the crossroad for two interstate national highways... I 15 and I 40. These busy highways intersected just outside the main gate of the

Marine Base. Young, long haired hitch-hikers thronged this area. I hit upon the idea of challenging our chapel congregation to confront these men with the gospel. Our plan was to take sandwiches and cold drinks to the intersection for free distribution. We also offered New Testaments to those who wanted one. Women from the chapel congregation prepared the sandwiches and a few volunteers manned the distribution site. I don't think the General was enthused about his Christian marines reaching out to the "hippies" but he never interfered. When the first General was transferred, the new Commanding General was very much in favor of what we were doing. He actually commended me for this ministry.

My office was next door to the physical fitness center. A female marine who was assigned to the fitness center often came by to talk. She was a lesbian trying to survive in a military culture that didn't countenance her life style. She knew I didn't approve of her sexual conduct but she knew I accepted her as a person of great worth. Sometimes she would open up and talk about her struggles and invite feed-back from me. This gave me an opportunity to share the good news of Christ's love, grace and power to transform. Eventually, I was transferred and never saw her again. Imagine my surprise when some years later I received a letter from a Women's Rehab Center in Pennsylvania operated by Teen Challenge. A former woman marine was enrolled there who was seeking help to break free from her lesbian life style. She gave credit for her motivation to a chaplain Brown who had befriended her when she was stationed in Barstow. God moves in mysterious ways.

The greenest spot on the face of the earth around Barstow was the MCSC golf course.

It was kept luxuriantly verdant by abundant water from the Mohave River.

The strange thing, the river bed of the Mohave, that went along the golf course, was dry as a bone. All of its water flowed twelve feet or so beneath the ground and had to be pumped to the surface. Since the golf course was an oasis in the midst of vast vistas of barrenness I spent a lot of free time roaming its fairways. I actually joined the Golf Association and faithfully recorded my scores so as to maintain an accurate handicap.

Two or three events stand out in my mind when I think of golf at Barstow. My second year there I was voted "the most improved golfer" and was presented a trophy by the Commanding General. This only testifies to how bad I was to begin with. Another memory has to do with a tournament. The golf team at the huge marine base at Twenty Nine Palms challenged our MCSC team to play on their home course. As it turned out, I had a fantastic day and shot considerably below my handicap. It was one of the very few times I ever shot below 80. I scored a gross 79 and, with my 14 handicap, a net 65. I actually had the best score in both categories and contributed to our team victory. And then there is the bad memory. Being the swinger that I was I inadvertently swung away my wedding ring. I searched again and again hoping to find my lost treasure but no luck. Actually, I did find a wedding ring but it belonged to someone else.

My pay check and status got a welcome boost in 1971 when I was promoted to full commander. The Commanding General made the presentation in a small ceremony and Donna pinned the silver oak leaves on my uniform. Although I never paid much attention to my "fitness reports" the promotion confirmed that the reports were strongly positive. I received another confirmation when the Chaplains' Corps selected me to join other chaplains for a concentrated month of training on the University of California campus at Berkeley. The field of study was "counseling" and the instructors were leading theorists in popular counseling approaches and techniques. I found it interesting but difficult to adapt the various theories to sailors and marines.

Classes normally ended about three p.m. and I escaped to the nearby golf course. Around four-thirty p.m. a dramatic bank of fog began to roll in from the Pacific ocean. The temperature suddenly dropped, probably thirty degrees, and a sweater or jacket was needed. I had a new appreciation for the person who said, "The coldest month I ever spent was a July in San Francisco." The chaplains at Berkeley were visited near the end of the course by a senior chaplain from the Chief of Chaplains office. He spoke briefly to me, indicating that my career was being followed with interest. I wasn't sure what that meant but I took it to be a positive affirmation.

Since the Lord seemed to be blessing my professional career as a Navy Chaplain I decided to apply for selection to the Senior Chaplain's Course in Newport, R.I. This was a course designed for chaplains who had reached the rank of commander and were good candidates for future promotion to captain. To my delight I was selected for the school year of 1973-74. Our three year assignment to the Marine Corps Supply Center was completed in the summer of 1973. God had blessed our ministry on the barren Mojave desert but all of us were ready for "greener pastures". I had much the same feeling for the Mojave as was expressed by a marine wife who remarked to me shortly after I arrived in Barstow: "They tell me the desert grows on you but if I see it growing on me I'll cut it off".

My classmates in the Navy Chaplains Senior School in
Newport, R.I., 1973-4. A great bunch of guys. I wonder
how many of them are still alive after forty years?

CHAPTER 22

THE SENIOR COURSE AT NEWPORT, R.I.

As the time approached for us to depart the Marine Corps Supply Depot we began to plan our trip to Newport, R.I. in earnest. I didn't do as much research as I should have and made a strategic error of judgment. Rather than move our furniture and rent a house for less than a year I thought it made sense to buy a house trailer and live in it. Wrong, wrong, wrong. I seriously underestimated how cold Rhode Island winter weather could get. I would have to learn the hard way.

John told us of a nice used 28 footer in Oshkosh that we decided to buy. We also purchased a big used 1969 Chrysler to provide ample power for pulling the trailer.

We thought it would be fun to go north from Oshkosh across northern Michigan and enter Canada at Sault Ste. Marie. We had never visited Canada so this seemed like a good chance to visit our neighbor to the north. We planned to continue to Toronto and reenter the United States at Niagara Falls. With our trip planned we were eager to begin our cross-country trek.

In addition to the Chrysler Newport (fittingly named) we still had our 1968 Rambler. We decided to drive both to Newport. We also had a pop-up camper that we would pull and use until we reached Oshkosh. No doubt I spent far more on the camper and trailer than the best motels would have cost. I just liked the sense of freedom and adventure that went with having a home on wheels. Maybe it was linked to my childhood adventures in the old model-T truck house that took us from Kansas to North Carolina.

We left Barstow as a small caravan. I drove the Chrysler pulling the camper. Donna, Celia and Peter Pan, our little Chihuahua-terrier, followed in the Rambler. I haven't mentioned Peter Pan before but he was Celia's pet and very much a member of our family. He would keep us amused for hours as he chased his tail in endless circles. I recall that Peter Pan made a lasting impression on the new Catholic chaplain who was assigned to MCSC. He paid a courtesy call to our home and was greeted by Peter Pan who immediately asserted his turf rights. He lifted his leg and baptized the chaplain's foot. The young priest took it in good humor and acknowledged that he had a dog in his quarters whose scent had prompted Peter Pan's action.

Our caravan wound its way toward Denver where we visited family and friends. From Denver we headed to Kansas for an overnight visit with Uncle George and Aunt Dora. They were always great fun and wonderfully hospitable. From Kansas we went northeast to Oshkosh for another enjoyable visit with Johnny and Bernie and their children.

We left our little pop-up camper in Oshkosh, hooked up the travel trailer and proceeded north through Green Bay to the U.S./Canada border crossing at Sault Ste. Marie. When the Canadian border guards stopped us they gave me some forms to fill out. On the form was a list of items which were illegal to bring into Canada which included firearms. To my dismay I suddenly realized that I had brought a small, single shot souvenir pistol from Brazil that Charley had given me to give to Johnny. I had forgotten to give it to John and only remembered about it when prompted by the questionnaire.

I told the border agent about the pistol and he asked me to let him look at it. That's when the fun started. I had no idea where I had put it. I looked in the Chrysler and searched high and low in the travel trailer without finding the pistol. Finally, I searched the Rambler and I found it hidden away in the trunk. I fully expected to have it confiscated by the Canadians. Of course the border agents had inspected my documents and knew that I was a U.S. Navy chaplain. When I finally produced the weapon one agent called to his partner and said, "The padre found his souvenir pistol. What do you think we should do with it? His reply surprised me "Padre, just keep that pistol out of the cars. Hide it securely in the travel trailer and be on your way." I followed their instructions and thanked them. With a friendly smile they waved us on. I can't imagine such an outcome in the post 9/11 climate.

It was a hot August day when we arrived in Toronto. Up to this point the vehicles had run well but suddenly on a busy thoroughfare the Chrysler just died. We had plenty of gas, the battery was strong but the engine was unresponsive. Not knowing what had caused the engine malfunction we just sat for awhile and watched the traffic stream around us. I am sure we prayed for guidance but there was no sudden inspiration as to what to do so we sat sweltering in the hot sun. While we soaked up the August heat the engine was gradually cooling down. I don't know if a cooler engine influenced what happened next. Anyway, I turned the switch key and the engine started right up and we continued on our way. This was the first of several phantom engine failures. This happened again soon after we got to Newport. I took it to a garage and they claimed to have found and fixed the trouble and charged us accordingly. Unfortunately, the "phantom" continued to strike at the most inopportune times. Finally, the trouble was traced to a faulty wiring harness.

From Toronto we crossed the border back into the United States at Niagara Falls. Our visit to these great falls was awe-inspiring. My imagination ran wild as I pictured Houdini doing his thrilling acts of balance on a swaying line high above the falls. In the nearby museum one could see the actual line on which Houdini had performed his sensational feats. One of my favorite sermon illustrations dealing with Christian belief centered on Houdini's Niagara Fall's act. It is purported that after Houdini pushed a wheelbarrow on a high line above the Falls he asked the crowd below, "Who believes that I can have a man get in the wheelbarrow and push him across the Falls?" Many shouted enthusiastically that they believed he could do it. Houdini then pointed to one of the shouters, "Please, sir, come get in the wheelbarrow." The man slunk back quickly into the crowd. The point being, of course, that belief in Jesus involves trusting your very life to him.

From Niagara Falls we continued on to Newport. The first task was to locate a mobile home park where we could locate our house on wheels. We found one in a convenient location and quickly got the water, sewer and electricity connected. The bad news was that no pets were allowed in the camp. Fortunately, the Hewetts, good friends from Iceland, had settled in Rhode Island, not many miles from Newport. They agreed to keep Peter Pan, our delightful little chihauhau terrier. We took care of the other preliminary things involved in our ten month "camp-out". While I was getting enrolled in the Senior Chaplain's course Donna got Celia enrolled in her first year of High school. We visited a few churches and settled on worshipping with the Evangelical Friends.

There were thirty or so chaplains enrolled in school about a third of whom were Roman Catholics. The administrative staff were senior chaplains (Captains) who had minimal teaching assignments. Most of our professors were from "ivy league" universities such as Harvard or Yale or other quality schools. I found many of the classes intellectually stimulating and I actually stayed awake in most of them. One of the required assignments was to learn a practical skill that would enhance one's ministry to sailors and marines. I chose to learn to play the guitar. I procured a guitar and instructor and practiced my lessons faithfully. It must have been quite trying for Donna and Celia, revealed occasionally by snide remarks, particularly when I sang along. Regrettably, I didn't continue practicing after leaving Newport so lost what little skill I had.

My poor decision about living in a trailer really became evident as winter approached. We discovered that winters can be very cold in Rhode Island. To prevent our water supply pipe from freezing I used electric heating tape. When our entry door latch kept freezing shut I knew it was time to look for more suitable housing. We found a pleasant two bedroom furnished cottage which we happily rented for the remaining months of the school year. I only have one bad memory associated with our sojourn in this house. There was no garage so we parked the cars in the front yard. One night I left the keys in the Rambler and it was stolen. We notified the police and hoped for the best. In a day or so the car was found abandoned in an open field, non-the-worse for its unauthorized absence. Apparently some kids had taken it for a "joy ride."

The infamous gas shortage of 1973-4 erupted while we were at Newport. Long lines at the pumps became commonplace and prices rose alarmingly. I purchased a bicycle and attempted to devise a battery powered motor for it. I had some plans that were supposed to help me but the project was a fiasco. After wasting hours in my futile gas saving attempt I bit the bullet and waited in line at the pump. The perceived gas shortage produced the usual moans and groans about our dependence on foreign oil. It was an ideal time to push for national action that would lead to developing other sources of energy. Unfortunately, when the crisis eased people forgot their concerns and little was done.

As summer approached, Celia and I were wrapping up our academic endeavors. From my perspective it had been a good year. We had enjoyed our association with the Evangelical Friends (Quakers) and I think they appreciated us. The Narragansett Bay area is very attractive, historically and scenically. The lavish mansions built by the super rich a century ago made for interesting tours. Furthermore, we had family living in New York whom we were able to visit occasionally.

But duty called. I had received orders to the largest U.S. Marine Corps base outside the United States, Camp Hansen, Okinawa. I was scheduled to be the senior chaplain, serving on the staff of the Base Commander. Unfortunately, this was to be an unaccompanied tour, meaning that Donna and Celia would remain in the U.S.

We had decided that we would settle them in the San Diego area again. It was a delightful area and we still had friends there who would welcome them. My school concluded before Celia's so I decided to take a few days, fly to San Diego and buy a house. I found a nearly new house in a development in southeastern San Diego. It was located at the end of a cul-de-sac and looked like a safe area for Donna and Celia to live while I was in Okinawa. House prices in San Diego were still reasonable although probably thirty percent higher than when we first purchased in 1968.

We departed Rhode Island in June, 1974. My orders to Okinawa included the provision for shipping an automobile from the east coast. We left the Rambler at the Army port in New Jersey for processing for shipment to Okinawa. We proceeded westward pulling our trailer behind the Chrysler. Our itinerary to San Diego included visits to Brown family relatives in Kansas and then Wirth and Brown/Bluhm relatives and friends in Colorado. We drove south from Denver to Albuquerque to spend some time with Donna's brother, Lanny, and his family. These welcome stops made our cross country jaunt all the more enjoyable.

We left Albuquerque early one summer morning driving west on US 40. By early afternoon we were through Flagstaff and making good progress toward Needles, California where we would likely spend the night in an RV park. I had driven all the way across country up to this point, reluctant to have Donna assume responsibility for pulling the trailer. But driving across the Arizona desert in mid-afternoon I became overwhelmingly sleepy. Rather than halt our progress we decided that Donna should drive while I took a short rest. Big mistake!! The mistake was not in letting Donna drive but letting her drive without giving her any instructions about braking in case of an emergency.

I went temporary brain dead, turned the car over to Donna without instruction, and went soundly asleep. Sometime later I was suddenly awakened by a careening car followed by a wildly "fish-tailing" trailer. Donna was desperately trying to gain control but it was a losing battle. The next thing we knew the car, flipped upside down by the cavorting trailer, was sliding along on its roof. Donna and I were secured by our seat belts. Celia had been sleeping in the back seat and she was tossed around a little bit since she had no seat belt.

Once the vehicles concluded their gyrations we tentatively considered our predicament. Was anyone injured? was our first consideration. Amazingly, no one was hurt except for a few bumps and bruises. I extricated myself and helped Donna and Celia escape from the wreck. Devastation from the destroyed trailer littered the highway. Donna explained she had lost control of the car and trailer when a strong desert wind had swept across the highway and forced the trailer into fishtailing action. This is not an uncommon occurrence on dessert roads as we observed when living in Barstow. If I had shown her how to use the braking system to help control the swerving action the accident may never have occurred. Despite the accident we had so much to be thankful for. God had protected us from serious injury and we rejoiced in His goodness.

The accident occurred near Kingman. It just so happened that the pastor of the local Assembly of God church was a preacher whom I had known when we were young men in Denver together. I phoned him, explained our predicament, and he graciously volunteered to come rescue us. The Arizona afternoon heat was fierce so the first priority was to get Donna and Celia located in an air-conditioned motel. That accomplished, the next order of business was to rent a vehicle large enough to transport all of our clothes, books and other personal gear salvaged from the trailer. The van we were able to get was large enough but uncomfortable and without air-conditioning. But it had four wheels and could get us to our destination. With the help of my pastor friend I was able to negotiate a deal to have the wreckage removed and assigned for salvage. The only insurance we had was collision so we had little compensation. Another big oversight on my part.

The four-hundred mile trip from Kingman to San Diego was miserably hot until we neared the city by the sea. What a relief to get back to San Diego. The first order of business was to introduce Donna and Celia to our new house. I was gratified to see they were pleased with my purchase. Our second order of business was to buy another car to replace the one we left wrecked in Arizona. We soon settled on a 1973 Ford sedan bought from Hertz. And it did have air-conditioning.

Here's what it is all about. I am giving baptismal instructions
to six Marines who are about to go with me into the South
China Sea off the coast of Okinawa to be baptized.

1975

CHAPTER 23
OKINAWA

Donna and I had prepared ourselves mentally, emotionally and spiritually for an extended separation. The Marines had some assignments overseas that permitted dependents to accompany the service member. The Third Marine Division in Okinawa was not one of those favored assignments. My send off to Okinawa was much more private than when I had embarked aboard ship. There were no bands or large crowds. There was just Donna and Celia to share hugs and kisses as we said our good-byes at the airport.

The flight from California to Okinawa was long and tiring but uneventful. It was hot when we landed but the temperature was not much different from California except more humid. The initial reports I received after reporting to Camp Hansen were not encouraging. The Camp Commander was an immoral scoundrel living illicitly with a local woman in the nearby village. Moral was low and black-white racial relationships were dangerously volatile. On the positive side, the current Camp Commander was rotating back to the States and a new Commander was arriving within the week.

Colonel Gray, the new Camp Commander, was a straight shooter. He met with me and other senior staff members as well as subordinate unit Commanders and presented his plan for restoring order and morale to the Camp. Much racial conflict took place in the many bars and nightclubs lining the streets of Kin, the nearby town. Col. Gray ordered all the unit commanders and special staff officers, including chaplains, to form teams and patrol the streets of Kin each night. The teams were instructed to specifically invade every nightspot and make their presence known to all the Marine patrons. In addition, Col. Gray himself made regular inspections of the bars and clubs. On base, he inspected barracks and mess halls, demonstrating genuine interest in the thousands of men under his command. Also, he was seen frequently in Protestant chapel services.

As a result of Col. Gray's decisive action and positive leadership the moral atmosphere at Hansen remarkably improved. Racial relationships remained dicey. The Black Power movement was popular at this time and there was a significant chapter among the African-American Marines at Hansen. Their leaders asked me if they could use the chapel for their meetings. I conferred with Col. Gray and his reply demonstrated his wisdom. "Tell the Marines I don't tolerate racial prejudice. They can have their meetings in the chapel only if it is open to all Marines." When I relayed this to the Black Power leaders they lost interest in using the chapel.

In addition to Col. Gray's outstanding leadership, there were other memorable events during my year in Okinawa. I received permission to conduct an old-fashioned outdoor revival aboard the base. A Marine tent was erected, a sound system was installed as well as a piano. Other chaplains helped with preaching, including Army chaplain Chuck Adams from the Army hospital. His wife, Peggy, played the piano.

I can't forget the wild ping-pong matches at the Christian Servicemen's Center just outside Hansen's main gate. The Center director was a good player and we had some hotly contested games but I modestly remember that I usually prevailed. He was a staunch Baptist and anti-Pentecostal. Imagine my surprise when years later I received a letter from him stating he had been filled with the Holy Spirit. I don't remember if I ever told him any of my reservations concerning some of the Pentecostal doctrines. He has retained his relationship with the Baptist church so I am sure he never publicized his Pentecostal experience. The Southern Baptist leadership has zero tolerance for such. But the Holy Spirit cannot be controlled and only God knows how many "closet" Pentecostals are in Baptist churches.

I met regularly with a group of Marine officers for Bible study. One of the members, a senior colonel who commanded the MAW (Marine Air Wing), impressed me for two reasons. First, he was a devout Christian who loved the Lord and loved to study His word. Second, he was a member of the Reorganized Church of Jesus Christ of Latter Day Saints. In my mind, the two were incompatible. I was not familiar with the Reorganized LDS with headquarters in Independence, Missouri. (Since 2001 known as Community of Christ). I discovered it was markedly different from the LDS headquartered in Salt Lake City. The RLDS rejected a plurality of gods and believed in one God manifested as a Trinity of Father Son and Holy Spirit. They rejected polygamy from the beginning, unlike the Utah LDS. Although they still held to some teachings from the Joseph Smith era, they were much closer to mainstream Protestant churches than to Mormanism.

My colonel friend's commitment to Christ was inspirational to all of us. You can imagine our shock and sorrow when we got the word that his jet fighter had flamed out on a routine training flight. He was forced to bail out into the Sea of Japan and perished. His death was a tremendous loss to the Marine Corps, to his Christian brothers and especially to his family back in Missouri. I wrote his wife a letter, sharing my admiration for her husband and expressing sorrow for her great loss. Words are so inadequate at such a time.

Halfway through the Okinawa tour I was given a brief leave to go home. Needless to say, it was a welcome respite. We were together again, at least for a few days. It was relaxing just doing normal family things...shopping, visiting the zoo and taking trips. We took a week-end drive to Chatsworth to visit my sister Carol and her family. A significant decision Donna made while I was in Okinawa was paying dividends. Celia had been strongly opposed enrolling in a San Diego public high school. Donna was able to enroll her in an excellent private Christian high school. Celia responded positively to the high moral and academic standards. Her grades were excellent and she blossomed socially and spiritually. The money spent for her tuition was one of the best investments we ever made. One incident tarnished the leave. While entering a double lane of traffic from a shopping center I was blind-sided by a speeding car in the second lane. Unfortunately, the driver who hit me was an uninsured visitor from south of the border. While our car was getting repaired we rented a small green Pinto for local running around. All too soon my leave was over and once again we said our good-byes. It was a long flight back to Okinawa.

The Christian world had been surprised by the rapid growth of Christianity in Korea. One of the great Korean Christian leaders was a Seoul pastor named David Yonggi Cho. His church was reputedly the largest Christian congregation in the world. Our executive officer, Lt. Col. White, invited me to accompany him for a four day jaunt to Korea. We were able to get a "hop" on a Marine plane. We flew into Inchon and from there took a wild taxi trip to Seoul. I visited the Assembly of God Servicemen's Center in downtown Seoul. Later, Colonel White and I shopped for souvenirs.

The highlight of our brief trip was attending a Sunday service at pastor David Yonggi Cho's huge church. At the time of our visit the congregation met in a church building seating ten thousand worshippers (Today a new church seats twenty-five thousand). In order to accommodate the more than one hundred thousand members (in 1975, today almost one million) multiple services were conducted. We attended the eleven o'clock service. As we filed into the huge auditorium we were met by an usher. He led us to the area where earphones were provided for an English translation, one of several languages translated for visitors. After the hour long service we were approached by an English-speaking Korean couple who insisted we permit them to take us to lunch. They were so friendly and gracious we couldn't refuse them. They escorted us to a lovely upscale restaurant where we were seated, Korean style, on soft mats on the floor. As we conversed we learned that our host was in the banking business. He expressed his love for America, grateful for the American sacrifices made in behalf of South Korea. The food was delicious, typically spicy, eaten leisurely much as Jesus must have eaten, reclining on the floor.

I was deeply disappointed to learn that Pastor Cho brought disgrace upon himself and his church in recent years. He conspired with his son to embezzle many millions of dollars from his huge church. He was convicted in 2014 of embezzling twelve million dollars (possibly much more) and sentenced to three years in prison. He is only the latest of numerous Assemblies of God "stars" to fall from the firmament. Why, why, why? I believe part of the answer is that a major doctrine of our church is founded on an experience rather than the clear teaching of scripture. All the stars that have fallen were vehement proclaimers of this experience of speaking in tongues as being evidence of Spirit baptism. Think of the false teaching my church has spawned... the prosperity doctrine, the "super faith" heresy, the cultic leadership models, etc. I am reminded of David's mournful cry upon learning of the death of king Saul and prince Jonathon. Three times David lamented, "How the mighty have fallen!" May God help his Church to reflect the character of Jesus.

Another memory, more significant to me personally than my visit to the huge Korean church, is that of baptizing Marine converts in the warm waters of the surrounding Pacific Ocean. To see these young Marines publicly declare their commitment to Jesus Christ was inspiring and a great testimony to believers and unbelievers alike. These new converts couldn't escape the ungodly environment surrounding them. Their lives were constantly scrutinized by critical fellow Marines. They had to walk the talk or lose their influence as Christians. The Christian Servicemen's Center, directed by Ralph and Wilma Porter, did a great job of helping disciple and provide fellowship for these new Christians.

I was not entirely without family while in Okinawa. My uncle Del, mother's oldest brother, was a U.S. Army auditor and was stationed at an Army base in another part of the island. We were able to meet occasionally and really enjoyed our times together. I believe the bond we formed in Okinawa was a factor in Del being receptive as I shared the gospel with him years later.

Another significant historical event took place while I was in Okinawa. The armed forces of South Vietnam were rapidly deteriorating in the face of strong communist attacks. The American public was strongly opposed to providing the South Vietnam forces any more support and our government decided to withdraw and leave them to their fate. Colonel Al Gray, my skipper, was chosen to be in command of the final withdrawal of American military and civilian personnel from Saigon. Most of his staff remained at Camp Hansen. We had daily staff meetings and were briefed concerning events coming to a head in Saigon. April 30, 1975 was a sad day as we heard the report of the last American helicopter departing while the abandoned Vietnamese wailed in despair.

Col. Gray was an outstanding military leader evidenced by the fact that a few years after we were together in Okinawa he was wearing four stars and was Commandant of the Marine Corps. However, he had a reputation for disliking administrative paperwork. Each year a commanding officer has to submit an evaluation on his immediate subordinates. This evaluation is called a "fitness report" and the evaluation determines whether an officer is promoted or not. As I neared the end of my tour I reminded the Colonel that my fitness report was due. He surprised me by replying, "Chaplain, you prepare your fitness report and I'll sign it." I was so surprised I didn't really know how to respond. I mumbled something like, "Yes, sir, if that's what you want."

I didn't feel very comfortable evaluating my own performance so I asked the advice of a senior chaplain. He said in
essence, "If Colonel Gray has any reservations about recom-
mending you for promotion he wouldn't have asked you to prepare your fitness report. Give yourself good marks that reflect
an outstanding performance. That is what he expects you to
do." So I followed his advice. With an assured outstanding
fitness report for a year's ministry with Marines in Okinawa I
was ready for my next duty station. My new orders sent me to
Moffett Naval Air Station in Mountain View, California.

Awaiting sunrise as we begin the Easter Sunrise service at
Naval Air Station, Moffett. C.M.Morris, renowned Assemblies
of God radio evangelist, was our guest preacher. His head
barely appears on left side just above the pulpit. Chaplain
Schall, a super Methodist chaplain, stands on platform also.

1977

CHAPTER 24
MOFFETT NAVAL AIR STATION

When we knew we were going to Moffett, Donna contacted a realtor. Our house in San Diego sold quickly while I was still in Okinawa. The Navy packed up our household goods and put everything in storage. Donna and Celia were able to stay with good friends while awaiting my return. Since I would not be returning home until the end of July, Celia decided to enroll in summer school. She took typing and driver's education, both practical courses that continue to pay dividends for her.

When I flew home in late July, Donna and Celia again met me at March Air Force Base. Since our house had already sold, we quickly prepared to depart on vacation. We loaded our 1973 Ford sedan and drove to Denver where Donna's parents and brother lived. We traveled some of the same desert that we had crossed the previous year, then in a stifling van without air-conditioning. This time we enjoyed the comfort of an air-conditioned car. We always enjoyed visiting Denver. Donna had grown up there and I had graduated from college and seminary there. In addition my uncles Arley and Elmo lived there with their families. Also, I had served several years as the youth leader at Calvary Temple, a leading Denver church for many years.

After enjoying a few days with family and friends in Colorado we flew to New York for a very special family reunion. Mom, dad and all my siblings with their families were meeting at Camp Champion, for a much anticipated family reunion. Camp Champion was affiliated with Teen Challenge and was the site for summer recreation for inner city kids. My sister Faith was one of the leaders of this program and helped procure the Camp for our use. The 1975 Brown family reunion was especially significant. This was the first of many bicentennial reunions that have continued in some form down to the present. Mom, dad and we nine siblings were all together for the first time in many years. As of this date (January 17, 2015) Mom, Dad and sisters Faith and Norma and brother Charley, are no longer with us. Little sister Aillene and kid brother Phil had died as youngsters in 1934 and 1954 respectively. We anticipate a great family reunion with all of them in our Lord's own good timing.

We returned to California in August and I reported to Moffett Naval Air Station as the senior Protestant chaplain. We decided to live in Navy housing aboard the base.

All the other chaplains lived in civilian housing in one of the nearby cities. The Commanding Officer preferred to have at least one chaplain to live on base so he was pleased that we agreed to do so.

Moffett was an historic Naval Air Station. It was home to the submarine patrol bombers that combed the Pacific ocean and kept tabs on any foreign subs discovered. Two huge, towering Moffett hangers were regional landmarks. Back in the 1930's these mammoth hangers had housed the gigantic dirigibles that the Navy employed for submarine patrol. The largest of the two sometimes had its own mini-atmosphere. I have seen small clouds floating near the ceiling, high above the hanger deck.

I was scheduled to be stationed at Moffett for three years. This meant that Celia could complete her last two years of high school in Mountain View, the little city just outside Moffett's main gate. Memories of my own high school trauma, when our family moved three times during my junior year, made me happy that Celia would be in the same high school for her junior and senior years. She had adjusted well to changing schools between her freshman and sophomore years but the last two years are more critical.

As senior Protestant chaplain my assignment was much like being pastor in a civilian community. The chapel congregation consisted of active duty military personnel and retirees who lived in nearby cities. The military personnel and families changed constantly but the retirees were stable members. The chapel choir as well as the ushers were primarily retirees. The chapel had a paid choir director and organist both of which had been on staff for years and were quite competent. Donna and I sang in the choir and enjoyed it immensely. We had an active Sunday School which was administered by a paid, part time Christian Ed director. In the summer we conducted Vacation Bible School for children living in military housing. On July fourth 1976 the chapel sponsored an outdoor musical celebration of our 200th anniversary of national independence.

An unexpected opportunity came to us while at Moffett. The large Coast Guard Station on Kodiak Island in Alaska, at the recommendation of their chaplain, requested that the Command at Moffett permit me to conduct a week long Religious Emphasis Week at the Kodiak Station. The Coast Guard would pick up the transportation tab for Donna and me. Moffett granted Kodiak's request and in early May, 1977 Donna and I found ourselves at the Coast Guard Station. The Coast Guard command gave us a warm welcome unlike the weather which was still quite cold. I preached a series of sermons, some good, but none particularly outstanding if I remember correctly.

The Coast Guard personnel were hardy souls performing their life-saving skills to seafarers off the Alaskan coast. We enjoyed our time with them and I appreciated the opportunity to minister for the week. Our scheduled return flight back to San Francisco was cancelled because of bad weather, including high wind and snow. According to the locals, this was not an infrequent situation. Since Alaska Airlines only flew to Kodiak once a week we were forced to wait a couple of days for a flight on a small local airline that flew us to Anchorage. From there we got seats on an airliner into San Francisco. It was about 1 a.m. before we got our luggage and secured a taxi. The taxi ride from the airport to Moffett was wild. The cab driver was extremely sleepy and kept dozing off. Fortunately, traffic was light at this time of night and we arrived home safely and gratefully.

Mother had been diagnosed with a serious heart problem in 1975. Dad decided to retire from the pastorate so as to relieve mother from the demands upon a pastor's wife. I had never been stationed near family members and I wanted very much to be able to visit my parents at this stage of their lives. I knew dad would never be able to adjust to the wild traffic of the San Francisco Bay area so I decided to look for a small farm within easy driving distance from Moffett. We began to investigate property near Turlock, a thriving town of about 20,000 people. It was seventy-five miles away from the congestion of the Bay area yet close enough for an easy drive. We found a small eleven acre farm with two houses and five acres of mature almond trees and six acres of pasture and open land. It had excellent irrigation and the price was reasonable. We bought it and upgraded the three bed-room house with new carpet and paint, getting it ready for mom and dad's arrival.

In the spring of 1976 mom and dad left Nebraska and moved into the farm house near Turlock, California. I went to Beaver City to help them make the trip. Dad drove pick-up truck loaded with some furniture and household goods. We helped them get settled in. Dad and I inspected the farm and I introduced him to the old Case tractor that came with the farm. I had already started a garden because I knew dad and mom would want one. The soil was extremely sandy but fortunately we had plenty of water for irrigation. I hoped they would enjoy rural life in sunny California. I know I was delighted to have them living less than two hours away.

Throughout the following year we made numerous trips to the farm and it was always a joy to be greeted by mom's welcoming smile and dad's warm handshake. After about fifteen months on the farm dad informed me that he and mom had decided to go back to their house in Nebraska. Mom explained that she didn't like the depressing fog that invaded California's central valley each winter. Dad explained his motivation this way, "Son, when one is your age you look for a place to live. When you are my age you look for a place to die." Dad clearly wanted to spend his declining years closer to his roots. I helped them make the move back. It was a sad day for me when I bid them good-bye. I'll always treasure the memory of our time together.

The summer and fall of 1977 was painfully life changing for Donna and me. In July after serving as a Commander for over six years I was being considered for promotion to Captain. This is the top of the promotion ladder for chaplains unless you are selected as the Chief of Navy Chaplains or Deputy Chief. The Navy had early in my career selected me as a future senior chaplain. I was selected as a Regular Navy officer rather than a reserve officer during my first sea duty in 1961-62. I had multiple assignments as senior chaplain on bases where I supervised other chaplains. In addition the Navy had prepared me for further promotion by choice educational assignments including a year at Princeton Seminary and another year at the Senior Chaplains' Course in Newport.

Although I had never made a practice of reviewing my annual "fitness reports", I knew they were good because I had never failed promotion. The fitness report is an official document that Commands submit to the Chief of Chaplains office which weighs the performance of an individual chaplain. These performance reports are used as the primary basis for choosing who gets promoted and who does not. Of course, the closer you get to the top of the ladder the more competitive it becomes.

I had the utmost confidence that I would be selected for promotion. You can imagine my surprise and disappointment when I was not on the promotion list. For one of the few times in my career, I asked to see my fitness report and I was provided a copy. To my consternation I discovered the Catholic chaplain had submitted a report filled with untruths which he used to justify a report that would keep me from being competitive for promotion.

I knew it was imperative that I write an immediate rebuttal. Both the Commanding Oficer and the Catholic chaplain were retiring in September. The lies of the chaplain were so blatantly false that I had no difficulty refuting them with factual data. I wrote a point by point by point rebuttal and submitted it to the Commanding Officer. After he reviewed it he called me to his office and said he was sending an amended fitness report to Washington to replace the one previously submitted. Unfortunately, I would have to wait a whole year for another promotion board to take the amended report into consideration.

I could not understand why the Catholic chaplain had perjured himself in order to recommend a fitness report that would deny me an expected promotion. I had not confronted him for an answer but rather went directly to the Commanding Officer for redress. Joe (the Catholic chaplain) was a surly, unfriendly guy but I had always tried to be civil. I suspected that he may have been jealous because the Protestant chapel program was alive and flourishing in marked contrast to his own. But that was his problem, not mine. It was a relief to know that he would soon be retired and out of my hair in September.

One day shortly before Joe retired he came by my office and asked if he might speak with me. I invited him to come in, curious as to what he wanted to say. He began to relate an astounding story. He said that several years ago he had been passed over for promotion to Captain because a senior Protestant chaplain had recommended that he be given a low fitness report. He admitted he became very bitter and vowed that if he ever got a chance to retaliate against a Protestant chaplain he would do so. "Glenn," he said, "you came along and I saw my chance to get even. I submitted a recommended fitness report to the Commanding Officer that was full of falsehoods. Glenn, I'm sorry, I really am. I've come here to ask you to forgive me. Can you, will you forgive me?"

I looked into his eyes and there were tears running down his face. As I pondered his question I knew I must forgive him. I dare not let bitterness erode my own soul as it had his. At this very moment the Spirit of Jesus Christ entered my office. I felt the warmth of His love and compassion as I looked into the tear-stained face of this repentant Catholic priest. I arose from my chair and took Joe in my arms. We wept together as I assured him that I forgave him. The compassion I felt for Joe was a miracle not of my doing. I knew God had entered my office and we were standing on holy ground. Joe left my office and I never saw him again. I heard that he retired somewhere in Idaho and died suddenly two years later. I hope that I see him again in heaven.

Joe's confession and plea for forgiveness presented me with a dilemma. I was reasonably sure that if I revealed what this Catholic priest had planned and carried out it would practically guarantee my promotion the following year. The new Commanding Officer was a straight-shooting Roman Catholic. He would be extremely supportive of me if he knew what had happened. Should I tell him or should I keep it to myself as a sacred secret. I decided to keep the matter confidential and to seal my decision I decided to retire from the Navy. It was decision that I later came to regret.

In retrospect I was not thinking very clearly when I made the decision to retire. The shock of not getting a fully expected promotion had shaken my psyche severely. The additional shock of the priest's confession of perjury had also impaired my judgment. But one thing I knew. God had wonderfully taken away every bit of bitterness nor was there the slightest desire to get revenge. I didn't want to do anything that would imperil that gracious gift. Also, another factor influenced my decision. I (mistakenly) thought Donna wanted me to get out of the Navy. In late August I submitted my official letter to the Navy Chief of Chaplains requesting retirement. Soon after I received a phone call from a chaplain in the Chief's office imploring me to change my mind.

Later, when I was thinking more rationally, I realized I should have changed my mind. My decision not to reveal the confession of the priest was a bad decision for the following reasons. It would not have hurt him since he was retiring. Furthermore, it would show our assignment desk the danger of assigning a Protestant scheduled for promotion under the supervision of a disgruntled Roman Catholic who had been passed over for promotion. The Navy should never have permitted that as my situation clearly demonstrated.

The Chaplain Corps had invested a lot of time and money in my education and preparation for a longer ministry as a senior chaplain. If I had been thinking clearly I would have recognized that my moral obligation to fulfill the ministry to which God had called me and for which the Navy had helped prepare me took precedence over keeping silent. I robbed myself and the Navy of fifteen more years of ministry as a senior chaplain. It was a bad decision for the family finances. If I had continued in the chaplaincy another fifteen years the additional retirement pay would have been substantial. I carry some guilt for depriving our family of this. Not that God hasn't wonderfully provided for us for He has. Retirement as a Navy Commander with its attendant medical coverage has been a blessing for which I am very grateful. And, if I am honest, the most painful of all was to my ego. Other chaplains thought that I had retired because I was angry about not getting promoted. Disappointed, yes. I really wanted to have the captain's eagles pinned on my uniform. Angered, no. I never explained my decision to retire because it would have necessitated explaining about Joe's perjury and I refused to do that.

Although my own life was in turmoil there were other important family matters going on. Celia had graduated with honors from high school in the spring of 1977. She had spent months going through various college and university catalogues. The only limitation we had laid down was that she choose a creditable Christian institution. She chose Seattle Pacific University. In September we loaded our bubble top van with Celia and her paraphernalia along with Cindy Miller and all her gear and took off for Seattle. Cindy was the youngest daughter of J C and Edith Miller, close friends from my days in Hawaii who now lived in Washington. We got Celia ensconced in her dorm at Seattle Pacific and then took Cindy to her parents in Mulketeo. Then we drove north to visit my cousins Jenny Carlson and husband, Rod and Debbie Koop and husband, Abe who lived near Vancouver, B.C. From there to Sand Point, Idaho to visit old friends formerly stationed at

Moffett. Touching base with good friends was balm for my wounded spirit.

We returned to Moffett to wind up the remaining three months of my service. Another Roman Catholic chaplain had been ordered in to replace the retiring Catholic chaplain. We were both Commanders but I out ranked him by a year so I was his senior. He was an out-going, friendly fellow: a breath of fresh air compared to his predecessor. I knew he would come into the zone for promotion the next year. Unknown to him, I made it a point to write him a good report and recommend his promotion. Indicative of the rapport developed between us in the few months we had together, he asked me to preach the sermon for the mid-night Christmas mass. Preaching at this solemn but joyful occasion was a first for me.

My retirement ceremony from the Navy Chaplains Corps was a bitter-sweet occasion. The Commanding Officer had some flattering comments to make about his high regard for my ministry as a chaplain. Joe Gearhart, Northern California/ Nevada District Superintendent of the Assemblies of God and a good friend, represented my endorsing denomination. Friends from the Moffett chapel congregation and other Navy friends were there to wish Donna and me well and to express their appreciation for my ministry and service. In an hour or less it was all over. On the afternoon of December 30, 1977 I walked away from a ministry that I loved to begin a new chapter of service.

There are many great memories connected with our nearly 14 years serving Faith Chapel. One of the best is celebrating our 25th wedding anniversary with Faith Chapel friends and family members from across the nation June, 1983

CHAPTER 25
THE FAITH CHAPEL
YEARS IN PLEASANTON,
CALIFORNIA

I was truly like a fish out of water when I walked away from the Navy Chaplains' Corps. Since dad and mom had moved from the farm we decided to live there until we resolved where to settle. I was relatively young, having just turned fifty a week after retiring. There was no question in my mind but that I would seek a civilian pastorate. God had called me to preach and I knew I could not play Jonah and run from that call. Donna was very supportive and willing to go wherever God would lead us.

Celia, a freshman at Seattle-Pacific University, had flown home for Christmas. We decided to drive her back to Seattle. Now that I was retired I wanted to investigate ministry opportunities in the state of Washington. We visited the Assembly of God Northwest district headquarters in Kirkland. I talked to the district superintendent regarding churches in his district that were without a pastor. I shared with him my ministry experience and educational background. He looked at me and said, "Chaplain, we have a church I think would be ideal for you. You have had an active life in the chaplaincy. This church would provide you an opportunity to relax and take life a little easier. It's located in farming country with a stable, mature congregation. It has no financial problems. Those farmers take good care of their pastor. There is a beautiful almost new parsonage that your wife will love."

The good Superintendent didn't know that I wasn't looking for a place where I could "take it easy". I wanted some place with growth potential, never mind if it wasn't an ideal situation. The District Superintendent must have observed that I wasn't too excited with his recommendation. He said, "We have a church without a pastor in Port Townsend. It's located on the northeast corner of the Olympic Peninsula just across the strait of Juan de Fuca from Victoria, British Columbia. Let me give you the address in case you want to explore that area." Donna and I decided to visit Port Townsend and look around. We located the church, a small, unpretentious building. The door into the vestibule was unlocked so we walked in and looked around. It was rather dreary with a few church notices tacked on a bulletin board. Neither Donna nor I sensed this was a place where we wanted to invest our lives. We were open to God's call, wherever that would lead us. We did not sense he was leading us to Port Townsend. We returned to Seattle, said good-bye to Celia, and drove back to our eleven acre ranch in California. It was late January when we returned and to our surprise the almond orchard was in full bloom. This usually happens later in February.

Early February found us back in our travel van on our way to southern California, Arizona, and New Mexico. It was a beautiful, unhurried trip combining the pleasure of visiting old friends and relatives and preaching in San Diego, Newport Beach and Albuquerque. The highlight of the trip was our involvement in a conference on the Holy Spirit at the beautiful Albuquerque Christian Center pastored by my good friend, Ron McConnell. Ron had asked me to be one of the speakers. I was surprised when a man approached me after my sermon and told me his name. He was a retired Air Force sergeant who had been my boss when I was a young Air Force photographer in Hawaii in 1948-49. I didn't recognize him. What a difference thirty years makes. Donna's brother Lanny and family lived in Albuquerque and they hosted us. Going and coming we spent quality time with Glenn's Uncle Del and Aunt Betty in Arizona.

We settled into our farm house near Turlock while we explored other opportunities for ministry. I heard the Assembly of God church in Santa Clara was looking for a pastor. I submitted my resume and met with their search committee but nothing came of it. One of my Princeton Seminary classmates, now a prominent Presbyterian pastor in Alabama, wrote and asked if I would consider pastoring a Presbyterian church in his area. He gave me the name and address of the elder to contact. I was mildly interested and wrote to the church representative a time or two. However, I knew in my heart that I wasn't a good fit for a Presbyterian church. There were certainly charismatic Presbyterian pastors and churches. That wasn't so much an issue as their Calvinistic doctrine and baptism of infants.

While back on the farm I received a call from Bob Pirtle, assistant district superintendent of the Northern California/ Nevada District. He said, "Glenn, I want to talk to you about assigning you as pastor of one of our District home mission churches. I think you are the man we want and need. Can I meet with you and tell you about it?" I agreed so we set a dinner date at one of the Turlock restaurants for later in February. Donna and I listened as Bob told us about First Assembly of God in Pleasanton, California. It wasn't a particularly inspiring story. First Assembly had begun as a home missions project by the Youth Ministries department in 1968. The founding pastor had an affair with one of the church members and left with the congregation in turmoil. The District was able to appoint a fine minister to replace the first pastor. The congregation rallied around the new pastor who won their love and trust. Things were looking up for the church when suddenly the beloved pastor resigned and took another church. Projects that he had pushed were suddenly stalled. The third pastor was young and enthusiastic but apparently lacked good judgment. He had to be dismissed because of financial irregularities with church funds. The fourth pastor was still living in the church parsonage in Pleasanton although he had been "relieved of command" to use military jargon. The congregation, never large, had dwindled to a handful. He apparently had been ineffective and driven the church deeper in debt. I'm not sure what I would have done if I had known just how deeply in debt the church was.

Donna and I promised Bob we would pray and think about his offer. I had wanted a challenge but I wasn't sure I wanted to become the fifth pastor in ten years of a church with multiple problems. Donna and I knew little about the town of Pleasanton although we had passed by it a few times. We decided we should at least go and look at the church and survey the town. Pleasanton was a pleasant bedroom community of about twenty five thousand located on the east side of San Francisco Bay area between San Jose and Oakland. There were numerous ranches in the surrounding area and the town had a western atmosphere which I liked. One of the stores on main street which catered to the ranch trade had a life-sized horse model which they parked in front of the store during business hours. There was only one good restaurant in downtown so I guess the horses were better served than people. But you could get a good sandwich at the cheese factory.

The church was situated on five acres about two miles from downtown. It was actually under the jurisdiction of Alameda county rather than the city. The church was surrounded on the north, east and west by farm land. Across the road on the south were several homes. We went inside the church and casually looked around. The sanctuary was pleasantly lighted with a platform that could accommodate a small choir, organ and piano. The padded pews could comfortably seat 150. There was an attractive nursery, a small kitchen, several Sunday School and office spaces and two rest rooms serviced by a septic tank and drain field. Since city water was unavailable the church had its own well and water system. The church did have a parsonage in town but the previous pastor was still living there so we didn't intrude.

We went back to our farm to mull over the Pleasanton situation. I had not sensed any definite leading from God, pro or con, regarding a decision. Donna was amenable to whatever I decided we should do. While we waited and prayed I received another call from Bob Pirtle. The District had invested hundreds of thousands of dollars in the Pleasanton project and it would be a financial disaster if it ceased to exist as a viable congregation. (I discovered this later.) This, of course, weighed on the District officials. And there were even more important spiritual implications. The community needed a church that proclaimed that God's supernatural gifts were still operating in the church today. There were hurting people in the community that desperately needed Divine intervention. They needed to know about God the Holy Spirit who is active among disciples of Jesus Christ today as surely as He was two-thousand years ago. This unique contribution of Pentecostal churches is needed in our materialistic, mechanistic society. I told Bob I would accept the pastorate of the Pleasanton church.

We had our initial service in Pleasanton's First Assembly of God on Sunday, March 12, 1978. We were commuting from the farm since the former pastor was still living in the parsonage. As we drove into the big parking lot only a handful of cars marred its emptiness. The empty seats in the sanctuary reflected the empty parking lot. Counting children there were possibly twenty-five present. But they were a friendly group and welcomed us cordially. I am sure they had some unvoiced questions such as "Can we trust this guy?" "Will our new pastor stick with us doing this difficult time?"

One member of the congregation was a sprightly widow who invited us to her home for lunch and a place to rest until the evening service. She burnt our ears with church gossip and gave us her prescription for bringing life to the church. Unfortunately, her formula promoted legalism and separatism and I had no plan to promote either. But we listened, expressed our gratitude for her hospitality and went back to the church. Thirty years ago most evangelical churches had Sunday evening services as well as morning services. In addition there was usually a mid-week prayer and teaching service. This was in marked contrast to the chaplaincy. It would take some getting used to.

We were handicapped for more than two months since the former pastor insisted that he was unable to vacate the parsonage until he obtained another residence. We continued to commute from our farm south of Turlock, a distance of one hundred and sixty miles round trip. Since the congregation was so small we were able to get well acquainted with each family even though we were in the community only two or three times a week. I can still remember most of the core families that had remained in the church: Gustafsons, Pearl Collins, Higgins, Mays, Prices, and Warks. The "sprightly widow" I mentioned earlier was part of the congregation but when I didn't accept her suggestions she soon left. More than thirty years later Gus Gustafson, Higgins, and Warks remain active in the church.

The former pastor finally found another house and we were able to move into the parsonage in June. It was an attractive three bedroom small ranch style house in a pleasant neighborhood. We had our furniture delivered from Navy storage and settled into our new home. The long commute to the church was now reduced to three miles.

Celia came home for the summer. She and I along with my brother John, his son Phil and some of their Wisconsin friends had long planned a week long mountain hike and fishing trip across the Bear Tooth mountains of Montana. Chris Wark, the seventeen year old son of Jim and June Wark, was an ardent fisherman and I invited him to come along. Donna flew to Denver to visit her folks while we went mountain climbing. We drove my bubble-top Ford camper van across country to Columbus, Montana where we rendezvoused with John and Phil. The next day we drove one vehicle to the terminus of the hike. The other we drove to Cooke City, just across the north border of Yellowstone, where the trail head began. We put on our back-packs loaded with fishing gear, tents and food.

It was August and there was lots of day-light but nights were cold in the high country. Celia and I slept in a tube tent that I had bought because it was cheap. It was no bargain as Celia and I discovered. We did much more hiking than fishing although there was one lake where we caught quite a few grayling. The fish made a pleasant addition to our store bought food supplies. By the time we completed our trek we were tired, dirty and ready for the comforts of civilization. We checked into a motel and luxuriated in hot showers and comfortable beds.

It had been twenty-five years since I had visited Yellowstone Park and others had never been there. We decided to spend a few days viewing the wonders of this national treasure. My camper van became our headquarters when we wanted to relax. This model Ford van had a gear shift lever that was attached to a tubular rod running along the steering column. This tubular rod controlled the gear shifting mechanism under the engine cover. While in Yellowstone we suffered a major catastrophe. The torque placed on this small hollow metal rod when gears were repeatedly shifted caused the rod to break. With the broken rod, it was now impossible to shift gears and we had a long trip ahead of us.

You could manipulate the gear shift mechanism by accessing the engine cover when the engine was not running but you couldn't shift while driving. The only way one could make progress was to put it in a gear and proceed in that gear. It was a three speed transmission so we put it in second and proceeded to a large auto parts store just outside Yellowstone. I didn't know what I was specifically looking for but hoped to find something that would secure the two broken pieces of the shift rod into a single solid rod. I finally saw a clamp device that looked like it might have promise. I bought a couple and firmly attached one, overlapping and securing the broken ends. Eureka !! It worked. We were mobile again and ready for our trip back to Pleasanton. I'm not sure if Celia and Chris were enthused about the trip but I enjoyed it immensely and returned refreshed and ready to get to work.

One of the first things I wanted to do was to change the image of Pleasanton First Assembly of God. The rapid changeover of pastors was one image problem. Another, and more difficult to erase from some memories, was the poor credit reputation the church had developed. The District paid the indebtedness with the proviso the church would repay the District when funds were available. I decided since the Assemblies of God had been given a black eye in the community perhaps we should change the name of the church. We had a congregational meeting at which I proposed we consider another name for our church. The folks agreed this was a good idea but what should we call ourselves? I asked for suggested names and several were submitted. We took a vote and Faith Chapel was selected. We replaced the old sign with a new one featuring FAITH CHAPEL. We hoped the new name symbolized a fresh beginning.

I wish I could report that we experienced quick, dramatic growth but it wasn't to be. We were encouraged by some families returning who had left the church. A retired Navy pilot and his wife who had been part of our Moffett Naval Air Station congregation surprised us by commuting to Faith Chapel each Sunday. The financial situation was a real challenge. Those who attended were very generous but we needed to win more people to Christ and build the congregation. I knew that if we won people to the Lord the financial situation would be solved. In the meantime my Navy retirement pay covered our living expenses and my pastoral salary could be applied to church expenses.

One of the big problems in reaching people was the location of Faith Chapel. We were in a rural area about two miles off a main thoroughfare. How could we get our church before the community? In the chaplaincy I always had a ready-made community prepared for me. Not so in the civilian pastorate. You had to win your community. To do this you had to contact people. The Lord led me to initiate a two-pronged effort. One was personal, door to door evangelism and the other was a mailer that covered about three thousand homes. I encouraged our people to reach out to friends and neighbors. I went "cold turkey" to some areas and actually found a few who were open to the gospel. The six page newspaper format mailer reached some we would never have touched otherwise. More visitors began to appear, including families with teens and younger children. We engaged part-time a young man and his wife who had experience ministering to young people. The wife with her pleasing personality and administrative skills agreed to serve as church secretary. Her husband helped develop a small but enthusiastic youth group.

The church parsonage was owned by the bank and the District but Faith Chapel was responsible for the monthly payments. These payments placed a sizeable drain on our resources which could be far better used elsewhere. I proposed to our deacon board that we sell the parsonage in the city and use the equity to help build a new parsonage on our own church property. Jim Wark and Gus Gustafson, influential board members, agreed it was worth considering. We approached the District officials and they agreed it was a good idea to have a parsonage owned by the church. However, if the present parsonage were sold the resulting equity would be insufficient to finance the building of a new parsonage even if volunteer labor was used. At least twenty-thousand dollars additional were needed. Donna and I agreed to withdraw that amount from our savings and make a zero interest loan to the District. The District agreed and we were now ready to present the proposal to the congregation.

By this time our outreach efforts had produced results. New people were coming to Faith Chapel. Some were new converts, others were unattached Christians looking for a church home. We presented our proposal of selling the current parsonage and using the equity to help finance the construction of a new parsonage. I explained that I would serve as general contractor and volunteers from our own congregation would do much of the labor. We were encouraged by the positive response of our people. The church board members agreed that since the congregation approved we should go ahead with the project. Donna and I perused house plans and finally decided on an attractive three bed-room, two bath ranch style with large living room, family room adjoining the kitchen and a two car garage. We ordered the detailed plans and presented them to the Alameda County Building department. After the plans were inspected and approved we were ready to begin construction as soon as the parsonage was sold.

Actually, we thought we had the parsonage sold. The young man and his wife who had been working part time with our youth group had resigned. I became acquainted with another young couple who had been working with an Assembly of God church near Modesto in the area of personal evangelism and discipleship training. The husband was commuting to a job in a town near Pleasanton. They wanted very much to sell their Modesto home and buy a place nearer his job site. I saw this couple as an answer to two prayers; a buyer for our town parsonage and a replacement for the couple who had resigned. The young man, Bill Booth, had a contagious enthusiasm for sharing the gospel and leading converts into Christian maturity. I approached them about buying the parsonage and they were both very open to that. When I discussed with Bill the church's need for a leader with his skills and experience he lit up like a Christmas tree. He was enthusiastic about getting involved in the church.

We agreed on a price for the parsonage. They wanted to move in as quickly as possible since they had young children to enroll in school. This was taking place in the spring of 1979 and we had been at Faith Chapel just over one year. There was a problem in allowing Bill and his family to move into the parsonage immediately. The new parsonage had not been built and we had nowhere to live. Mel May, the chairman of our deacon board, suggested a solution. He had recently bought a beautiful thirty-four foot motor home and offered it to us to live in while the new house was constructed. Donna agreed we could do that. We situated the motor home behind the chapel and moved in. Our furniture, not needed in the beautifully furnished motor home, was stored in the rear of the church educational wing.

With our own temporary housing problem resolved we were able to let Bill and his family move into the parsonage. We agreed on a price for the house and signed a contract contingent upon the sale of their Modesto house. They would make the mortgage payments until the sale was finalized. It appeared to be a win-win situation.

Unfortunately, the Modesto housing market was very slow and there was no action on its sale. Bill could not afford two house payments so they reluctantly had to move back to Modesto. What a disappointment, for us and them. We immediately put the house in the hands of a realtor. Pleasanton was a choice bed-room community for the Bay area and a sale was soon pending.

Our loss of the Booth's was disappointing but about this time God compensated us with David and Sophia Grajeda and family. Sophia agreed to serve as church secretary and soon became an invaluable asset. Thirty-five years later Sophia still serves as church secretary. David contracted cancer and the Lord called him home far sooner than we had hoped. His beautiful Christian testimony in the midst of painful adversity powerfully impacted all who knew him.

We had sufficient funds to begin some of the important preliminary work while we waited for proceeds from the sale of the parsonage. We had the septic system installed, the perimeter was staked out and the foundation was formed up and concrete poured. We were on our way. When the parsonage sale was finalized we had funds to order lumber and other building materials. We had men in the church who had some construction experience. These were augmented by men who were willing to work if someone told them what to do. We organized the projects so that major jobs were scheduled for week-ends when we could muster a large work crew. It was wonderful to see the enthusiasm of the men, and some women too, as they gathered to work.

The volunteers did most of the framing and much of the plumbing and installation of natural gas and water lines. We got the shake roof installed and the interior was protected from the autumn rain. We installed the windows and doors and a professional crew applied the exterior stucco. By November we were ready for the final inspections. A slow leak was detected in the gas line that ran under the house. For obvious reasons we didn't dare move into the new parsonage until the leak was discovered and repaired. I made several slow excursions under the floor exploring all the soldered joints. I carried a spray bottle of liquid soap and water and sprayed some on each joint. I would know I had found the leak when a bubble appeared at the joint. After numerous, frustrating tries I finally found the illusive joint partially hidden by a concrete overhang where the foundation joined the garage. I shined my flashlight on the suspected joint and applied the soapy liquid. Eureka ! The slowly expanding bubbled signaled my search was over. The joint was repaired and the next inspection confirmed the gas line was secure.

We moved in November before the sidewalks were installed. What a mess. It was the rainy season and the sticky black clay relentlessly clung to shoe bottoms. Fortunately, we could bring our household goods in through the garage. As the rain continued for days the ground became saturated and water began to pour down the hill behind our five acres. Soon our backyard was inundated. There was no place for the water to escape except to cascade through our garage. But no harm was done and the garage floor got a thorough washing. Later I was able to construct a berm that directed the water around the garage instead of through it.

After living in a thirty-four foot motor home for a few months we really rattled around in the commodious parsonage. But we had a great sense of satisfaction knowing that we had reached one of our goals. Faith Chapel now had a parsonage on its property that would serve pastors for years to come. The congregation was growing, not dramatically but steadily. I sensed that I needed an associate that had ministry gifts that would augment my own. I had met Dean Bohl, a young minister in San Diego, who had marvelous gifts in ministering to children and was also a talented musician. I had kept in touch with the Bohl's and knew he was thinking of leaving the church where he served as associate pastor. I talked to him about the Pleasanton challenge and asked him and Judy to think and pray about coming and helping us. He agreed to do so.

In the late fall of 1979 Dean Bohl became our associate pastor for children's ministry. He was a skilled ventriloquist and the kids loved his skits with the dummy. Dean and his family moved into a duplex in town. His ministry helped bring young couples with children into the church and we rejoiced. However, the income of the church did not rise appreciably and finances were tight. Judy took a job in a local business to augment their income. In retrospect, perhaps we should have put the Bohl's in the parsonage while Donna and I bought a small house for ourselves. Without rent payments the Bohl's may have been able to stay with us longer. Dean and I had a wonderful relationship and it was fun to work with him. I knew a minister with Dean's gifts would not stay with us long unless we could pay him an adequate salary. Unfortunately for us, Dean resigned after a little over a year. He made a positive contribution to Faith Chapel during the short time he was with us. We still keep in touch.

My nephew Phil Brown graduated from seminary in 1980. In view of Dean's imminent departure I invited Phil to come and lead our youth ministry. He was single, had a great outgoing personality and loved the Lord and people. We couldn't pay him nearly what he deserved but we offered him room and board at the parsonage, a small salary and lots of experience in a developing home missions church. He agreed to come and we had the joy of sharing our home with him for several months. Donna discovered that Phil would eat anything she prepared...as long as he could baptize it with ketchup. We jokingly called him "the garbage can" because he would obligingly devour all the left-overs.

Celia spent five weeks of her summer vacation at home and the remainder working at a church camp with her Aunt Faith in New York. She was a senior, majoring in sociology. Donna and I spent our vacation backpacking in the Beartooth Mountains along with my brother John and wife Bernie, Phil and his fiancée, Lynn, plus some of their Oshkosh friends. The women did remarkably well keeping up with the men although Donna suffered swollen feet and ankles.

Phil and Lynn were married in October and they moved into an apartment in the neighboring city of Livermore. In addition to being an effective youth pastor Phil had tremendous skills working with wood. He made wonderfully functional cribs for the church nursery which amazed me. Later, after leaving Faith Chapel, he would use his uncanny skill to launch a professional career.

1981 was filled with significant family events. In February mother's oldest brother Delbert died. Uncle Del and I had developed a close relationship as our paths crossed in Germany in 1965-66 and in Okinawa in 1974-75. Donna and I visited him and Betty twice when they lived in Green Valley, Arizona. Shortly before he died I visited him in the hospital and had the privilege of sharing the wonderful truth of God's love and forgiveness through Jesus Christ. We prayed together and I believe he responded in faith to God's offer of salvation. In March we lost beloved grandma Bluhm, just days shy of her ninety-eighth birthday.

Celia graduated Magna Cum Laude from Seattle Pacific University in June with a BA degree in sociology. Donna and I proudly watched along with grandmother Wirth. Shortly after graduation Celia, along with seven other students from SPU, signed up with Food for the Hungry International to serve six months in refugee camps in Somalia. These young people raised their own support and some curtailed their college education. Celia had always loved to travel so the trip to Somalia was a dream come true for her. The group had a ten hour layover in Hong Kong, a week in Bangkok and two weeks in Nairobi. After arriving in Somalia Celia spent three months working in a camp helping direct the supplemental feeding for underweight children, pregnant women and nursing mothers. For her final months she was assigned a job in the FHI office in Mogadishu, Somalia's capital.

Our 1981 summer vacation began with a Brown family reunion at Eagle River, Wisconsin. It had been years since we had all been together and the only grandchild missing was Celia. It was a fun week of canoeing, swimming, eating, talking and playing games. On the return trip we visited Donna's folks in Denver. After leaving Denver we teamed up with my brother John and his family in Cheyenne and then caravanned to California. I think Phil and Lynn were part of the caravan as well. We spent a wild night just across the Utah border in Nevada. There were no motels available so we put the women and children in our travel van. John and I tried to pitch a tent but the wind was too ferocious. Stinging sand was swirling throughout the night making it difficult to breathe. Dawn brought an end to our miserable night and we were glad to be on our way to Pleasanton. We enjoyed a pleasant week together before John, Bernie and children headed back to Oshkosh. Visits with family were always very special to me.

We didn't expect Celia to return from Somalia until late January but she surprised us and came home a week before Christmas. We enjoyed three weeks with her before she went back to Seattle and got a job while she awaited graduate school. She had made application for admission to the American Graduate School of International Management in Phoenix and had been accepted for the class beginning in June, 1983.

Donna underwent hysterectomy surgery in February at the Naval Hospital in Oakland. She stayed in the hospital for a few days, three I think. She made a good recovery and soon returned to her busy schedule at church and home.

Celia joined us for our vacation trip in September (1982). She wanted to get in touch with her roots so we visited family in Denver, Kansas, and Nebraska. While in Nebraska we helped her grandpa Brown celebrate his eightieth birthday.

Leaving Denver we toured Mesa Verde and then visited the campus of her graduate school in Phoenix. In twelve days we drove four thousand miles and went from snow in Colorado to stifling heat in Phoenix. It was great being together, touching base with numerous relatives and helping Celia explore her roots.

Phil and Lynn welcomed John Michael into their family in September. Lynn's mother came out from Kansas City to help Lynn and welcome her grandson. Like a good grandmother she told Lynn and Phil they needed to live in the mid-west, closer to little Johnny's grandparents. Phil was feeling the pressure of fatherhood, youth pastor and limited finances. The church income was too limited to pay him what he deserved or needed so I was not surprised when he resigned.

1983 was an exciting year for us as a family and as a church. In June we had the biennial Brown family reunion in California. My sister Carol and family were living in San Jose so some spent nights there. Charlie's family stayed in his motor home parked near our house. The remainder hung out at our place. It so happened that the reunion coincided with the twenty-fifth wedding anniversary of Donna and me. We had a delightful celebration with our extended family. Ladies from Faith Chapel prepared and hosted a delicious buffet. It was a happy, joyous occasion. Also in June, Celia enrolled in the **American Graduate School of International Management** at Phoenix. It was a demanding curriculum and required learning a foreign language. She chose French.

The church was growing and we needed more space, particularly for Christian education and social functions. We obtained architectural plans for a sixty by forty foot addition. The "red tape" involved in getting all the building permit requirements satisfied delayed start of construction until September. In November record breaking rains began which halted construction for much of the winter. As the wet weather receded in 1984 we were able to proceed with construction. We had an experienced carpenter in the congregation who was able to provide professional oversight to our volunteer work force. Sizeable groups of men gathered on Saturdays to work. Women provided noon meals. With the increased manpower now in the church almost all the construction was accomplished by volunteers. Offerings increased so that we could purchase building materials as needed. Amazingly, the addition was completed a year after construction begun – debt free. We dedicated it in October with great thanksgiving and praise to God. Another cause for thanksgiving was the exciting growth of our youth department. Pedro Abeyta, our new youth pastor, provided excellent leadership. The youth loved him and his unique ministry style.

In May 1984 Celia completed a year of graduate school and got a break before completing her final summer session. We timed our vacation plans to coincide with her break. We picked her up in Phoenix and drove on to Carlsbad Caverns in New Mexico. We continued on to Van, Texas and spent a week with my parents and visited families of sisters Shari, Barbara and Gayle who lived in east Texas.

Celia graduated from AGSIM in August. The intense heat in Phoenix at this time of year was intolerable for Donna so I represented us both at Celia's graduation ceremony. I was one proud dad, especially when Celia was awarded honors for graduating at the top of her class. No small feat as there were students there from all over the world. Our drive back to Pleasanton in her old VW warmed our hearts as well as the rest of our anatomies. Driving across the desert in a vehicle without air conditioning will do that. Celia spent the rest of the summer at home exploring the job market and enjoying some leisure time after her demanding graduate studies. In October she flew to Wheaton, Illinois to accept a position as project accountant with World Relief. She monitored the finances for a multi-million dollar water and agriculture development project in Senegal, Mali and Upper Volta. Her residence in Dakar provided plenty of opportunity to practice her French language and cross cultural skills.

For the first time since I had retired from the Navy, Donna and I took a whole month off for travel and vacation. We visited friends and relatives in southern California, Colorado, Kansas, New Mexico and Texas. We attended the Assembly of God General Council in San Antonio. My friend Howard Ryan, former pastor in Chula Vista, was there selling computers with software designed for churches and I ordered one to be delivered to the church. From San Antonio we joined the Brown family reunion in Galveston. Wow, was it hot in Galveston! Everyone spent a lot of time in the nearby ocean. Unfortunately, a recent oil spill polluted the beach so you had to watch out for sticky tar blobs.

The Galveston days were torrid but the late evenings were pleasant. I'll never forget our final evening together. We sang favorite songs and choruses and shared some memories. The most memorable moment came when dad seated next to mom turned to her and sang "Let Me Call You Sweetheart." It was a tender moment and brought lumps to throats and a few tears. I'm sure dad sensed this was probably his last family reunion this side of heaven. Although he never complained, he was suffering from colon cancer and an exotic lung disease transmitted by birds. This deadly combination took his life less than a year later.

In March 1986 Donna, a few members from our church and I made a ten day trip to Israel and Jordan. The weather was perfect and we had a marvelous guide. Donna had made a trip to Israel while I was enrolled in the Senior Chaplain's course in 1973-74 at Newport. I had visited there in 1954 while stationed in Germany but this was our first trip together. This was in great contrast to my trip twenty-two years previously. In 1954 barbed wire was in place between the Israeli and Palestinian areas of Jerusalem. The chaplain with whom I was traveling and I spent the night in a Palestinian "bed and breakfast" sort of place before crossing over to Israeli territory the next day. The host and hostess were lovely people until something about Israel entered the conversation. They made no effort to hide their deep hatred for the Jews.

Not long after our return from Israel I received word that dad was very ill. I flew to Texas and met him and mother in the hospital. I was with dad when he was being prepped for an MRI. He seemed absolutely overwhelmed by all the modern medical technology. I felt so sorry for him and wished there was something I could do help him through the ordeal. While dad was in the hands of the medical people mom and I slipped away to the hospital cafeteria. She knew that her beloved Bob with whom she had shared more than sixty years was soon to leave her. She was a tower of strength for all her children although her heart must have been breaking. We knew the source of her quiet confidence in the midst of death's raging attack. The Lord Jesus Christ had been her constant companion for more than seventy years and she had no doubt that he would walk with her during this ordeal.

Dad rallied briefly and he was allowed to go home. On one of my three trips to Van during dad's dying ordeal, Johnny and I were there at the same time. Dad was still mobile though very weak. We were sitting around just talking when dad indicated he would like us to drive him around the East Texas countryside before he left it for the last time. We didn't drive far or long as dad tired quickly but he obviously enjoyed his tour.

Barb and Jimmy took a huge load off mama's shoulders and heart when they had dad moved into their home. There he was able to live out his final days in dignity with loved ones at his side. Thank you, Barb and Jimmy. Even though cancer and a lung fungus were performing their deadly dance within dad's body, his heart remained strong. But even dad's valiant heart could not sustain the battle against the forces of death. On May 23, 1986 God called him home. After he had greeted and thanked his Lord, I think I know what dad's first request must have been. "Can I see Alliene and Phil, the children I loved so much and lost so soon."

Celia was in still in Senegal, Africa when her grandfather died and she was unable to attend his funeral. She sent him a letter before he died, expressing her love and regrets that she could not visit him. She came home in October for a two week visit. Her contract will be fulfilled in May, 1987 so when she returns she will start training her replacement.

Dad's death left an empty space in our hearts. Sometimes something would happen and I would think to myself, "I sure wish I could share that with dad." I was grateful that I had been able to have mom and dad on the almond farm in California. It was a treat to be able to drive to see them frequently or have them come visit us at Moffett Naval Air Station. I was disappointed when they decided to move back to Beaver City. But as Dad explained to me previously, "Son, when you are your age you look for a place to live. When you are my age, you look for a place to die."

Donna decided to enlarge her horizons and enrolled in the H & R Block basic tax class. It was challenging but she stuck with it and later became one of their agents. I made a decision that proved to be far less productive than Donna's. In 1986 houses were steadily increasing in price. I bought a 40,000 square foot building site in an exclusive development not far from the church. My plan was to secure a contractor to build the house and then sell it at the time of my retirement for a nice profit to provide added financial security. Gil Borgardt, a retired Navy captain in our congregation, expressed interest in being a partner in this endeavor and we agreed on a partnership.

A series of poor decisions, mostly on my part, coupled with a collapsing housing market, resulted in our hopes and plans coming to a disappointing end. My first major mistake was to employ a contractor that was attending our church. It's not good to attempt to be a boss and pastor at the same time. Worse, the contractor, supposedly a recovering alcoholic, reverted to his addiction. The crew he hired were also given to imbibing on the job. Before the framing was completed it became obvious that the contractor and crew were incompetent to build a luxury home such as the plans called for. I eventually had to fire them all.

We were desperate to secure a competent general contractor. The Lord was merciful and we did eventually hire a professional who knew what he was doing. Much of his time initially was spent correcting mistakes by his incompetent predecessor.

The superstructure of the house was imposing as it took shape. Sitting on the upper level of a prominent ridge, it towered above the other houses in the area. It had five thousand square feet of living area plus a large four car garage. In one upstairs wing we got city approval to build a "mother-in-law" unit with full kitchen, bedroom, living room and separate entrance. In the main house there were five bedrooms and five bathrooms. We sure hoped some wealthy guy would like it when it came time to sell.

1986 and 1987 were banner years for Faith Chapel. There were over two-hundred faces pictured on our photo directory. Pedro Abeyta, our Youth Pastor, was impacting the young people for the Lord and the number was increasing. I thought it might be a good time to add an Associate Pastor to our staff. Without praying and seeking God for guidance I invited a retired Assemblies of God chaplain to be our Associate Pastor. There's an old saying: "Decide in haste, repent in leisure." I have experienced the truth of this more than I would like to admit.

We moved out of the parsonage so we could house the new Associate Pastor and family and rented a house in Dublin. Problems quickly arose because our new Associate and our Youth Pastor had diametrically opposed personalities. Our Youth Pastor was a free spirit with lots of enthusiasm and sanctified imagination, demonstrated in his ministry style and his dress. The young people loved him. Our Associate was a "spit and polish", tie and jacket sort of guy with legalistic tendencies. I'm sure there were churches where he would have found an effective ministry but it wasn't in Faith Chapel. Belatedly, I found out that one of his goals was to change our Youth Pastor's life style and image. I intervened but much too late.

The wounds from this conflict, and my inability to resolve the issue, resulted in both men departing in the summer of 1988.

My extended family consisting of my mother and seven siblings suffered a terrible tragedy in July, 1988. Our beloved sister, Faith Lavon, succumbed to brain cancer while ministering in NY City. All the family gathered in NYC to be near her while she transitioned from earth to heaven. After God called her home a celebration of her life was conducted in a great black church in Harlem where she ministered and served on staff

I continued serving as sole pastor for over six months with volunteer help from members of the congregation. Sophia Grajeda, Church Secretary, and June Wark, Church Counsellor, as well as the deacons, helped retain close contact with the congregation and were a tremendous encouragement to me. Nevertheless, the Deacon Board and I agreed that we needed an Associate Pastor to help shepherd the flock. Some candidates were interviewed but none were deemed a fit for Faith Chapel. One candidate who interested us was serving as an Associate Pastor at an Assemblies of God church in Tracy, a town about forty miles away. Deacon Gus Gustafson was commissioned to attend a Sunday service in the church where the candidate led worship and give a report to the Board. The candidate's name was Bud Adcock. His wife, Becky, was a skilled musician and teacher. They had two golden haired young daughters.

Deacon Gustafson gave a very positive report on Bud's ministry after observing him lead the congregation in worship. He admired his people skills and thought we should interview him regarding the position of Associate Pastor. We arranged for both Bud and Becky to meet with our Board and we liked what we saw and heard. On May 28, 1989 we introduced Bud Adcock, with his family at his side, as our new Associate Pastor. I don't remember if it was ever officially discussed but in my own mind I was thinking of Pastor Bud as the next senior pastor. We had already vacated the parsonage and moved into the ground floor of our new house. The Adcock's were able to immediately occupy the parsonage.

Although the installation of the Adcock's reduced some of the external pressures there were internal pressures that I could not share with my new Associate Pastor. I was opposed to a central doctrine of my denomination's tradition but had revealed this only to the District and National leaders of the Assemblies of God. Despite knowing this, the District officials had urged me to become pastor of Pleasanton's First Assembly of God after four failed pastoral appointments in ten years. As explained previously, the doctrine for which I could find no biblical support was the rigid insistence that there was no valid Spirit baptism unless evidenced by speaking in tongues. I knew that this teaching led to a spiritual caste system. It had fathered serious doctrinal aberrations relating to "health and wealth." It has been the cause of an impenetrable wall of division in the body of Christ

Earthquakes are common in California and in our 21 years living there from 1968 to 1989 we had experienced several. But the Loma Prieta that hit the Bay area of Northern California in October 1989 was the most powerful we had ever experienced. I was mowing the lawn just after five o'clock in the afternoon of October 17. I felt the ground roll and looked up in time to see my van dancing on the drive. It made some nice moves and then sedately came to rest. Due to the strict building codes of our area our new house suffered no damage. Many in the Bay area were not so fortunate. Sixty three lost their lives and more than thirty-seven hundred were injured by this 6.9 magnitude quake. The Bay bridge connecting Oakland and San Francisco suffered severe damage and had to be rebuilt.

Almost exactly three years after we had broken ground for construction of our spec home in August 1987 we completed the project in 1990. We put it up for sale but the housing market was stagnate...and falling. They say in real estate, "The three most important things for sales are location, location and location". We had a choice location. That was not the problem. Something else can be just as important as location and that is timing. If you have an excellent location and a quality home and sufficient capital you can ride out the downward dips in the market. Our weak link was insufficient capital to sustain us during a year or more of the downward trend. Despite the trend our bank still gave us a loan evaluation of close to a million dollars. We received an offer of eight hundred thousand dollars but my partner wanted to hold out for something closer to the loan evaluation. I think we were both too inexperienced to know that was a good offer in the current market so we agreed to not accept it. It was a poor decision on my part.

In 1991 I definitely decided to retire from the pastorate. Pastor Adcock and Becky had been warmly received by the people and I was sure Bud would be elected to replace me. Like the housing market, our growth had started to decline with the loss of young people, following the departure of Youth Pastor Abeyta.

There was a relatively new charismatic church in town that was an outgrowth of the Jesus Movement that had sprung up during the 1970's. They had been renting a meeting place but it was no longer available. I was sure their doctrine was compatible with the Assemblies of God. The thought came to me, "Why not combine our two congregations. Faith Chapel has space and a mature, seasoned congregation. The Charismatic church body has a younger congregation but no space. The pastors of both congregations could serve as co-pastors of the merged congregations."

I presented the idea to the board and they thought it was worth pursuing. Pastor Adcock had some misgivings as he rightly foresaw that serving in a co-pastor relationship might present difficulties. Nevertheless, he was willing to cooperate if it would strengthen Faith Chapel. I received approval to talk to the Charismatic pastor and to the officials of the Northern California/Nevada District of the Assemblies of God. The Charismatic pastor saw some merit in the idea and agreed to meet with a delegation of leaders from the NCal/Nev District.

A time was arranged for the two delegations to meet at the District headquarters in Santa Cruz. I did not attend but heard a report of the meeting from the Charismatic pastor. The District delegation extended an extremely warm welcome to the pastor and his delegation before they discussed Assemblies of God polity and doctrine. They then proceeded to overwhelm them with assurances of how they would benefit by an association with the Assemblies of God. The Charismatic pastor interpreted this as an effort to advance the denomination rather than an effort to advance the kingdom of God. As a result, the Charismatic church decided not to pursue the merger and later merged with another Pentecostal church. We had prayed for God's will to be done and we accepted this as such.

In July, 1991, the Brown family biennial reunion was in Winter Park, Colorado. Dad had died several years previously but mother was very much alive, a sprightly 84 year old. We had a wonderful time in the rarified atmosphere of the Rocky Mountains. A highlight for Donna and me was visiting nearby Granby, Colorado where we had begun our married life.

While in Seminary God had nudged me to pioneer a new church in Granby. I worked hard, God blessed, and a church was established. I served as pastor from 1955 until 1960, when I was called to serve as a Navy Chaplain. I graduated from Denver Seminary, was ordained by the Assemblies of God and married Donna, all within a short time period in 1958. We established our residence immediately in Granby where we continued to serve until I entered the chaplaincy.

We drove to the Granby church one Sunday morning in July, 1991, our first visit in thirty-one years. God apparently had blessed in the intervening time. An attractive new church building and parsonage had been constructed. The congregation worshipped with joy and enthusiasm. We looked for a recognizable face but saw no one that looked even vaguely familiar. As we chatted with the people after the service a lady came up and introduced herself. She had been one of our teens and was now a grandmother. We remembered her and her family well. Jackie was our last link to the original congregation. Many were now with the Lord, awaiting another great family reunion around a symbolic marriage feast in heaven.

Our daughter Celia had become engaged to Steve Browne, a young man in Seattle, and the wedding was planned for August 3, 1991. She asked her dad to help officiate. It was a beautiful wedding conducted on the shores of lake Washington. Celia had planned it all, including the dinner following the ceremony. All the numerous friends of her and Steve had been invited to bring a favorite dish to share. We had a veritable feast at no expense to the father of the bride. I highly recommend this arrangement.

On the last Sunday in November, 1991, I preached my farewell sermon to the beloved Faith Chapel congregation and helped install Bud and Becky Adcock as the new senior pastor team. There were many more present than at my first service thirteen years and nine months previously. I regrettably noticed there were fewer present than gathered three years ago. I knew I had to accept the major responsibility for the bad if I accepted any plaudits for the good. I felt relieved of the constraints that hindered me from addressing doctrinal issues that, in retrospect, may have impeded our growth.

We traveled extensively during the month of December, visiting relatives and friends in Colorado, Kansas, New Mexico, Arizona and Texas. We helped Donna's mother in New Mexico celebrate her 80th birthday on December 19th. We spent Christmas with my mother and sister near Tyler, Texas.

We began 1992 back in our beautiful new home in Pleasanton. We had plans to relocate but all were based upon when our house sold. Our hopes were raised briefly when we had an offer which we quickly accepted. It was contingent upon the sale of the buyer's house. When that didn't happen the offer was withdrawn and we were back to square one.

I turned 64 on January 7, 1992 and decided to enroll a year early for social security although, in retrospect, that was probably a poor decision. Donna and I were in good health and we both wanted to continue in ministry. However, neither of us had any idea what God wanted us to do or where He would have us serve. We agreed to seek God for direction and both concurred that when we got divine direction we would obey wherever it led us. We determined not make a hasty decision but to wait for the Lord to reveal his plan.

Although 1992 was a year of waiting it was not a year of idleness. I served as interim pastor at a neighboring church in Hayward. I preached as guest minister at several other churches. In addition I served as a chaplain with the Pleasanton Police and Fire Departments. When not ministering elsewhere or traveling we sat in the pew at Faith Chapel and encouraged pastor Bud.

We were not sure where we would settle once our home was sold but planned to depart Pleasanton. We considered several regions, including Colorado. But when I remembered the cold winters and shoveling snow I regained my sanity. Celia urged us to consider the Seattle, Washington area. I demurred, sure that I could not adjust to the rain and gray days characteristic of western Washington. Also, the traffic was very congested and could pose a problem. At this point Celia recommended we visit Sequim, a little town 70 miles WNW of Seattle on the Olympic Peninsula. We did so and liked what we discovered.

Sequim sits in the "rain shadow" of the Olympic Mountains, which means that most of the prevailing rain is captured by the peaks. The town and surrounding area only get 18 inches of rain annually, less than Pleasanton. It seldom gets snow in winter and usually no air conditioning is needed in summer. Its dry climate makes it remarkably free of mosquitoes. Victoria, British Columbia is easily viewed across the strait from Sequim. Building sites were available with water views or mountains; some with both. We liked what we saw and heard and decided Sequim might be the answer to our search. After several trips to Sequim looking for a suitable building site we purchased a 1.26 acre site just out of the city limits. I had two primary requirements in a site: One was a good view the other was good soil suitable for gardening. Our choice contained both. We had our house plans and a contractor but couldn't start construction until our Pleasanton house sold.

About a month after I preached my farewell sermon, Mikhail Gorbachov, President of the Soviet Union, gave the speech that resulted in the collapse of the Communist Empire. New democracies were catapulted into existence as the iron curtain crumbled. As a result, Western visitors, long denied entry into the Soviet bloc nations, were pouring across newly opened borders. Many of these visitors were Christian missionaries taking a message of hope to people long deprived of the gospel. Donna and I were intrigued at what God was doing in these various countries.

One day in prayer as I was pondering God's activity in Eastern Europe, I sensed the Lord was laying that region on my heart. I knew it was not realistic and tried to dismiss it. I knew nothing about the region except that the USSR had been our cold war enemy for many years. I couldn't speak Russian nor did I understand their funny looking alphabet. I knew practically nothing about their history or culture. I would be a "fish out of water" anywhere in E. Europe, a total misfit.

The more I tried to dismiss E. Europe from my mind and heart the more it persisted. Finally I decided to share my ridiculous perception with Donna. Her reply surprised me. "Glenn, as I was praying about our future ministry I sensed God had something in mind for us in E. Europe. I didn't say anything because I had no idea where in E. Europe we should go or what we could possibly do in any of those nations. So I just continued praying and waiting."

My conversation with Donna convinced me that I wasn't imagining things after all. The Holy Spirit was actually leading us to do something somewhere in the former Soviet Union. But where in that vast region would the Lord direct us? And what could we possibly do there? We had no answers so all we could do was pray and wait. Throughout 1992 heaven was silent. Near the beginning of 1993 God began to bring together a series of events that astounded me. People I didn't know began to impact my life and very quickly the "where" and the "what" unfolded.

To my utter amazement, in the first week of June, 1993 I found myself in the office of General Zoblotny, Commanding General of a huge military complex in far western Ukraine near the Hungarian and Slovakian borders. I was accompanied by retired Army Chaplain Jim Ammerman and Missionary David Clark, two of those people I did not know previously whom God had used to get me to General Zoblotny's headquarters in Mukachevo, Ukraine. The General was looking for a retired American military chaplain who could assist in introducing Christianity to his troops as a replacement for their previous religion…godless communism. He asked me if I would return and demonstrate to his Command how American chaplains minister in the military environment. I was in awe and humbled by what God was doing, totally unforeseen, totally unexpected. I knew this was my Macedonian call and I dared not refuse General Zoblotny's invitation. I assured him I would return and did so later that year. Thus began a spiritual adventure that has continued for more than twenty years.

What God did in Ukraine, as the result of obedience by Donna and me, is a separate story deserving another book which I have written. However, I want to include some highlights of what God has done in W. Ukraine because it is an important part of my story. It is by no means just my story. It is more the story of Christians in America who reached out with me to help introduce the gospel to the Ukrainian armed forces and then to bring assistance and encouragement to the poverty stricken civilian community. What God did in Ukraine was not what I envisioned or planned. It was much better because it was obviously the result of God doing what was far beyond my ability to accomplish. There were times when I simply marveled as I watched God do His work. I was grateful just to be along for the ride.

Here is a summary of what I watched God do in Ukraine during my sojourn there:

1. Provide a vibrant Christian witness aboard military bases, especially the Artillery base in Perechin, that persisted until the base closed about 2000.
2. Raise up major conferences that brought together military and religious leaders to do necessary groundwork for a future Ukraine chaplaincy. I helped organize one such international conference and spoke at several.
3. Introduced immensely popular Christian conferences for women.
4. Helped organize and spoke at various pastor's conferences.
5. Raised funds to buy buildings that were converted into churches. Also helped other churches complete their building projects.
6. Ministered to the Gypsies and helped provide funds for the Seredne village Gypsy church. Also raised funds to pay for the construction of modern toilet facilities for the Gypsy school in Mukachevo, the largest Gypsy village in Ukraine.
7. In 2003 my family joined me in raising funds to purchase a house that would become a home for orphans.

As a result, Lasma Balyuk gave her blessing to naming this house after our mother who had died in 2001. Hence, the **Eunice Brown Home for Children** came into being in 2003. It has become a model for this type of home across Transcarpatia.

8. I have had the privilege of preaching numerous times in a variety of churches; Pentecostal, Baptist, Methodist, and Charismatic. I have had the further privilege of participating and speaking at various conferences with Ukrainian Orthodox, Roman Catholic, Greek Catholic and various Protestant denominations represented. I have learned much from them.

9. Our Eunice Brown Home Ukraine Mission (EBHUM) entered into a partnership with Bishop Balyuk and Ukraine Christians in 2014 to establish another orphanage near Kiev. We are also attempting to raise funds to alleviate the suffering of refugees from Eastern Ukraine who are fleeing Russian brutality. I have purchased a ticket to return to Ukraine in May, 2015 and view firsthand the needs of refugees who have fled to our region.

10. Perhaps our most significant and lasting legacy of twenty plus years invested in Ukraine will be the boys and girls whose lives were impacted by Jesus Christ as they lived in the Eunice Brown Home in Mukachevo. Under the supervision of the House parents, they experienced love, security and godly discipline. God grant that this be the experience of those who will live in the new Children's Home in Kiev.

To God be the glory for what He has done..and continues to do!

EPILOGUE

You can read the remarkable account of God at work in Ukraine in a book I have written called **BIBLES, BORSCHT AND BULLETS.** It is published by **PORT HOLE PUBLICATIONS** and is available from the publisher. It also can be ordered on line from Amazon and Barnes and Noble and from me. The publisher has all rights to the book and sets the selling price so I don't have a lot of "wiggle room" but I can wiggle a little. If you wish to order a signed book from me you can contact me at my web site or email address.

Website....www.pentecostrevisited.com

Email.......rglennb@olypen.com

At my age, I will very likely soon stand before my Lord and give an account for what I have said and written. As one called to preach and teach, I take seriously the words of James: "**Not many of you should act as teachers, my brothers, because you know that we who teach will be judged more strictly.**" (James

3:1) The Scripture has clearly spoken concerning the purpose of "tongues" that accompanied the outpouring of the Holy Spirit at Pentecost and subsequently. Human experience is not a basis for doctrine; human assumptions have no authority. The Spirit inspired purpose and meaning, described by the prophet Joel as quoted by Peter, authoritatively describes the purpose and gives meaning to the tongues at Pentecost. Tongues were not to give evidence of valid Spirit baptism but rather to serve as an oral reminder that the gospel was to be proclaimed to every language group on earth. Speaking in tongues is a legitimate spiritual gift but has a far more noble and loftier purpose than my church assigned. I am compelled to bear witness to Scripture. I can do no other.

As God continues to endue me with health and strength I am open to conduct seminars or teach and preach as doors open. I can be contacted through my email address.